Getting Prices Right

Getting Prices Right

The Debate Over the Consumer Price Index

DEAN BAKER, EDITOR

ECONOMIC POLICY INSTITUTE

M.E. Sharpe
Armonk, New York
London, England

Cover design by Kim Arbogast.
Cover photographs © 1997 PhotoDisc Inc.

Library of Congress Cataloging-in-Publication Data

Getting prices right : the debate over the
consumer price index / Dean
Baker, editor.
p.   cm.
Includes bibliographical references and index.
ISBN 0-7656-0221-0 (alk. paper). —
ISBN 0-7656-0222-9 (pbk. : alk. paper)
1. Consumer price indexes—United States.
2. Prices—United States.   I. Baker, Dean, 1958–
HB235.U6G46   1998
338.5′28′0973—DC21   97-17606
CIP
Printed in the United States of America

The paper used in this publication meets the minimum requirements of
American National Standard for Information Sciences—
Permanence of Paper for Printed Library Materials,
ANSI Z 39.48-1984.

MV (c)   10   9   8   7   6   5   4   3   2   1
MV (p)   10   9   8   7   6   5   4   3   2

To Helene Jorgensen, Fulton, and Elecktra,
who have put up with more talk about the CPI
than any person or canine should be forced to endure.

Table of Contents

Acknowledgments

In the preparation of the response to the Boskin Commission report, Eileen Appelbaum, David Bernstein, Patrick Jackman, Helene Jorgensen, Larry Mishel, Janet Norwood, John Schmitt, and Mark Weisbrot gave helpful comments on earlier drafts. Terrel Hale, the librarian at the Economic Policy Institute, provided valuable assistance by quickly finding reference materials. The first appendix was prepared by Jim Perkins.

Kim Arbogast and Patrick Watson did a great job putting this book together while working under a tight deadline. Kim designed and laid out the book; Patrick copyedited. They had to work with material that was much further from completion than it should have been, and they managed to turn it around quickly and make it readable and accessible. Patrick, along with Eileen Appelbaum, Nan Gibson, and Diane Schwartz, deserve credit for carrying through the logistical arrangements that made this book possible. Linda Ellis, Elizabeth James, and Stephanie Scott-Steptoe have worked hard to distribute the material contained in this book, and related work, to a wide audience.

Introduction

by Dean Baker

The construction of government statistics is not ordinarily a topic that draws much attention. Even most economists would rather not be bothered with the details of how statistical agencies assemble the data that is vital to economists' research. The release of the Boskin Commission report in December 1996 changed all this. Suddenly press conferences on the accuracy of the consumer price index (CPI) were drawing overflow crowds. Newspapers and television reports were filled with late-breaking stories on the CPI. The report itself became one of the hottest documents in Washington.

Why the sudden interest in the CPI? Two years earlier, Federal Reserve Board Chairman Alan Greenspan told Congress that he thought the CPI overstated the true rate of consumer inflation by at least 1.0 percentage point annually. Furthermore, he suggested that Congress take this overstatement into account in setting indexation formulas for government benefits and income tax brackets; under current law, both are adjusted each year by the rate of inflation reported by the CPI. After 10 years, the cumulative impact of lowering the indexation formulas by 1.0 percentage point a year would be a reduction in the federal debt of $700 billion.

The Senate Finance Committee proceeded to hold hearings on the accuracy of the CPI in the winter and spring of 1995. Fifteen economists gave their assessments, and in June the Finance Committee appointed five of these economists to a commission to determine the extent of any bias in the CPI and to recommend improvements in the index's accuracy. The five economists were Ellen Dulberger, a research economist at IBM; Robert Gordon, a professor at Northwestern University; Zvi Griliches and Dale Jorgenson, professors at Harvard University; and Michael Boskin, a professor at Stanford University. Boskin, who also served as head of President Bush's Council of Economic Advisors, was selected as chairman.

In its interim report, released in September 1995, the Boskin Commission set a range of 0.8-2.0 percentage points for the amount that the CPI overstated the annual rate of consumer inflation; it set 1.0 percentage point as its best point estimate. This report began to prompt questions about the CPI, but the political impact of the preliminary report was limited.

By the time the final report was to be released in December 1996, shortly after the presidential election, the main topic of political discussion had turned to the federal budget, specifically the budget deficit. Both President Clinton and the Republican congressional leadership had committed themselves to eliminating the deficit by 2002, but both had also made commitments that foreclosed options for reaching that goal. For example, the Republicans had promised that they would not raise taxes or cut the military budget, and President Clinton was committed to protecting Medicare and Social Security.

For the policy makers and legislators caught in the middle of this dilemma, the anticipated findings of the Boskin Commission's report offered a way out. Spending on Social Security and other government benefits could be reduced billions of dollars below what had been projected, but without any cut for beneficiaries *in real terms*. Because tax-bracket thresholds would be lower than projected, more taxpayers would rise into higher brackets. Tax revenues would rise, but without any *real* added burden on taxpayers. By the weekend before the release of the report, news stories were presenting accounts of how the report would provide the solution to the budget impasse. Reporters, some of whom were learning about the CPI for the first time, were chasing down economists to explain the various ways in which bias might creep into it. On the day before the release of the Boskin Commission's report, Katharine Abraham, the commissioner of the Bureau of Labor Statistics (the agency that produces the CPI) held a press conference to explain her view of the problems in the CPI and the steps her agency had taken to correct them. The crowd of reporters spilled out into the hallway. When the report was released the next day, the Boskin Commission press conference was so crowded that people were actually turned away. The CPI had become big news.

The Boskin Commission report, which appears in its entirety in the first section of this volume, identified four distinct sources of bias in the CPI. Each of these, in the commission's view, led the index to overstate inflation by a cumulative amount of 1.1 percentage points. These biases are:

1. *Substitution bias* — Because the CPI monitors the prices in a fixed basket of goods and services, it does not pick up the extent to which consumers are able to save by switching to items that rise less rapidly in price. The commission estimated the size of this bias as 0.4 percentage points annually.

2. *Retail outlet substitution bias* — The CPI compares prices in the same store through time. But if consumers save by switching to discount stores that charge lower prices, then the CPI will overstate what shoppers are actually paying. The commission estimated the size of this bias as 0.1 percentage points annually.

3. *Quality bias* — The commission argued that the CPI fails to fully account for all the quality improvements in goods and services through time. If this is the case, then the CPI will wrongly report that items have risen in price when in fact consumers are really paying more to get a better product. The estimated size of this bias is combined with the new goods bias below.

4. *New goods bias* — New products are not incorporated fully into the CPI immediately after they are introduced. Consequently, when their price falls, as is often the case with new products (e.g., hand calculators, cellular phones), the CPI will miss the price decline and thereby overstate inflation. New goods, like videocassette recorders or the Internet, may also provide qualitatively new opportunities to consumers, the benefits of which are not picked up in the CPI. The commission estimated the size of the quality and new goods bias together at 0.6 percentage points annually.

The second section of the book, which analyzes the Boskin Commission report, disputes each of these estimates. It makes the case for a lower estimate for substitution bias, and argues that even this bias should decline in the next few years as BLS alters its procedures. It makes a similar argument regarding retail outlet substitution bias, and points out that the CPI may have missed a recent deterioration in the quality of retail service, causing the index to understate inflation in this sector.

The issue of quality and new goods bias is the largest area of disagreement between the two essays. The Boskin report, relying on a variety of sources and methodologies, presents estimates of quality and new goods bias for 27 different areas of the CPI. The critique raises questions about the way in which the Boskin estimate was derived, and offers reasons for believing that the CPI may currently overadjust for quality and therefore understate the true rate of inflation by as much as 0.44 percentage points annually. When all the different types of possible bias are added up, the analysis concludes that *the CPI may slightly understate inflation.*

There are other areas in which the two essays differ as well. The Boskin report evaluates the CPI as a measure of the cost of living, an extremely difficult concept for economists to quantify. The analysis of the report argues that the Boskin Commission has examined only one side of the issue, finding ways in which the cost of living might be lower than indicated by the CPI but ignoring factors that might cause the cost of living to rise more rapidly than the CPI.

The two analyses also differ as to whether all groups experience the same rate of inflation. The Boskin Commission notes the limited research in this area, and it concludes that there is little reason to believe that groups such as the elderly or poor experience more rapid rates of inflation. However, research from BLS suggests that the elderly may experience a somewhat higher rate of inflation than the population as a whole. Furthermore, there may be reasons to believe that inflation rates differ across income groups, with the poor experiencing a higher rate of inflation than the population as a whole and the wealthy a lower rate.

The response to the Boskin report also explores the implications for economic research and policy of a significant CPI overstatement. This is an area largely unexamined by the Boskin Commission, since such an examination was not one of the tasks assigned it by the Senate Finance Committee. Applying the Boskin Commission's findings back through time and forward to projections for the future, the analysis asserts that many of the implications about the past are implausible, if not impossible. It also argues that the implications of the commission's report for the future require serious rethinking of basic economic priorities.

In addition to the Boskin Commission's report and the critique, this volume also includes three shorter pieces intended to provide additional perspective to the debate over the accuracy of the CPI. The first is a paper prepared by Katharine Abraham, the commissioner of the Bureau of Labor Statistics, discussing some of the problems in the consumer price index and the steps that BLS is taking to correct them. The second piece presents testimony delivered to the Senate Finance Committee in January 1997 by Barry Bosworth, a senior fellow at the Brookings Institution and one of the most prominent critics of the Boskin Commission's conclusions. The third piece presents testimony given before the same committee by Martin Feldstein, a professor at Harvard University and president of the National Bureau of Economic Research. Professor Feldstein is one of the most prominent supporters of the Boskin Commission's conclusions.

The Boskin Commission's report came to public attention in the context of a battle over benefits and taxes. However, this is only the beginning of the story. Whatever is decided about these indexation formulas, economists and policy makers will have to grapple with the fact that the accuracy of the basic data we use to understand the world has been called into question. It is imperative that the issues raised by the commission be fully examined and understood within the profession. Until these issues are resolved, economists will not be able to answer the most basic questions about whether wages and living standards are rising or falling.

PART I

Toward a More Accurate Measure of the Cost of Living

Final Report to the Senate Finance Committee from the
Advisory Commission to Study the Consumer Price Index

DECEMBER 4, 1996

Michael J. Boskin, Chairman
Ellen R. Dulberger
Robert J. Gordon
Zvi Griliches
Dale Jorgensen

Executive Summary

1. The American economy is flexible and dynamic. New products are being introduced all the time and existing ones improved, while others leave the market. The relative prices of different goods and services change frequently, in response to changes in income and technological and other factors affecting costs and quality. This makes constructing an accurate cost of living index more difficult than in a static economy.

2. Estimating a cost of living index requires assumptions, methodology, data gathering and index number construction. Biases can come from any of these areas. The strength of the CPI is in the underlying simplicity of its concept: pricing a fixed (but representative) market basket of goods and services over time. Its weakness follows from the same conception: the "fixed basket" becomes less and less representative over time as consumers respond to price changes and new choices.

3. There are several categories or types of potential bias in using changes in the CPI as a measure of the change in the cost of living. 1) Substitution bias occurs because a fixed market basket fails to reflect the fact that consumers substitute relatively less for more expensive goods when relative prices change. 2) Outlet substitution bias occurs when shifts to lower price outlets are not properly handled. 3) Quality change bias occurs when improvements in the quality of products, such as greater energy efficiency or less need for repair, are measured inaccurately or not at all. 4) New product bias occurs when new products are not introduced in the market basket, or included only with a long lag.

4. While the CPI is the best measure currently available, it is not a true cost of living index (this has been recognized by the Bureau of Labor Statistics for many years). Despite many important BLS updates and improvements in the CPI, changes in the CPI will overstate changes in the true cost of living for the next few years. The Commission's best estimate of the size of the upward bias looking forward is 1.1 percentage points per year. The range of plausible values is 0.8 to 1.6 percentage points per year.

5. Changes in the CPI have substantially overstated the actual rate of price inflation, by about 1.3 percentage points per annum prior to 1996 (the extra 0.2 percentage point is due to a problem called formula bias inadvertently introduced in 1978 and fixed this year). It is likely that a large bias also occurred looking back over at least the last couple of decades.

6. The upward bias creates in the federal budget an annual automatic real increase in indexed benefits and a real tax cut. CBO estimates that if the change in the CPI overstated the change in the cost of living by an average of 1.1 percentage points per year over the next decade, this bias would contribute about $148 billion to the deficit in 2006 and $691 billion to the national debt by then. The bias alone would be the fourth largest federal program, after Social Security, health care and defense. By 2008, these totals reach $202 billion and $1.07 trillion, respectively.

7. Some have suggested that different groups in the population are likely to experience faster or slower growth in their cost of living than recorded by changes in the CPI. We find no compelling evidence of this to date (in fact just the opposite) but further exploration of this issue is desirable.

8. The commission is making over a dozen specific recommendations to the BLS. These include the following:

    i.   The BLS should establish a cost of living index (COLI) as its objective in measuring consumer prices.

    ii.   The BLS should develop and publish two indexes: one published monthly and one published and updated annually and revised historically.

    iii.   The timely, monthly index should continue to be called the CPI and should move toward a COLI concept by adopting a "superlative" index formula to account for changing market baskets, abandoning the pretense of sustaining the fixed-weight Laspeyres formula.

    iv.   The new annual COL index would use a compatible "superlative-index" formula and reflect subsequent data, updated weights, and the introduction of new goods (with their history extended backward).

    v.   The BLS should change its procedure for combining price quotations by moving to geometric means at the elementary aggregates level.

    vi.   The BLS should study the behavior of the individual components of the index to ascertain which components provide most information on the future longer-term movements in the index and which items have fluctuations which are largely unrelated to the total and emphasize the former in its data collection activities.

    vii.   The BLS should change the CPI sampling procedures to de-emphasize geography, starting first with sampling the universe of commodities to be priced and then deciding, commodity by commodity, what is the most efficient way to collect a representative sample of prices from which outlets, and only later turn to geographically clustered samples for the economy of data collection.

viii. The BLS should investigate the impact of classification, that is item group definition and structure, on the price indexes to improve the ability of the index to fully capture item substitution.

ix. There are a number of additional conceptual issues that require attention. The price of durables, such as cars, should be converted to a price of annual services, along the same lines as the current treatment of the price of owner-occupied housing. Also, the treatment of "insurance" should move to an ex-ante consumer price measure rather than the currently used ex-post insurance profits based measure.

x. The BLS needs a permanent mechanism for bringing outside information, expertise, and research results to it. At the request of the BLS, this group should be organized by an independent public professional entity and would provide BLS an improved channel to access professional and business opinion on statistical, economic, and current market issues.

xi. The BLS should develop a research program to look beyond its current "market basket" framework for the CPI.

xii. The BLS should investigate the ramifications of the embedded assumption of price equilibrium and the implications of it sometimes not holding.

xiii. The BLS will require a number of new data collection initiatives to make some progress along these lines. Most important, data on detailed time use from a large sample of consumers must be developed.

9. The Commission is making several recommendations to the President and Congress. These include the following:

xiv. Congress should enact the legislation necessary for the Departments of Commerce and Labor to share information in the interest of improving accuracy and timeliness of economic statistics and to reduce the resources consumed in their development and production.

xv. Congress should provide the additional resources necessary to expand the CES sample and the detail collected, to make the POPS survey more frequent, and to acquire additional commodity detail from alternative national sources, such as industry surveys and scanner data.

xvi. Congress should establish a permanent (rotating) independent committee or commission of experts to review progress in this area every three years or so and advise it on the appropriate interpretation of then current statistics.

xvii. Congress and the President must decide whether they wish to continue the widespread substantial overindexing of various federal
spending programs and features of the tax code. If the purpose of
indexing is accurately and fully to insulate the groups receiving
transfer payments and paying taxes, no more and no less, they should
pass legislation adjusting indexing provisions accordingly.

This could be done in the context of subtracting an amount partly or
wholly reflecting the overindexing from the current CPI-based indexing. Alternatively, a smaller amount would need to be subtracted from indexing based
on the new revised annual index if and when it is developed and published
regularly, to more closely approximate the change in the cost of living.

We hasten to add that the indexed programs have many other features and
raise many other issues beyond the narrow scope of a more accurate cost of
living index. We also wish to express our view that these findings and their
implications need to be fully digested and understood by the BLS, the Congress, the Executive Branch and the public.

I. Introduction[1]

Accurate measures of changes in the cost of living are among the most useful and important data necessary to evaluate economic performance. The change in the cost of living between two periods, for example 1975 and 1995, tells us how much income people would have needed in 1975, given the prices of goods and services available in that year, to be at least as well off as they are in 1995 given their income and the prices of goods and services available then. For example, if a family with a $45,000 income in 1996 would have needed $15,000 in 1976, the cost of living has tripled in the interim.

If the American economy was quite static, with very few new products introduced, very little quality improvement in existing products, little change in consumers' income, and very small and infrequent changes in the relative prices of goods and services, measuring changes in the cost of living would be conceptually quite easy and its implementation a matter of technical detail and appropriate execution. Fortunately for the overwhelming majority of Americans, our economy is far more dynamic and flexible than that. New products are being introduced all the time and existing ones improved, while others leave the market. The relative prices of different goods and services change frequently, in response to changes in consumer demand, and technological and other factors affecting costs and quality. Consumers in America have the benefit of a vast and growing array of goods and services from which to choose, unlike consumers in some other countries or our ancestors many decades ago.

But because the economy is complex and dynamic is no reason to bemoan the greater difficulty in constructing an accurate cost of living index. Major improvements can and should be made to the various official statistics that are currently used as proxies for changes in the cost of living, such as the well-known Consumer Price Index (CPI).

The Consumer Price Index measures the cost of purchasing a fixed market basket of goods and services. Based on surveys of households from some base period, the index sets weights (expenditure shares) for different goods and services. The weights reflect average or representative shares for the groups surveyed.[2] Keeping these weights fixed through time, the CPI is then calculated by attempting to measure changes from one month to the next in prices of the same, or quite closely related, goods and services.

But through time consumption baskets change, in part because of changes in the relative prices of goods and services, and therefore the weights from the base period no longer reflect what consumers are actually purchasing. Representative purchases also change as discount coupons, buyers' clubs and other marketing devices determine the best value and alter buying patterns. This failure to adjust for the changes in consumer behavior in response to relative price changes is called substitution bias. It is a necessary result of keeping the market basket fixed. Because the market basket is updated only every decade or so, as we get further away from the base period, there is more opportunity for relative prices to diverge from what they were in the base period, and for consumption baskets to change substantially.

Just as there are changes in what consumers purchase, there are also trends and changes in where purchases are made. In recent years, there has been a transformation of retailing. Superstores, discount stores, and the like now comprise a large and growing fraction of sales relative to a decade or two ago. As important as keeping up with the basket of goods that consumers actually purchase is keeping up with the outlets where they actually purchase them, so that the prices paid are accurately recorded. The current methodology suffers from an outlet substitution bias, which insufficiently takes into account the shift to discount outlets.

Many of the products sold today are dramatic improvements over their counterparts from years ago. They may be more durable and subject to less need for repair; more energy efficient; lighter; safer; etc. Sometimes, at least initially, a better quality product replacing its counterpart may cost more. Separating out how much of the price increase is due to quality change rather than actual inflation in the price of a standardized product is far from simple, but is necessary to obtain an accurate measure of the true increase in the cost of living. To the extent quality change is measured inaccurately or not at all, there is a quality change bias in the CPI.

The same is true with the introduction of new products, which have substantial value in and of themselves — not many of us would like to surrender our microwave ovens, radial tires, and VCRs — as well as the value of greater choice and opportunities opened up by the new products. To the extent new products are not included in the market basket, or included only with a long lag, there is a new product bias in the CPI.

Finally, in a dynamic, complex economy like the contemporary United States, there are literally many thousands of goods and services consumed. Price data are collected at a considerable level of disaggregation and how the price changes are aggregated into an overall index involves quite technical issues that can lead to a formula bias in the CPI.

Even if no federal program on either the outlay or revenue side of the budget were indexed, it would still be desirable to improve the quality of measures of the cost of living from the standpoint of providing citizens a better and more accurate estimate of what was actually going on in the economy, a way to compare current performance to our historical performance or to that of other countries. For example, the most commonly used measure of the standard of living is real income or output per person. To measure changes in real income requires the separation of nominal income changes from price changes. Obviously, that requires an accurate measure of price changes. The

Commerce Department uses the component indexes of the CPI as inputs in estimating inflation and real GDP, and thus some of the bias from the CPI is transmitted to the national income accounts.

But numerous federal, state, and local government programs and tax features are "indexed" for changes in the cost of living by the changes in the Consumer Price Index. The CPI is also used to index, formally or informally, a large number of private sector contracts, including wages in collective bargaining agreements and rents, to name obvious examples that affect millions of Americans. Currently, slightly under one-third of total federal outlays, mostly in retirement programs, are directly indexed to changes in consumer prices. Several features of the individual income tax, including the tax brackets, are indexed; the individual income tax accounts for a little under half of federal revenues.

Congress indexed these outlay programs and tax rules in order to help insulate or protect the affected individuals from bearing the brunt of increases in the cost of living. Yet the Bureau of Labor Statistics, the agency responsible for compiling and presenting the Consumer Price Index, has explicitly stated for years that the CPI is not a cost of living index, presumably for some of the reasons mentioned above. If the Consumer Price Index as currently produced, and as likely to be produced over the next few years, is not an appropriate cost of living index for the task Congress had in mind, then it is desirable to consider alternative measures.

The consequences of changes in the Consumer Price Index overstating changes in the cost of living can be dramatic. For example, if use of the CPI is expected to overstate the increase in the cost of living by one percentage point per year over the next dozen years, the national debt would be about $1 trillion greater in 2008 than if a corresponding correction were made in the indexing of outlays and revenues.

This report proceeds as follows: Section II discusses the historical and prospective budgetary implications of changes in the CPI overstating changes in the cost of living. Section III presents an overview of how the CPI is actually constructed. Section IV details why the CPI is not a true cost of living index and discusses substitution bias. Section V describes in greater detail the current procedures employed by the BLS to adjust for quality change and presents a survey of the studies and the Commission's judgment on the bias from quality change and new products. Section VI summarizes the Commission's findings on the size of the bias by type, plus the range of plausible overall bias. Section VII discusses the issue of separate price indexes for different groups and of aspects of the quality of life that fall primarily outside the market-based consumption focus of cost-of-living measures. Section VIII presents the Commission's detailed recommendations of ways to produce and to use more accurate cost-of-living measures. The Conclusion offers a brief perspective and some cautionary notes on the use of the findings of the Commission.

II. Indexing the Federal Budget

The issue posed for fiscal policy makers by an upward bias in the CPI has been stated with admirable clarity by the Congressional Budget Office (1994):

> The budgetary effect of any overestimate of changes in the cost of living highlights the possibility of a shift in the distribution of wealth. If the CPI has an upward bias, some federal programs would overcompensate for the effect of price changes on living standards, and wealth would be transferred from younger and future generations to current recipients of indexed federal programs — an effect that legislators may not have intended.[3]

Social Security is by far the most important of the federal outlays that are indexed to the CPI. However, Supplemental Security Income, Military Retirement, and Civil Service Retirement are significant programs that are similarly indexed. Other federal retirement programs, Railroad Retirement, veterans' compensation and pensions, and the Federal Employees' Compensation Act also contain provisions for indexing. The Economic Recovery Tax Act of 1981 indexed individual income tax brackets and the personal exemption to the CPI.

How important have the budgetary consequences of upward bias in the CPI been historically? Obviously, a precise answer to this question would require extended study, taking into account the timing of the bias, the parallel development of indexing provisions in specific federal outlays and revenues, and interest on the accumulation of debt that has resulted. An indication of the potential size of these effects can be inferred from one important historical example of one clearly identified source of bias. A careful study of this type, which focuses on the most important federal program affected by indexing, namely, Social Security benefits, has been conducted by the Office of Economic Policy (OEP) of the Department of the Treasury.

On February 25, 1983, the Bureau of Labor Statistics (BLS) introduced an important technical modification in the Consumer Price Index for All Urban Consumers (CPI-U). This altered the treatment of housing costs by shifting the costs for homeowners to a rental equivalent basis. The new treatment of housing costs was incorporated into the Consumer Price Index for Urban Wage Earners and Clerical Workers (CPI-W), used to index Social Security benefits, in 1985.

The rental equivalent measure of housing costs was a conceptual improvement and has been retained in subsequent official publications. However, housing costs in preceding years employed a "homeownership" measure " . . . based on house prices, mortgage interest rates, property taxes and insurance, and maintenance costs."[4] The treatment of housing costs prior to 1983 was not modified in publishing the revised CPI-U, so that the new treatment of housing introduced a discrepancy in the conceptual basis for the CPI-U before and after 1983. Similarly, housing costs in the CPI-W prior to 1985 have not been modified.

BLS developed an "experimental" price index, CPI-U X1, based on a rental equivalent treatment of housing extending back to 1967. This provides the basis for the OEP assessment of bias in the CPI-W. The bias for 1975, the first year that Social Security was indexed to the CPI-W, was 1.1 percent. This bias mounted over subsequent years, reaching 6.5 percent by 1982 and then declining to 4.7 percent in 1984.[5]

Overpayments of Social Security benefits resulting from the bias in the CPI-W mounted through 1983, reaching a total of $8.76 billion or 5.55 percent of benefits paid in that year. These overpayments have resulted in a lower balance in the OASI trust fund and a larger federal deficit and debt. OEP estimates interest costs associated with these deficits at the rate of interest paid or projected to be paid on the OASI trust fund. Beginning in 1984 interest costs predominate in the total. In the current fiscal year the total cost is $21.79 billion, of which $17.64 billion is interest. The cumulative effect of just this one source of bias in the CPI-W via this one program on the federal debt amounts to $271.0 billion, as of 1996.

In summary, the BLS made two decisions in revising the treatment of housing costs in the CPI-W in 1985. The first decision was to change the treatment of housing costs to a rental equivalent basis beginning in January 1985. The second was not to revise the treatment of housing costs for 1984 and earlier years. As a consequence of these two decisions the level of the CPI-W is 4.7 percent above the CPI-U X1, a measure of the cost of living based on the same primary data sources and similar methodology, but with a consistent treatment of housing costs.

The increases in federal outlays resulting from the bias in the CPI-W cannot be justified as cost of living adjustments. These increases are the consequence of an inappropriate treatment of housing costs before 1985 and have resulted in large transfers to beneficiaries of the OASI program that are devoid of any economic rationale. The overpayments have continued up to the present, but are declining in importance. However, the resulting decline in the OASI trust fund continues to mount due to rising interest costs and now contributes more than two hundred billion dollars to the federal debt.

Of course, nobody would suggest retroactively undoing the overindexing due to this or any other source of bias. The point of this discussion is to demonstrate how important it is to correct biases in the CPI as quickly and fully as possible before their consequences mount, indeed compound.

What would be the effect of an upward bias in the CPI on future budget deficits? More than half of federal spending of $1.5 trillion is now attributable to entitlements and mandatory spending programs. In January 1995 the annual Congressional Budget Office (CBO) outlook for the economy and the federal budget showed that this proportion is projected to rise to almost two-thirds of federal spending during fiscal year 1998. Cost-of-living adjustments at a projected rate of 3.0 percent will contribute $43 billion to total spending on mandatory programs in that year and $80 billion in fiscal year 2000.[6] This is 6.8 percent of projected spending on mandatory programs in fiscal year 2000.

Testimony presented by the CBO to the Committee on Finance shows the impact of a hypothetical correction (reduction) of 0.5 percentage point in cost of living adjustments for fiscal years 1996-2000. Federal outlays would decline by $13.3 billion in fiscal year 2000, while revenues would rise by $9.6 billion. The decline in debt service resulting from reduced deficits in fiscal years 1996-2000 would be $3.3 billion, yielding a total contribution to deficit reduction of $26.2 billion in fiscal year 2000.[7] This is more than ten percent of the deficit projected by CBO in that year.

The CBO has provided the Commission with updated projections of the impact of hypothetical corrections (reductions) of 0.5 and 1.0 percentage point in cost of living adjustments for fiscal years 1997-2006.[8] With a reduction of 0.5 percentage point the total contribution to deficit reduction rises to $67.5 billion in 2006. Of this amount, an increase in revenue accounts for $22.3 billion and reductions in outlays, including debt service, amounts to $45.3 billion (of which debt service is $13.1 billion).

CBO projections for the impact of a hypothetical correction (reduction) in cost of living adjustments of 1.0 percentage point are, of course, even more dramatic. The total change in the deficit in the year 2006 is $134.9 billion. Federal revenues would be increased by $44.5 billion and federal outlays reduced by $90.5 billion; of the reduction in outlays $26.1 billion can be attributed to lower debt service and $64.4 billion to lower outlays on indexed programs. (See Appendix Figure A-1 for detail.)

Stated differently, if the change in the CPI overstated the change in the cost of living by an average of one percentage point per year over this period, this bias alone would contribute almost $135 billion to the deficit in the year 2006. That is one-third the projected baseline deficit (which assumes no policy changes such as the current balanced budget proposals). More remarkably, the upward bias by itself would constitute the fourth largest federal outlay program, behind only Social Security, health care, and defense. By 2008, the increased deficit would be $180 billion and national debt $1 trillion.

In summary, an upward bias in the CPI would result in substantial overpayments to the beneficiaries of federal entitlements and mandatory spending programs. In addition, such a bias would reduce federal revenues by overindexing the individual income tax. In short, the upward bias programs into the federal budget every year an automatic, real increase in indexed benefits and a real tax cut. Correction of biases in the CPI, while designed to adjust benefits and taxes for true changes in the cost of living more accurately, would also contribute importantly to reductions in future federal budget deficits and the national debt. These reductions can be attributed to higher revenues, lower outlays, and less debt service. Lower outlays — cuts in indexed federal spending programs and reduced interest payments — account for over two-thirds of the long-run deficit reduction, while higher revenues account for the rest.

III. How the CPI Is Constructed: A Brief Introduction

Knowledge of how the CPI is constructed is needed to understand the reasons that biases occur and the rationale for our recommendations for improvements and changes. This section provides a brief description of the BLS methodology highlighting the places where biases and key issues are likely to arise. We refer the reader to BLS documentation for more detail on data collection procedures and index construction methodology, as well as to recent articles by Armknecht (1996), and Shapiro and Wilcox (1996b). [9]

As could be inferred from the discussion above about the complexities of a modern dynamic capitalist economy, the CPI program is a complex and difficult undertaking. To make it manageable, the BLS applies a simplified view of the marketplace and consumer behavior. This simplified view is reflected throughout the CPI approach. It takes expenditures for a fixed market basket of goods and services at some point in the past, called the base or reference period, and estimates what it would cost today to purchase the same market basket. The formula used to construct the CPI, called Laspeyres, assumes that purchases are made in fixed quantities based on decisions from some previous period's experience. In other words, the CPI attempts to answer the question, "what is the cost, at this month's market prices, of purchasing the same market basket actually purchased in the base period?" Since the Laspeyres formula does not allow for the substitution of products or services in response to current prices and choices, it is an "upper bound" to a cost of living.

The market basket consists of total expenditures on items directly purchased by all urban consumers, that is, food, clothing, shelter and fuels, transportation, medical services, and other goods and services that people buy for day-to-day living. The BLS uses scientific sampling techniques to select specific items. The BLS measures the price changes in these items over time. The sample design involves a multistage process for sampling by geographic area, retail outlet, item category, and individual goods and services within an outlet and category.

Several samples are used to try to make the CPI representative of the prices paid by consumers: urban areas selected from all U.S. urban areas, consumer units within each selected area, outlets from which these consumer units purchased goods and services, specific items — goods and services — purchased by these consumer units, and housing units in each urban area (for the shelter component of the CPI). The key sources of information used to determine the items which comprise the market basket and the outlets at which prices are to be collected are the Consumer Expenditure Survey (CES) and the Point-of-Purchase Survey (POPS).

Each month, prices for approximately 71,000 goods and services are collected from 22,000 outlets, in 44 geographic areas.[10] Separately, information is collected each month from about 5,000 renters and 1,000 homeowners for the housing components of the CPI.[11] The price quotations are combined, that is, aggregated, into the overall CPI. The determination of representative items to be priced, the procedure for collecting prices at the outlets, and the levels at which the prices are combined into indexes and the indexes are combined into higher aggregates, are all based on a fixed structure or system in which a number of key assumptions are embedded.

The item structure has four levels of classification beginning with major groups such as food and beverages, transportation, and medical care. The seven major groups are made up of 69 expenditure classes (ECs), for example, fresh fruits (EC 11) and hospital and other related services (EC 57). The expenditure classes are in turn divided into 207 groupings called item strata, the lowest level at which indexes are constructed.[12] Two examples of item strata are apples, and nursing and convalescent home care. It is important to note that while the item categories are mutually exclusive and exhaustive for all consumer expenditures, this does not mean that new goods and services are automatically brought into the sample if they were not available during the reference period. It just means that every good and service can be classified within an existing stratum and there is no need to create a new stratum for when a new good or service is introduced. (This is made possible in part by numerous item categories called "other.")

Within each item stratum, entry level items, called ELIs for short, are defined. Indexes are not constructed at this level. Many strata have only one ELI, for example, Apples. The ELIs are the lowest level sampling units for items. They are the level of item definition at which the data collectors begin item sampling within each sample outlet. For example, prices for Brand "X" fever thermometers for babies, model 41303 41082, 4 3/10 inches long with plastic case, sold by "Y" Foods, Inc. in West Terre Haute, Indiana, might be collected for Medical Equipment for General Use, ELI 55032, within Nonprescription Drugs and Medical Supplies, item stratum 5503, within Nonprescription Drugs, EC 55, within the Medical Care Commodities component of the Medical Care major expenditure category.[13] A schematic of the item structure is shown below in Figure 1.

Outlets within geographic areas are sampled, too. The probability of selection for any given outlet is proportional to that outlet's share in total expenditures in the survey area for the item category in question. This is done so that the price quotes for selected items are obtained at outlets which are representative of the places that consumers made their purchases and also because

FIGURE 1
CPI Hierarchy Structure

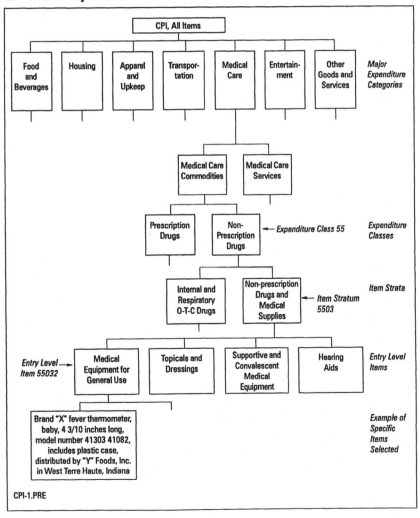

the outlet is assumed to be an important characteristic of the purchase and component of price change. It follows from this assumption that differences in prices of the same item in different outlets must represent differences in aspects of the purchase such as quality of service or convenience of location and that consumers will pay the same proportional difference over time for these other aspects. When this assumption does not hold, such as when some outlets grow faster than others, the methodology will prevent adequate accounting in two ways: the current methodology will not adequately provide for obtaining more price quotes or give more importance to the more favored outlets, nor does it provide for direct comparison of the quality differences in purchasing the same item at two different places.

There is a process to "refresh" items and outlets sampled, called sample rotation, which generates a sample of specific items each of which had a probability of selection into the sample proportional to its share in recent consumer expenditures. Approximately 20 percent of the sample is rotated every year such that full rotation takes five years. The items rotated in are not directly compared to those they replaced. The procedure assumes that at the time of rotation, the original item and the one rotated in have the same quality adjusted price.

BLS procedure provides for selecting alternative items to be priced when the previously priced item is sold out, discontinued or otherwise permanently unavailable. The field agent is given guidelines to use in selecting the replacement or substitute item within the same ELI and a judgment is made as to the comparability of the specifications. (However, there is no provision to assure that the replacement is the product which has taken market share from the one that has disappeared.)[14] When the substitute is determined to be non-comparable, BLS most often assumes that the quality difference accounts for the price difference, net of the price change since the last pricing period for similar items.[15] In some cases, attempts are made to measure the quality differences. Notice that it is the disappearance of an item which triggers the mechanism to price a substitute.

Prices of new goods not falling within an established stratum, which are introduced after the base period and therefore not in the reference market basket, are not given special preference in item substitution and sample rotation, and consequently are often not included in the index until the subsequent decadal revision.[16] (Moreover, the impact of new goods is not measured retrospectively because the CPI is not revised historically.)[17] Frequently cited examples of important new products which were not introduced until many years after their introduction are air conditioners and VCRs.[18] Cellular telephones will be included in the 1998 revision of the CPI.

While the methodology does not ensure the introduction of new products until the market basket is updated, improving the timeliness through more frequent updates of the market basket solves only part of the problem. Direct comparisons of the quality of new products with those with which they compete is often difficult. Furthermore, proper accounting of the impact of new products often requires comparisons with products in other item groups. The current item structure prevents the CPI from fully capturing the effects of a drug replacing surgery, of electronic information services replacing newspapers, of automobile leasing competing with purchases, of video rentals replacing cinema attendance. Over time, price changes in successful products will be given greater weight in the CPI, but full measurement of the price impacts across item groups is not possible when close substitutes are in different item groups.[19] Although the item structure has several purposes, index estimation is the most important.

Prices for specific goods and services at specific outlets in specific locations are combined into item group-area indexes and these indexes are further aggregated by weighting them together either up through the item classification structure or by geographic area, to form a national CPI. The weights are derived from the Point-Of-Purchase Survey, the Consumer Expenditure Survey (which contains only modest detail) and from the statistical approach used in initiating specific commodities or services at the selected outlets. The design does not provide for collecting changes in quantities over time (since the market basket is assumed to be unchanged, this is not necessary to construct the CPI).

The use of arithmetic means to combine price changes within item groupings, for example, different types of apples, implements the restriction that quantity weights do not change when prices change.[20] The arithmetic mean fails certain commonsense tests, as discussed in the next section.

The greater the substitutability of the items whose prices are combined this way, the greater the resulting substitution bias in the index. An alternative to assuming no change in quantities is to assume no change in expenditure shares. This can be accomplished through the use of geometric means, which effects a price increase that is proportionally offset by a quantity decrease. For example, if a 10 percent increase in the price of Granny Smith apples were associated with a 10 percent reduction in the quantity purchased, geometric means would be the appropriate way to capture the market response. If there were no quantity change associated with the price increase then arithmetic means would be appropriate. In the case of Granny Smith apples, the availability of other varieties of apples may yield a market response to quantities that more than offsets the price increase. When this happens, the use of geometric means understates the market response.

It is worth noting that the published geographic indexes do not provide comparisons of the price level across geographic areas; rather, they provide comparisons of rates of change in the CPI. Clearly, if the rates of change are different, then the levels must also differ at some point. Indeed, the differences in levels would be of significant interest as a comparison of the cost of living across geographic areas. Yet the methodology does not provide such comparisons. Geographic areas play an important role in the sampling design, however, geographic area indexes as they are constructed today serve no other purpose than a step in aggregation, en route to a national CPI.

In summary, sampling techniques are used to determine which items are priced at which outlets. The methodology requires allegiance to the concept of a fixed market basket which by design does not change item category weights until the market basket is updated, historically every ten years or so, and hence fails to capture some new products. Neither does it make direct comparisons of the purchase experience at different outlets, by assumption not capturing the lower prices to which consumers respond making some outlets grow faster than others. The most detailed level at which price indexes are constructed is for 207 item groups for each geographic area. Geographic area price indexes are constructed to provide estimates of price change in specific geographic areas en route to the national CPI, but they do not provide inter-area comparisons of the cost of living. Price indexes are successively combined into broader categories until a national CPI is reached.

In conclusion, improving the CPI as a measure of the cost of living requires addressing a range of issues beginning with revisiting critical assumptions, adjusting resource optimization criteria, and abandoning the Laspeyres index formula. The Commission's recommendations are presented in Section VIII.

IV. The Consumer Price Index and a Cost of Living Index: Measurement Issues

A cost of living index is a comparison of the minimum expenditure required to achieve the same level of well-being (also known as welfare, utility, standard-of-living) across two different sets of prices. Most often it is thought of as a comparison between two points of time. As with any practical application of theory to index number production, estimating a cost of living index requires assumptions, a methodology, data gathering processes and index number construction.

There are two sets of potential biases in the CPI: biases relative to an "ideal" cost of living index and biases which arise within its own terms of reference. The strength of the CPI is in the underlying simplicity of its concept: pricing a fixed (but representative) market basket of goods and services over time. Its weakness follows from the same conception: the "fixed basket" becomes less and less representative over time as consumers respond to price changes and new choices.

Consumers respond to price changes by substituting away from products that have become more expensive and toward goods whose prices have declined relatively. As the world changes, they are faced with new choices in shopping outlets, varieties, and entirely new goods and services, and respond to these as well. These changes make the previously "fixed basket" increasingly irrelevant.

In trying to keep true to its concept in a rapidly changing world, the current CPI procedures encounter difficulties. Biases result when they ignore some of these changes such as the appearance of discounters, and also when they try to do something about them such as when items are rotated out of the sample and replaced with new items. Attempting to capture the changes in a way that tries to mimic the pricing of a "fixed basket" within a rather patchwork framework just cannot be done without introducing other problems into the resulting index. These different biases overlap and have been discussed under a number of headings: substitution bias; formula bias; outlet substitution bias; quality change; and new product bias.

The "pure" substitution bias is the easiest to illustrate. Consider a very stylized example, where we would like to compare an initial "base" period 1 and a subsequent period 2. For simplicity, consider a hypothetical situation where there are only two commodities: beef and chicken. In period 1, the prices per pound of beef and chicken are equal, at $1, and so are the quantities consumed, at 1 lb. Total expenditure is therefore $2. In period 2, beef is twice as expensive as chicken ($1.60 vs. $0.80 per pound), and much more chicken (2 lb.) than beef (0.8 lb.) is consumed, as the consumer substitutes the relatively less expensive chicken for beef. Total expenditure in period 2 is $2.88. The relevant data are presented in Table 1. How can we compare the two situations? Actually, there are several methods, each asking slightly different questions and therefore, not surprisingly, giving different answers.[21]

TABLE 1
Hypothetical Example of Substitution Bias

	Price in Period 1	Quantity in Period 1	Price in Period 2	Quantity in Period 2	Price Relatives		Relative Weights	
					P2/P1	P1/P2	1	2
Beef	1	1	1.6	0.8	1.6	0.63	0.5	0.43
Chicken	1	1	0.8	2.0	0.8	1.25	0.5	0.57

The simplest comparison is to ask "How much more must I spend in my current situation (period 2) to purchase the same quantities that I purchased initially (in period 1)?"[22] This is the question asked by the CPI. The price index for period 2 relative to period 1 uses the initial period 1 basket of consumption as the weights in the computation. To buy 1 lb. of beef and 1 lb. of chicken in period 2 costs $2.40. The price index for period 2 relative to period 1 is 1.20 (2.40/2.00), that is a 20% increase.

Intuitively, it is easy to understand why such a computation imparts an upward (substitution) bias to the measure of the change in the true cost of living. It assumes the consumer does not substitute (cheaper) chicken for beef. In the real world, as in the hypothetical example, consumers change their spending patterns in response to changes in relative prices and, hence, partially insulate themselves from price movements.

An alternative approach would be to ask the question "How much more am I spending in my current situation (period 2) than I would have spent for the same goods and services at the prices that prevailed initially (in period 1)?"[23] This price index compares expenditures in period 2 ($2.88) with what it would cost to buy the current (period 2) market basket at the initial prices ($0.80 for the beef plus $2.00 for the chicken equals $2.80). This price index is 1.03, that is only a 3% increase. This approach understates the rise in the true cost of living as it overstates substitution.

The idea underlying a cost of living index is to allow for the substitution that follows relative price changes. The question answered by a cost of living index is: "How much would we need to increase (or decrease) initial (period 1) expenditure in order to make the consumer as well off as in the subsequent period (period 2)." Although the answer to this question might appear to require detailed knowledge of a consumer's preferences, an excellent approximation can be obtained by using a "superlative" index formula instead of the traditional fixed weight index employed in the CPI.

The concept of a superlative index number was introduced by the American economist, Irving Fisher (1922), to describe index numbers that met certain reasonable criteria and thus agreed closely with his "ideal" index, described below.[24] This concept was generalized by the Canadian economist, Erwin Diewert (1976), and used to describe any index number formula that provides a satisfactory approximation to an underlying economic index, such as a cost of living index.[25] The CPI is based on a fixed weight index formula that does not provide such an approximation, fails to meet these sensible criteria and worse yet is known to be biased upward. A superlative index requires the same information on prices and quantities as a fixed weight index, but involves interpolating between the two periods rather than treating one of them as the "base" period. There are two ways of doing this.

The first approach to interpolating between time periods is to use the geometric mean of the two fixed weight indexes — using the initial period and the subsequent period as "base" periods. The geometric mean is the square root of the product of the two indexes. This is the ideal index originated by Irving Fisher (1922) and now called the "Fisher ideal index" in his honor. In our example, this comes to 1.11, an 11% increase. By comparison the CPI-type fixed weight index, treating period 1 as the "base" period, is biased upward by 9% (1.20 minus 1.11). Alternatively, a fixed weight index with period 2 as the "base" period is biased downward by 8% (1.03 minus 1.11). The Fisher ideal index is employed by the Bureau of Economic Analysis in compiling data on the U.S. national income and product accounts.

An alternative approach to interpolation is to use a weighted average of the growth rates in prices with relative weights equal to the average of the weights in the two periods. This is called the "Tornqvist" index in honor of one of its originators, the Finnish statistician Leo Tornqvist (1936).[26] In our example, this is 1.10, a 10% increase. We conclude that the two superlative index formulas yield very similar approximations to the cost of living index. Estimates of the biases of the two fixed weight indexes are also similar. The BLS has compared a fixed weight index with the Fisher ideal and Tornqvist indexes to assess the bias in the fixed weight index as a measure of changes in the cost of living.

How large are substitution biases in the CPI? To answer this question we must take into account the hierarchical nature of the construction of the CPI described above. It is useful to focus initially on Upper Level Substitution Bias, which occurs when indexes for the 207 item groups and 44 areas are aggregated to form the CPI. The BLS uses a fixed weight index for this purpose (with weights derived from the Consumer Expenditure Survey [CES], a survey of household expenditure patterns), and hence ignores substitutions of chicken for beef, apples for oranges, etc. The BLS has measured this form of substitution bias by comparing a fixed weight index with an index generated by one of the interpolation methods we have described. Estimates are presented in Section VI.

The second type of substitution bias in the CPI is Lower Level Substitution Bias, which occurs when prices for the approximately 71,000 goods and services and information on housing costs are used to form indexes for the 207 items and 44 areas. This part of the index construction involves probability sampling with probabilities derived from the CES and the Point-of-Purchase Survey (POPS) of retail establishments in order to reflect the likelihood of purchases of individual items at specific retail outlets. It is useful to think of this as an alternative fixed weight index with probabilities playing the role of expenditure weights. Since 1978 the formula at the lower level of index construction has been closely analogous to the fixed weight index at the upper level. The use of arithmetic means to aggregate the price changes assumes no substitution to changes in the relative prices of the specific commodities or services within the lowest grouping, e.g., when the price of Granny Smith apples rises, it assumes no substitution, of say, delicious apples. The BLS has measured Lower Level Substitution Bias by comparing this fixed weight index with a geometrically weighted average of prices at the lower level.

A major difficulty with a fixed weight index at the lower level of index construction is the failure of time reversibility. This simple and intuitive requirement or "test" for an index number is that the index should remain the same if the underlying prices undergo a reversal. For example, suppose that the price of beef in Table 1 rises from 1.0 in period 1 to 1.6 in period 2, but then falls back to 1.0 in period 3, reversing the change that took place between periods 1 and 2. A fixed weight index increases by 60% between periods 1 and 2, but decreases by only 37.5% between periods 1 and 3, so that the increase in the "beef" index between periods 1 and 3 is 22.5% or 11.25% per period, rather than zero, as required for time reversal.

A geometric average satisfies the time reversal test, since it is based on the square root of the product of the price ratios between periods. In the example of the beef price from Table 1, the price ratio between period 1 and period 2 is 1.6, while the price ratio between period 2 and 3 is .625. The product of these two price ratios is one, as required for time reversal, so that the average price increase is zero per period. The time reversal property has led to widespread use of of geometric averages as a standard for comparison of different approaches at the lower level of index number construction. For example, Moulton and Smedley (1995) have compared the BLS fixed weight approach at this level with a weighted geometric approach.[27]

Diewert (1995) has provided a detailed review of the properties of alternative approaches to index number construction at the lower level.[28] These include time reversal, as well as other reasonable requirements for index numbers at the lower level. Shapiro and Wilcox (1996b) have provided an elegant rationale for the geometric approach based on the correlation of relative prices over time.[29] Provided that this correlation is small, a modification of the geometric mean is approximately unbiased for the underlying cost of living index, and this characterization does not require information about the underlying system of consumer's preferences.

Modified geometric means have been widely used as a standard for evaluating methods for index number construction at the lower level. Diewert (1995) gives a useful review of the empirical studies. In addition to the work of Moulton and Smedley (1995), Carruthers, Sellwood, and Ward (1980) have conducted a study of this type for the U.K., Schultz (1994) for Canada, Dahlen (1994) for Sweden, and Woolford (1994) for Australia.[30] These studies show that fixed weight indexes, like those used by BLS, are biased upward; the order of magnitude of the bias is similar to that suggested by the study of Moulton and Smedley (1995) for the U.S. These problems have led an increasing number of statistical agencies, such as Statistics Canada, to follow Irving Fisher's (1922) advice and jettison the arithmetic mean in favor of the geometric mean.

A relatively subtle problem developed in implementing the fixed weight index at the lower level. When sample items are replaced by substitute items for which no previous price observations are available, base period prices for the substitute items must be "imputed" to fill this gap. The procedure adopted by BLS for doing this had the effect of linking the weights for the substitute items to the prices used in the CPI and produced a bias that is an important component of Lower Level Substitution Bias. This problem also arises during rotations of items included in the sample of 70,000 prices for goods and services and the sample of housing costs.

An estimate of the overall Lower Level Substitution Bias is given by the difference between the fixed weight index and a geometrically weighted average, where the fixed weight index is based on the methods for price imputation introduced by BLS in 1978. In 1995 and 1996 BLS introduced new procedures based on "seasoning" the price estimates. Seasoning involves lengthening the period between a price imputation and the period when an item is actually introduced into the CPI. By lengthening this period the link between weights and prices for individual items can be broken and the bias reduced. However, the bias associated with the fixed weight formula remains.[31]

Our Interim Report anticipated that what we called "formula bias" and now refer to as Lower Level Substitution Bias would be eliminated by BLS. The BLS did alter its procedures by introducing "seasoning" where appropriate; while this eliminated bias due to methods for price imputation, it did not affect the bias due to the use of a fixed weight formula at the lower level. Accordingly, we have recommended below that BLS should replace the fixed weight formula by a geometrically weighted average. This has been tested and found to be feasible in an important study by Moulton and Smedley (1995).[32] Additional work is currently under way to extend the period of this study.

The introduction by BLS of a fixed weight index at the lower level of aggregation was viewed at the time as introducing consistency of indexing at both upper and lower levels of aggregation. However, the disadvantages of the fixed weight approach at the upper level carry over to the lower level. A superlative index formula is required to provide a satisfactory approximation to the underlying cost of living index at the upper level. This avoids the bias associated with the fixed weight index formula employed in the CPI. Similarly, lacking quantity or expenditure information at the lower level, a good approximation to the underlying cost of living index is obtained from a geometrically weighted average formula.

Just as consumers change the goods they purchase in response to changes in relative prices, as in the beef and chicken example, so do they change the location where they make their purchases. The opening of a new discount store outlet may give consumers the opportunity to purchase at a lower price than before. At present, the CPI procedures ignore such reductions that occur when consumers change outlets. However, if consumers cared only about obtaining goods at the lowest price, then we would observe all goods sold at the same price at all outlets. Instead, we observe low prices at discount stores and warehouse clubs at the same time as medium prices at supermarkets and higher prices at convenience stores. Evidently, consumers care not only about prices, but the level of services such as availability of clerks, wrapping services, and the distance between home and alternative outlets.

Current procedures in the CPI ignore price changes when consumers switch outlets. This incorporates into the CPI the implicit assumption that price differentials among outlets entirely reflect the differences in service quality. This approach would be legitimate if the economy stood still with a stable set of outlets providing alternative levels of service quality. However, there has been a continuous increase in the market share of discount stores as more efficient technologies of distribution allow low price outlets to expand while older, higher priced outlets have contracted and in some cases gone out of business. This shift in market share indicated that many consumers respond to price differentials and do not consider them to be fully offset by differences in service quality. Completely ignoring all differences in service quality by incorporating all such price reductions into the CPI would err in the opposite direction. Further research is required to disentangle true changes in prices from changes in service quality. This problem is analogous to the need to disentangle the changes in prices from changes in product quality.

Quality change and new goods present the most difficult problems for measurement. They include capturing the introduction of new products in a timely manner; making direct quality comparisons of new products with existing ones; making direct quality comparisons of new products with other products against which they compete (in other classification groupings such as a new drug and the surgical treatment it replaces); and capturing the combined impact of quality and substitution as these new products displace others within and across their classification grouping.

A well-known expert on price indexes has stated the general issue clearly: "...heterogeneity in economics pertains to transactions, and not just the physical description of the product. Whenever two transactions involve different bundles of explicit or implicit attributes, they differ qualitatively. Differences in terms of sale, services provided with the sale,...are exactly identical from the economics of the matter, to physical changes that we normally think of as 'quality change' " (Triplett 1990).

For example, it is not just what is purchased where (and how), but possibly also when that matters. There may also be a time of week bias. The BLS does not collect prices on weekends and holidays when certain items and types of outlets disproportionately run sales.[33] There appears to have been a sizable increase in the fraction of purchases made on weekends and holidays perhaps reflecting the increased prevalence of two-earner families. We know of no systematic study of this issue and urge the BLS to conduct the research necessary to examine it thoroughly, perhaps with scanner data.

A full treatment of these issues reinforces the problem of focusing on the "average" or "representative" consumer. Different consumers have different tastes and time costs, and hence value the appearance of new outlets and new products differentially, with some (the majority) becoming better off with supermarkets and others losing out as the corner grocery store disappears. The CPI is not equipped to account for special characteristics of different consumers or groups of consumers.[34][35]

There are still other issues that would in principle apply to obtaining a true cost of living index (COLI). Consider two examples: the negative effects of higher crime rates and the concommitant purchases of security devices and higher insurance premiums and the positive effects of improvements in information technology that permit a parent to work at home when a child is ill. Surely these would enter a calculation of "the minimum expenditure necessary to be at least as well off." Section VII below explores some of these problems.

V. Quality Change and New Products

INTRODUCTION

The difficult questions posed by quality change and the continuing arrival of new products have been called the "house-to-house combat of price measurement." In this section we will treat new product bias as a component of quality change bias and will not attempt to break down our overall bias estimate into the separate contributions of quality change bias and new product bias.

Quality changes have occurred at a rapid rate for some products but not others. The CPI has done a better job capturing the effect of quality change for some products than others. The CPI has introduced some new products faster than others. Because the magnitude of quality change bias differs so much across product categories, any overall evaluation of the magnitude of quality change bias must be conducted "down in the trenches," taking individual categories of consumer expenditure, assessing quality change bias for each category, and then aggregating using appropriate weights.

Further complicating the analysis is that quality change bias, assessed at the level of individual products, appears to have changed significantly over time. For instance, important improvements in BLS methodology largely or entirely eliminated an upward bias in the CPI for new automobiles prior to the mid-1960s and a downward bias for apparel after the mid-1980s. Likewise, an important source of downward bias in the CPI rent index was eliminated in the late 1980s.[36]

Previous evaluations of quality change bias, e.g., Shapiro and Wilcox (1996c) and Lebow, Roberts, and Stockton (1994) have tended to take bias estimates from earlier research on particular products, e.g., consumer appliances or automobiles, apply that bias estimate with the weight of those products in the CPI, and assumes that in the rest of the CPI the rate of quality change is zero. We do not view that approach as likely to emerge with a neutral evaluation of the bias, simply because the evaluation that the rest of the CPI is unbiased represents an extreme one-sided answer to the question as to whether the components of the CPI subject to relatively little research are biased. They may be as likely to be subject to the average rate of bias of those components which have been subject to careful research as to no bias at all. In this section we evaluate the CPI component-by-component and extrapolate research on bias from one category to another when the categories seem related. Nevertheless, we attribute bias estimates of zero to a number of categories which seem quite dissimilar to those categories subject to intensive research, or where unmeasured quality change and new products have been relatively unimportant.

While the problem of bias due to quality change and new products can be largely separated from the other forms of bias considered above, this is not entirely possible. Evidence on quality change bias developed in other studies, for instance Gordon (1990), is based on an attempt to measure prices directly from sources independent of BLS price quotations, using such sources as mail order catalogues and *Consumer Reports*.[37] However, any differences between these independent indexes and the CPI for the same goods may reflect not just quality change and new product bias, but also traditional substitution bias (since the mix of products and models shifts faster in the alternative source than the CPI), outlet substitution bias (since alternative price quotes are often an average of market prices which adjusts for the changing mix of discount stores), and formula bias (since the alternative indexes are free from the formula bias problems discussed previously).[38]

CONCEPTUAL ISSUES

The difficulty created by quality change in existing products, and by the introduction of new products, is highlighted by returning to the definition of a cost of living index: a comparison in two time periods of the minimum expenditure required to achieve the same level of well-being. What does the "same level" mean when the models of a given product available in the second time period embody different quality attributes than in the first time period? And, an even more profound difficulty, what does the "same level" mean when entirely new products are introduced that were unavailable in the first time period?

A pervasive phenomenon called the "product cycle" is critical in assessing the issue of new product bias in the CPI and applies as well to new models of existing products. A typical new product is introduced at a relatively high price with sales at a low volume. Soon improvements in manufacturing techniques and increasing sales allow prices to be reduced and quality to be improved. For instance, the VCR was introduced in the late 1970s at a price of $1,000 with clumsy electromechanical controls; by the mid-1980s the price had fallen to $200 and controls were electronic, with extensive preprogramming capabilities. Later on in the product cycle, the product will mature and eventually will increase in price more rapidly than the average product of its class. The sequence is easily visualized as a "U"-shaped curve — the price of any given product relative to the consumer market basket starts high, then goes down, is flat for a while, and then goes back up. To the extent that the CPI overweights mature products and underweights new products, it will tend to have an upward bias. Some recent academic research, notably Berndt, Griliches, and Rosett (1993) and Berndt, Cockburn, and Griliches (1996), computes alternative price indexes with the mix of prescription drugs actually sold and the limited and older sample contained in the CPI, and this research attributes a significant upward bias to the CPI on the grounds of its lateness in introducing the mix of models and varieties actually sold.

An important criterion for the assessment of quality change and new product bias is the evolution of market shares for particular models and products. When a new model is introduced that is more expensive than an old model, but it gains market share, we can conclude that it was superior in quality to the old model by more than the differential in price between the two.

The same criterion helps us deal with outlet substitution bias. When consumers shift from traditional supermarkets to new, more expensive specialized food markets offering an improved selection or variety of produce, we can deduce that consumers are better off. The fact that Wal-Mart both charges lower prices and has become by far the largest retail chain over the past 15 years indicates that consumers do not consider the lower Wal-Mart prices to be offset by inferior service, as implicitly assumed by the CPI, but rather that consumers view Wal-Mart to offer a superior combination of prices and service to the previously available mix of outlets. The fact that convenience stores like 7-11 both charge higher prices and have gained market share indicates that consumers view convenience stores as providing a value of extra convenience that is worth more than the extra price that they charge. Many consumers shop at both Wal-Mart and convenience stores, paying both lower and higher prices on particular items than with the previous mix of stores, and the shift in market share suggests that the new mix is an improvement. The same evaluation can be made of restaurants, where consumers have shifted toward low-priced fast food outlets like McDonalds, medium-priced franchises like Olive Garden and Red Lobster, and in some urban areas, sophisticated high-priced restaurants specializing in Tuscan, Thai, and other ethnic food specialties. An important strand of academic research on such diverse products as medical imaging devices (Trajtenberg, 1990) and breakfast cereal (Hausman, 1996) attributes substantial value to increases in product variety. Thus, the "value of variety" is critically important in our assessment both of outlet substitution bias and, in this section, of quality change and new product bias.

BLS METHODOLOGY

Our discussion of quality change and new product bias begins with a review of the methods used by the CPI to handle quality changes in existing products and then turns to problems posed by new products. The BLS has five different methods to cope with a model change for an existing product.

- The "direct comparison" method treats all of the observed price change between the old model and the new model as a change in price and none as a change in quality. There is no necessary bias, because quality can decrease as well as increase. But in practice most goods tend to undergo steady improvement, and often a better model is introduced with no change in price, causing the quality change to be missed entirely.

- The "deletion" method makes no comparison at all between the prices of the old and new model. Instead, the weight attributable to this product is applied to the average price change of other products in the same commodity classification. To the extent that the deletion method is used, the CPI consists disproportionately of commodities of constant quality which may be further along in the product cycle.

- The "linking" method can be used if the new and old model are sold simultaneously. In this case the price differential between the two models at the time of introduction of the new model can be used as an estimate of the value of the quality differential between the two models. As indicated above, this can lead to an understatement of quality change if the new model gains market share. Also, a quality improvement in the new model can occur even if it costs less or the same as the old model, as in the case of the VCR where the price fell continuously while programming capability and reproduction quality improved.

The "cost estimation" method attempts to establish the cost of the extra attributes of the new model. Problems in practice with the costing method have been its infrequency of use, and the fact that it has been applied disproportionately in the case of automobiles relative to other products. This raises the possibility that there is a spurious upward "drift" in the relative price of other products relative to automobiles due to an uneven application of the costing method. An emerging source of upward bias is that products like automobiles are benefitting from the improved quality of materials like steel (which does not rust as it once did) and tires (which last many more miles). To the extent that some of these inputs to the auto production process are experiencing quality improvements of their own in excess of differences in cost, these will not be picked up by the BLS cost-based quality estimation procedure.

- Thus far, the CPI has introduced only in its apparel category an alternative methodology called the "hedonic regression method" for estimating the value of quality change. The hedonic approach can be viewed as an alternative method to manufacturers' cost estimates in making quality change adjustments. It assumes that the price of a product observed at a given time is a function of its quality characteristics, and it estimates the imputed prices of such characteristics by regressing the prices of different models of the product on their differing embodied quantities of characteristics. Thus the hedonic approach is less a new method than an alternative to cost estimates to be used when practical factors make it more suitable than the conventional method.

  By their very nature hedonic indexes require large amounts of data. Given the thousands of separate products that are produced in any modern industrial society, the need to collect a full cross-section of data on each product presents a substantial obstacle to the full-blown adoption of the hedonic technique. But in many cases the data already collected by CPI field agents can be used for hedonic regression analysis; this is already done in the case of apparel.

  Another possible objection is that it is impossible to construct a hedonic index in the timely fashion required by the CPI, with its orientation to producing within a few weeks an estimate of month-to-month price changes that can never be revised. But this ignores the fact that coefficients can be estimated on the basis of historical data, and these previously estimated coefficients can be used to evaluate quality change when a new model is introduced. This approach would be particularly suitable for product categories subject to a rapid succession of new model introductions, notably TV sets and personal computers.

This list of BLS methods reveals at least four potential sources of upward bias: the use of the direct comparison method that does not address the quality issue at all, the use of the deletion method that bases price change on models that are unchanged in quality and may be further along in the product cycle, the use of the linking method when quality improvements are greater than the price differential across models, and the use of the cost method which may miss quality improvements achieved by those firms which supply better materials and inputs to producers of final goods.

A potentially greater difficulty is that the CPI makes no attempt to create systematic estimates of the value of quality improvements which increase consumer welfare without raising the price of products. For instance, many consumer electronic products and household appliances have experienced a reduction in the incidence of repairs and in electricity use, and few if any of these improvements have been taken into account by the CPI. The increased longevity of automobiles (cited below), appliances, and other products introduces a similar source of bias.

NEW PRODUCT BIAS

We turn now to the issue of new product bias. There is no debate regarding the reality of the product cycle, and nobody debates the fact that the CPI introduces many products late, thus missing much of the price decline that typically happens in the first phase of the product cycle. An extreme example involves room air conditioners, which were widely sold in 1951, but not introduced into the CPI until 1964, 13 years later. More recently, the microwave oven was introduced into the CPI in 1978 and the VCR and personal computer in 1987, years after they were first sold in the marketplace. As an even more contemporaneous example, there are currently 36 million cellular phones in use in the United States, but as yet the CPI has no price index for cellular phones. Thus none of the benefit to consumers of being able to keep track more easily of children, spouses, or of aged parents has yet received any credit in our national measures of inflation, real output, or productivity. Even more recently, there are more than 40 million cellular phone subscribers in the U.S., but the cellular phone has yet to be introduced into the CPI.[39]

A second aspect of new product bias results from a narrow definition of a commodity. When a new product is finally introduced into the CPI, no comparison is made of the price and quality of the new product with the price and quality of an old product that performed the same function. For instance, people flock to rent videos, but the declining price of seeing a movie at home, as compared to going out to a theater, is not taken into account in the CPI. Similarly, the CPI missed the replacement of electric typewriters by electronic typewriters and then PCs with word-processing and spell-checking capability, or CD-ROM encyclopedias that cost far less than old-fashioned bound-book versions and eliminate many trips to the library. Inevitably, however, many new products embody genuinely new characteristics that have no previous counterpart. Electronic mail that provides a new set of bonds and communication between parents and their children who are off at college and cellular telephones that make possible virtually continuous contact with a sick child or aged parent are but two examples.

This discussion of new products leads inevitably to deeper questions about changes in the standard of living of the average American. Positive changes made possible by consumer electronics need to be weighed against increasing crime, pollution, and other "bads." We return to these issues in Section VII below.

QUALITY CHANGE AND NEW PRODUCT BIAS BY PRODUCT CATEGORY

Because quality change bias differs in magnitude, direction, and timing across product categories, the only way to narrow the range of uncertainty of the magnitude of quality change bias is to examine the available evidence, category by category. Table 2 is designed to provide a guide to this assessment. The left-hand column lists each major product category within the CPI next to its "relative importance," i.e., percentage weight, in December, 1995. In this section we review the available evidence on bias related to quality change and new products, by category.

In some categories there is little if any published evidence that allows us to reach a determination. However, we do not follow previous research by assuming that in these categories the overall bias due to quality change and new products is necessarily zero. Instead, we discuss the likely direction of bias in the context of the definition of a cost of living index: a comparison in two time periods of the minimum expenditure required to achieve the same level of well-being.

1. **Food and beverages**. The most dramatic evidence of upward bias in the

food and beverages category was produced by Reinsdorf (1993), who found during the 1980-90 period an annual rate of change of average price paid for 50 narrowly defined commodities that was fully 2.0 percent per annum slower than the CPI for the same product categories. While Reinsdorf thought at the time that this difference reflected outlet substitution bias, in fact he later concluded that the difference represented a mix of formula bias and outlet substitution bias. Whatever the interpretation of Reinsdorf's study, it does not represent evidence on quality change, since his commodities were chosen to be identical to those priced in the CPI.

Besides his study, there is little if any published evidence on the food category, other than Hausman's (1996) attempt to establish the value for the introduction of a new variety of breakfast cereal. Perhaps more important than new varieties of packaged goods has been a wave of technological improvements that has greatly increased the variety of fresh fruits and vegetables available in the typical supermarket during the winter months, and a trend toward more services provided in supermarkets, eliminating the need to travel to small specialty shops, especially fresh fish markets and deli counters preparing fresh-cooked food. How much would a consumer pay to have the privilege of choosing from the variety of items available in today's supermarket instead of being constrained to the much more limited variety available 30 years ago? A conservative estimate of the value of extra variety and convenience might be 10 percent for food consumed at home other than produce, 20 percent for produce where the increased variety in winter (as well as summer farmers' markets) has been so notable, and 5 percent for alcoholic beverages where imported beer, microbreweries, and a greatly improved distribution of imported wines from all over the world have improved the standard of living. Increased variety and convenience in food away from home, in every price category from McDonalds to luxury restaurants (as discussed above), can also be credited with a 10 percent premium. The annual rates of bias in Table 2 are calculated by converting these assumed premia to annual geometric growth rates over the past 30 years.

2.   **Housing.** By far the largest single weight in the CPI is given to the housing component, and within that to shelter. The shelter component shifted to a rental equivalence approach in 1983, and the CPI-U-X1 index represents an attempt to provide a consistent treatment of housing using the rental equivalence concept back to 1967. The annual rate of change of the CPI shelter index exceeds that of the CPI residential rent index by 2.33 percent per annum from 1967 to 1983, and correspondingly the annual rate of change of the official CPI-U exceeds that of CPI-U-X1 by 0.52 percent per annum over the same interval.[40] The BLS has also shifted methodology in 1995 to correct

formula bias and in 1988 to correct an "aging bias" that resulted from pricing in successive periods housing units that were becoming progressively older. Randolph (1988) estimates this pre-1988 aging bias at 0.3 percent per annum, a concept that represents the effect of depreciation net of any maintenance and renovation expenditures.

First, we register our skepticism that the Randolph aging bias should be considered a bias in its entirety. Older units rent for less than new units for two reasons. First, they may physically deteriorate by more than is offset by repairs and maintenance. But, second, they may lose value as newer units come on the market containing amenities such as central air conditioning. Such economic obsolescence does not represent a decline in the quality of the service provided by the older apartments, but rather represents the result of the fact that the income elasticity of demand for shelter amenities is positive, and people expect higher quality in apartments and houses as the nation's per capita income increases. An exact analogy is the introduction of the jet plane, discussed in detail by Gordon (1990). The quality of the ride on a propellor-driven DC-7 did not decline when the pure-jet DC-8 was introduced in 1958. Rather, consumers valued the ride on the jet plane so highly that the demand for flights on the DC-7 vanished. The DC-7 was scrapped prematurely, within five to ten years after the introduction of the jets. Consumers gained the entire surplus from the transition from propellor to jet planes for long-distance air travel, and the declining rents of older apartments represent a less dramatic example of the same phenomenon.

Thus far there has been little investigation into quality change in the apartments included in the CPI rent survey. The "CPI methods hold most housing quality constant by measuring rent changes longitudinally for a cross-section of housing units" (Randolph, 1988, p. 359). That is, rent changes on a given unit are followed through time, and alternative units are rotated in, with the overlap handled by deletion. If there is a general tendency for more recently constructed units to have more and better appliances, central air conditioning, and other amenities that were not present in previous decades, there is the possibility of an upward bias in the CPI rental index if consumers value these amenities at more than their extra cost. The continuous movement of households to newer apartment complexes in suburbs and in the Sunbelt may be part of a process by which housing quality steadily improves. The "market share" test suggests that many households prefer new Sunbelt apartments to older types of apartment in central cities in the north central and northeastern states.

The U. S. Census Current Housing Reports report median monthly rent of all rental occupied units. The ratio for 1993 to 1976 is 2.92 ($487/$167). The CPI rental index ratio (not adjusted for formula or aging bias) for the same years is 2.46. The implied annual difference in growth rates for the CPI is -1.00 percent per year. An alternative comparison for 1973-88 yields a difference of -1.10 percent per year.[41]

While only limited data are available on the quality of rental units, there is evidence that rental units have improved in quality at approximately the pace of owner-occupied units, for which more data are available. Two key measures have persuaded us of the comparability of rental and owner units (the CPI uses rent indexes for both the rental and owner-occupied segments of housing, so these findings support the CPI choice). First, between 1970 and 1993 the mean number of rooms increased by 9.7 percent in all occupied units (of which about 1/3 were rental units), while the mean number of rooms in rental units increased by a similar 7.8 percent. Perhaps more important, the number of rooms per person increased by 30.2 percent in all units and 27.0 percent for rental units.[42] This set of comparisons supports the view that quality has improved at approximately the same rate in rental and owner-occupied units, and that we can use some of the available data on the totality of occupied units to reach a judgment on the extent of quality change.

While the best data are available for newly constructed units, some important data are available for the entire stock of existing units. For the entire stock of existing rental units alone, the mean number of bathrooms increased by 23.3 percent between 1970 and 1993. And for the entire stock of all units, the fraction containing central air conditioning increased from 10.8 to 41.7 percent.

Further indication of the change in quality standards is indicated by changing characteristics of new single-family houses completed in 1993 compared to 1976: median square feet increased by 30 percent, bathrooms from 2.0 to 2.4, percentage with central air conditioning from 49 to 78, percentage with one or more fireplaces from 45 to 63, and percentage with a garage from 72 to 84.[43]

We have already determined that between 1976 and 1993 the average rent paid in the U.S. increased 1.0 percent faster than the CPI rent increase. To conclude that the CPI is unbiased, we would have to determine that the quality of the average rental unit increased by 1.0 percent per year over that period, or 18 percent over the entire period. From the evidence we have examined, we believe that 20 percent is a low-end estimate of the increase in the average size of apartments, which would support the conclusion that the average rent per square foot has increased no faster than the CPI. But also, we find convincing evidence that the average quality of apartments per square foot has increased as well. The transition to central air conditioning proceeded at a rapid rate during the past two decades. Other amenities were added which increased the average quality of apartments, particularly swimming pools, health clubs, on-site free parking, and climate (since the mix of apartments shifted toward southern climates which reduced the impact of winter weather on tenants, particularly older tenants).

For the period since 1970 we find it plausible that the CPI accurately measures rent per square foot of apartment space, but its measure of shelter rent is upward biased by neglecting the increase in the quality of apartments per square foot. It is entirely natural that an increase in per-capita income would spill over into increased quality of housing, because there is no reason why housing size and quality should have an income elasticity of zero. The improved quality of appliances documented by Gordon (1990) applies to the shelter sector, since most apartments are now provided with relatively recent refrigerators, stoves or oven/cooktop combinations, dishwashers, and garbage disposals. The rental equivalent of these appliances must be substantial and they have been included in both new and older apartments mainly since 1955-60. A conservative estimate is that the total increase in apartment quality per square foot, including the rental value of all appliances, central air conditioning, and improved bathroom plumbing, and other amenities, amounts to 10 percent over the past 40 years, or 0.25 percent a year. Accordingly, Table 2 records an upward bias in the CPI of 0.25 percent per year for the shelter component, and this well may be an understatement.

For years before 1973, there is some evidence that the CPI rent index may be biased downward by more than can be explained by changes in quality. For instance, average annual rental expenditures for working class families in the CES increased from $444 in 1950 to $1803 in 1973, a ratio of 4.06, while the equivalent ratio for the unadjusted CPI rent index is only 1.93. This translates into a slower annual growth rate of the CPI of -3.24 percent per year. The same comparison for 1918 to 1950 yields an annual difference of -2.82 percent per year.[44] Without a measure of annual quality change per year, we cannot make a judgment on the magnitude of the bias, but the possibility that the CPI rental index incorporates a substantial downward bias prior to 1973 may help to explain the "Nordhaus thought experiment problem" identified above, namely that backward extrapolation of substantial CPI bias for a century or more yields implausibly low levels of the standard of living during the 19th century. Further judgment on this issue must await the development of quantitative measures of the change in apartment quality between 1918 and 1973, although we note that there has obviously been a major improvement in quality since 1918, when only 36 percent of apartments had bathrooms and only 61 percent had inside water closets (Brown, 1994, Table 3.6A).

Turning now to other components of housing expenditure, there is no reason to suppose that the CPI has measured the price of fuel or electricity inaccurately, since these commodities are homogeneous and among the easiest to measure of any goods or services. However, when we think of why people prefer to live in the modern age and would (in most cases) not willingly choose to go back to the conditions of 70 years ago, the change in the nature of household heating fuel surely enters the calculation. In 1918, 80 percent of American homes were heated with coal and wood, which had to be stored and carried, and produced a fire that had to be tended, used a stove that had to be cleaned, and smoke that polluted the air.[45] Because the transition from coal and wood heat to other sources of fuel had been largely completed by the early 1970s, we do not include this major improvement in the quality of life as a source of recent bias in the CPI.

The rest of the weight in the CPI on housing is applied to a myriad of expenditures, each having a relatively small weight, including telephone service, refuse collection, cable TV, curtains, furniture, bedding, video and audio products, major household appliances, and a large number of miscellaneous items. Most of the CPI weight on "other utilities" is applied to local and long distance telephone service and cable television. Even if the CPI correctly tracked the prices of each of these items, quality change would be missed. There has been continuous improvement in the quality of telephone service (e.g., reduction of static and improvement in clarity), improved convenience (credit card pay phones, itemized billing), and a great increase in picture quality and consumer choice achieved by cable television viewed as a new product. The fact that more than 60 percent of American households are now wired for cable TV, despite substantial monthly program fees, suggests that the development of cable TV has created a product yielding substantial consumer surplus. We conservatively estimate the quality bias connected with this category as 10 percent per decade, or 1.00 percent per year.[46]

The appliance and radio-TV category has been subject to more extensive research than any other category of consumer spending. Over the full period 1947-83 Gordon's detailed study (1990, p. 552), based on model-by-model comparisons from *Consumer Reports*, found an upward bias in the PCE deflator (which in turn is based on the CPI) of 3.22 percent per year for appliances and 5.94 percent for radio-TV. For the 1973-83 subperiod, the respective rates are 2.83 percent and 4.69 percent. These rates are applied in the CPI to a remarkably small fraction of consumption, just 0.8 percent according to Table 2. Consumer electronics alone, i.e., excluding electric appliances, recorded annual factory sales (i.e., net of retail markups) of $55.9 billion in 1994, which amounted to 1.25 percent of nominal personal consumption expenditures.[47] The 1995 share in PCE of final sales to consumers of audio and video equipment, including TV sets and VCRs, was also 1.25 percent, appliances contributed an additional 0.55 percent and personal computers an additional 0.33 percent, for a total weight in PCE of 2.13 percent, well over double the weight of the same products in the CPI.[48]

This small slice of personal consumption is the source of the largest annual rate of bias, with the possible exception of medical care. Our overall estimate of bias, based on Gordon's research, incorporates both quality change bias and also new product bias, since his estimates of the overall bias take account of the fact that the quality-adjusted price of the VCR was declining at 30-40 percent per year in the early 1980s, prior to the introduction of this product into the CPI in 1987. Similarly, in recent years the price of personal computers purchased by consumers has been declining by at least 25 percent per year, but this has no impact at all, because home purchases of PCs were negligible in the CPI base period of 1982-84.

Our estimate of overall bias in this sector is 3.0 percent for appliances, 4.0 percent for radio-TV, including VCRs and camcorders, and 15 percent per year for personal computers.[49] Applying respective current nominal weights of 0.8 percent for appliances, 1.0 percent for consumer electronics, and 0.4 percent for personal computers, this category contributes an annual rate of quality change and new product bias of 0.10 percent per year to the total CPI. The figure entered into Table 2 for this category is a weighted average of the bias estimate, but the bias figure for the total CPI is based on weights corresponding to current nominal expenditures, not the CPI weights displayed in Table 2. Also, prior to 1994 the bias figure is based only on appliances and radio-TV, since personal computers did not emerge as a significant product until that date.

Regarding housefurnishings other than appliances and video-audio products, there is no available research to provide guidance. The available range of furniture, draperies, etc., allows consumers to substitute among products, fabrics, and outlets along dimensions that are not captured by the CPI. There have been many new products in this area, including furniture and fabrics that are much less susceptible to damage by stains and children's accidents than was previously possible. This category also includes soap and cleaning products, where substantial progress has been made. We view a bias rate of 0.33 percent per year, or 10 percent over the past 30 years, as conservative.

3. **Apparel**. It is often assumed that there has been no quality change in apparel. But new apparel products are constantly introduced that improve consumer welfare, including denim jeans and shorts, advanced varieties of running shoes, iron-free synthetic fabrics, and lightweight but water-resistant raingear. Despite this, apparel is the other major area where the CPI is thought to have incorporated a downward bias. One source of downward bias occurred when the CPI price quotations followed the decline in price of an old model placed on sale, and then (using the deletion technique) made the transition to a new model without accurately recording the corresponding increase in price.

Reforms in the CPI in the mid-to-late 1980s eliminated this source of downward bias and shifted to the hedonic price technique for some quality adjustments within the apparel component.[50]

The CPI apparel index is relatively easy to assess by accumulating outside evidence from such sources as mail-order catalogues. While style changes in fashion goods are frequent, quality changes in utilitarian apparel products purchased by average urban consumers are sufficiently infrequent to allow careful price comparisons across identical models from mail-order catalogues. By limiting itself to a month-to-month measurement framework, without cross-checks based on yearly or decadal comparisons, the CPI is vulnerable to persistent drift that emerges from measurement flaws such as the treatment of products on sale, as discussed above.

In a new project Gordon (1996) has compiled an apparel price index from the Sears catalogue based on thousands of year-by-year comparisons of identical apparel items over the intervals 1965-93.[51] The ratio of the CPI relative to the Sears apparel index rose at an annual rate of +1.92 percent per year during 1985-93.[52] The rapid rate of increase of the CPI apparel index after 1985 relative to Sears is surprising, because Sears in those years was losing market share to Wal-Mart and other discounters. Thus there is reason to think that the Sears catalogue index might overstate the increase in true apparel prices faced by the average American consumer. Nevertheless, we shall take the conservative approach of cutting the implied bias rate from +1.92 percent suggested by the Sears index to a smaller 1.0 percent bias rate.

4. Transportation. The transportation component of the CPI consists of a wide variety of heterogeneous goods, including new vehicles, used vehicles, motor fuel, vehicle repairs, auto insurance and registration, and public transportation, mainly airline fares.

The most important questions to be addressed in the transportation sector are the valuation of mandated safety and anti-pollution devices, and the treatment of used cars relative to new cars. As documented by Gordon (1990, p. 364) for the period 1947-83, the actual price of new cars increased much faster than the CPI for new cars, and after 1967 almost none of this relative increase could be explained by increases in the dimensions included in the traditional hedonic regression equations for new cars. The key ratios of 1983 to 1967 prices were that actual prices had increased by a ratio of 289.9, the CPI for autos had increased by a ratio of 202.6, and that the difference had been more than explained by the contribution of CPI adjustments for safety and environmental quality and Gordon's adjustments for fuel economy.[53] The resulting upward bias in the CPI relative to Gordon's final auto index is 0.44 per year from 1967 to 1983.

However, Gordon accepted the CPI's treatment of anti-pollution devices as a quality improvement rather than a price increase. We are persuaded that mandated anti-pollution devices are analogous to an indirect tax. Gasoline taxes may be used to provide a benefit in the form of better highways, but a tax increase is treated correctly by the CPI as an increase in the cost of living. Anti-pollution devices provide a benefit in the form of cleaner air, but by analogy to taxes should be treated as an increase in the price of the car. Using the detailed information given by Gordon, we can calculate an alternative to his index that converts the CPI adjustment for anti-pollution devices from a quality change to a price change, and this results in the finding that the CPI for new cars was downward biased during 1947-83 by 0.94 percent per year. We do not make a similar adjustment for the value of quality change taking the form of safety devices such as seat belts and crash-resistant bumpers, since our feeling is that consumers see the connection between their own safety and the devices more directly than they do between anti-pollution devices and air quality. Subsequently we will adjust the 0.94 percent downward bias for an offsetting increase in automobile durability.

What has happened since 1983, the terminal year of Gordon's study? Berry, Kortum, and Pakes (1996) show that emission control standards for automobiles became markedly tighter in two stages, 1975 and 1979-81, but did not change thereafter through the conclusion of their study in 1990. They also develop a fuel efficiency index that adjusts for changes in the horsepower and weight of cars; this rises by 67 percent between 1972 and 1983 and then drifts down by 13 percent by 1990. An alternative study of fuel economy (Sykuta, 1996) extends the data to 1994 and concludes that "new car fuel efficiency reached a plateau by 1986 and has not since changed by more than 1 percent in any direction" (p. 12). He attributes the absence of a decline in fuel economy in response to lower fuel prices to the high cost of "switching back to older, less efficient designs and technologies." Thus it appears that neither changes in anti-pollution equipment nor in fuel economy have been important potential factors in creating a bias in the new car CPI since the mid-1980s.

However, neither Gordon's study nor the CPI have taken into account the increased service lifetime of the typical new car. The average age of automobiles in use increased at an annual rate of 2.1 percent per year during 1970-83, part of the period covered by the Gordon study, and at 1.3 percent per year during 1983-93.[54] The CPI should be pricing automobiles on a rental equivalent basis, parallel to their treatment of housing. If the useful life of a car is improved by technological change that raises quality, reduces maintenance requirements, and minimizes rusting and corrosion, then consumers benefit. The cumulative increase in the useful life of a car from 1970 to 1993 amounted to 48 percent. Consider an automobile costing $10,000 with a life of 10.0

years; this is equivalent to an annual cost of $1,000 per year. Now consider the same car with a life extended by 48 percent to 14.8 years; its annual cost has been correspondingly reduced to $676.

The reduction in automobile depreciation is only part of the user cost of owning a car. Many of the additional elements of cost, e.g., insurance and repairs, are priced separately by the CPI in the major category "Other Private Transportation," where we impute no bias at all. The remaining component of user cost, in addition to depreciation, is real interest expense. Balancing alternative methods of paying for cars, including cash, installment finance, and leasing, we think that 10 percent is a reasonable estimate of the real interest cost. The extension of automobile longevity has reduced user cost from roughly 20 percent per year (consisting of a 10 percent real interest cost plus 10 percent depreciation rate) to 16.7 percent (the same real interest cost plus a 6.7 percent depreciation rate), for an overall reduction in user cost of 16.7 percent, or a geometric rate of -0.79 percent per year over the period 1970-93.

Since the rate of increase of average age slowed after 1983, we distribute this effect accordingly, as contributing to an upward bias in the CPI at a rate of 0.95 percent per year during 1970-83 and 0.59 percent per year after 1983. For the 1970-83 period, we add the upward bias in the true price of cars due to increasing durability of 0.95 percent per year to our previous estimate of a downward bias of 0.94 percent per year, exactly cancelling out and yielding a net bias for zero. For the subsequent post-1983 period, we found no other reason to suppose the CPI is biased in either direction, so the durability adjustment is converted to a net upward bias of 0.59 percent per year.

In assessing these calculations, we recognize that some fraction of the durability effect may not represent a pure quality change, but rather may reflect other factors, such as an increased relative price of cars that induces users to hold onto cars longer, or an improved quality of highways. This might suggest that our durability adjustment is too large. However, an offsetting error may be more important and may represent an important source of quality improvement that is not taken into account in the CPI or in our adjustments — namely, the marked decrease in the incident of defects on both imported and domestic new cars, as measured by the J. D. Power survey and other evidence. This additional source of quality improvement, which we have not taken into account, suggests that our estimate of the CPI bias for new cars is probably conservative.

The CPI index for used cars has long been known to be upward biased, simply because no quality adjustments were applied to this category at all. The upward bias over the period 1967-87 is very large, amounting to 2.44 percent per year, if we take the difference in the growth rate between the new car and used car index to represent a measure of the bias.[55] Adding this to the new car upward bias of zero, we arrive at a total bias for used cars for 1967-87 of 2.44 percent per year. For the period since 1987 we apply the CPI durability bias to used cars as well.

Regarding other components of the transportation category, we regard motor fuel as homogeneous and easy to measure. However, numerous improvements in fuels and related products have contributed both to cleaner air and improvements in autos, such as increased durability. While the cleaner air is valuable in its own right (see Section VII), we treat the mandate for cleaner gasolines like an indirect tax, not quality change per se. The improvements to autos are counted there, but must be understood to result in part from improvements in fuels, lubricants, etc. The CPI treats full-service and self-service fuel as two different commodities, as in the case of full-service department stores and no-frills discount stores. The shift in market share from full-service to self-service motor fuel provides evidence of a type of outlet substitution bias, which we do not count here as quality change bias. For the past decade, when the transition to self-service was largely complete, we attribute a small upward bias of 0.25 percent per year to the CPI for ignoring the increased convenience and time-saving contribution of automatic credit-card readers built into gasoline pumps.[56]

"Other private transportation" expenditures, an important CPI category, consist primarily of automobile maintenance and repair and automobile insurance. We are not aware of any evidence of price index bias involving these areas and thus assign a zero bias. However, in the public transportation category, which is dominated by airline travel, it is well documented that prior to 1982 the CPI incorporated a substantial upward bias due to a failure to take discount fares into account. We take our estimate of this bias from Baily-Gordon (1988, p. 416) and multiply it by the weight (about 2/3) of airline fares in the public transportation category.

5. Medical Care. The medical care category may be the location of substantial quality change bias at a rate as rapid or more rapid than in appliances and radio-TV products, but its weight in the CPI is much greater. That weight is controversial in itself, since the 7.4 percent weight is based only on out-of-pocket expenses by consumers and does not include expenses paid for medicare, medicaid, or by employer-financed payroll deductions. Since one of the main uses of the CPI is to convert indexes of real income, compensation, and wages into "real terms," the current weight is wrong. Changes in medical care prices or technology should influence the CPI with the same weights that are relevant for total income and compensation, that is, they should include the total medical care bill, which in National Income and Product Accounts version of consumption amounts to 16 percent, not the much smaller 7.3 percent weight in the CPI.

The CPI weight of 7.4 percent is applied to three primary categories — drugs, professional medical services (i.e., doctors and nurses), and hospitals. There has been substantial recent research on prescription drugs. For instance, Berndt, Cockburn, and Griliches (1996) have studied prices of anti-depressant drugs. They find a substantial difference between an index based on BLS methods, which rises during 1993-96 at 4.6 percent per annum, and an alternative index based on their preferred methodology which rises at 1.1 percent per year. This alternative index uses an alternative (Divisia) weighting scheme, introduces new items much more promptly, and treats generic drugs as fully equivalent to proprietary brand-name drugs. In July 1995, the CPI shifted its treatment of generics, so that any decline in price when generic equivalent drugs become available is taken fully into account as a price change rather than being treated as a different good and hence "linked out" of the index. Based on the Berndt et al. research, and related research by Griliches and Cockburn (1994), we conclude that prior to 1995 there was a 3.0 percent annual bias in the CPI for prescription pharmaceuticals. The new CPI treatment of generic drugs after July 1995 reduces this annual rate of bias from 3.0 to 2.0 percent, and the remaining bias can be attributed (based on the previously cited research) to the late introduction of particular drugs into the CPI and the failure to attribute a positive value to newly introduced drugs that gain market share and thus appear to add value for consumers.

The major weight of the CPI medical care component is applied to medical care services, e.g., physician fees, and hospital costs. No attempt is made in the CPI to value health care "outcomes" as contrasted to "inputs." A hybrid approach is taken by the Producer Price Index (PPI), which also prices inputs but with different weights and increases by roughly 2.0 percent per year more slowly than the CPI in both the doctor and hospital category in the recent past (1995-96). Thus government indexes already provide important evidence that the CPI is upward biased by at least 2.0 percent per year, but that ignores many changes in medical care practice and technology that suggest a higher rate of bias. Cutler et al. (1996, Table 1) contrast input price indexes for the cost of heart attack treatment with alternative "outcome" indexes that take account of the cost of achieving a given increase in life expectancy. The authors contrast an "input" index of the type currently compiled by the CPI, which rises by 3.3 percent per year over 1983-94, with a final outcomes index that takes into account a conservative valuation for the extension of life expectancy attributable to new heart attack treatments and declines by 1.1 percent a year, for a net bias of 4.4 percent per year. Shapiro and Wilcox study cataract surgery for the period 1969 and 1993. Their "protypical" index that duplicates CPI methods increases by a factor of 9 while their preferred alternative index increases by a factor of 3, implying an annual rate of upward bias of 4.57 percent. The closeness in the Cutler et al. and Shapiro-Wilcox studies of quite different medical procedures is striking. In view of the fact that the CPI has been rising relative to the PPI for medical care (taking the input rather than the outcomes approach) by 2 percent per year in 1995-96, the rate of upward bias that we have assigned to the medical care category, 3.0 percent per year, is probably conservative. There is probably additional quality change taking into account the wide variety of new diagnostic and test equipment, the reduction of pain of routine procedures, the shortening of hospital stays, and also the quality of hospital rooms.

This new research by Cutler and others opens up the potential for a major improvement in our understanding of the economics of medical care. This category should receive a substantial component of the CPI's future research investment, and we strongly endorse a move in the CPI away from the pricing of health care inputs to an attempt to price medical care outcomes.[57]

6.   Entertainment. The entertainment category is divided roughly equally between commodities and services. Commodities consist of newspapers, magazines, sporting equipment, and toys. We assume that there is no bias in newspapers and magazines (although electronic news services provide convenience and timeliness to some) but that sporting equipment and toys are subject to a somewhat smaller bias than Gordon found for appliances, namely 2.0 percent per year as contrasted to 3.0 percent for appliances. This may represent an average of the rate of bias in electronic toys, e.g., Nintendo games, which may be close to the 15 percent rate we have applied to personal computers, and a bias rate of zero for other toys, including stuffed animals and non-electronic board games. Entertainment services consist of club memberships, admission fees, and lesson fees. There has undoubtedly been an improvement in the comfort of attending sports events, with domed stadiums and more comfortable seats, but we have not assigned any bias to the CPI measure of entertainment services prices.

7.   Other Goods and Services. While purchases of such products as cigarettes, toiletries, and cosmetics may have been subject to outlet substitution bias, there is no reason to think that quality change has been missed or that new product bias has been important. However, this category includes a small weight for small personal care appliances, e.g., hair dryers, and it is reasonable to suppose that these items are subject to the same magnitude of bias as large appliances, i.e., 3.0 percent per year. Much of the rest of the weight in the "other" category consists of school books and fees, primarily college tuition. However, about one-tenth of the weight in this category consists of personal financial services, which have been subject to rapid technological change, particularly with the widespread diffusion of ATM machines and all-in-one cash-management accounts. Taking a conservative 2.0 percent estimate of personal financial services and applying that to one-tenth of this category yields our 0.2 percent annual rate of bias.

CONCLUSION ON QUALITY CHANGE BIAS

Our final estimate of quality change bias, taking the weights and bias rates in Table 2, aggregates to approximately 0.6 percent per year. This is slightly higher than the rate of 0.5 percent per year for the combined categories of quality change and new product bias estimated in our interim report or 0.35 percent in Shapiro and Wilcox (1996c). Our higher estimate results from a much more extensive examination of the existing literature and consideration of factors that affect each of the 27 separate categories included in Table 2.

Table 2
Relative Importance of Components in the CPI-U, U.S. City Average, December 1995, and Estimates of Quality Change and New Product Bias for Selected Time Intervals

Major and Selected Minor Components	Relative Importance in Percent	Estimated Quality Change Bias at Annual Rate for Selected Time Intervals	
1. Food and beverages	17.332		
Food at home other than produce	8.543	0.30 (1967-96)	
Fresh fruits and vegetables	1.337	0.60 (1967-96)	
Food away from home	5.886	0.30 (1967-96)	
Alcoholic beverages	1.566	0.15 (1967-96)	
2. Housing	41.346		
Shelter	28.289	0.25 (1976-96)	
Fuels	3.792	0.00	
Other Utilities, incl. telephone	3.222	1.00	
Appliances incl. electronic	0.806	3.6[a] (1973-94)	5.6[a] (1994-96)
Other housefurnishings	2.639	0.30	
Housekeeping supplies	1.116	0.00	

(cont.)

Major and Selected Minor Components	Relative Importance in Percent	Estimated Quality Change Bias at annual rate for Selected Time Intervals		
Housekeeping services	1.482	0.00		
3. Apparel and upkeep	5.516	-0.95 (1965-85)	1.00 (1985-96)	
4. Transportation	16.953			
New vehicles	5.027	0.00 (1970-83)	0.59 (1983-96)	
Used Cars	1.342	2.44 (1967-87)	1.59 (1987-96)	
Motor Fuel	2.908	0.0[b] (1974-84)	0.25[b] (1984-96)	
Other Private Transportation	6.153	0.00		
Public Transportation	1.523	2.66 (1972-77)	4.60 (1977-82)	0.00 (1982-96)
5. Medical Care	7.362			
Prescription drugs	0.891	3.00 (1970-95)	2.00 (1995-96)	
Nonprescription drugs and medical supplies	0.391	1.00		
Professional medical services	3.465	3.00		
Hospital and related services	2.257	3.00		
Health insurance	0.358	0.00		
6. Entertainment	4.367			
Commodities	1.975	2.00		
Services	2.392	0.00		
7. Other Goods and Services	7.123			
Tobacco, smoking products	1.610	0.00		
Personal care	1.170	0.90		
Personal and educational expenses	4.342	0.20		
Total	100.000	0.612 (for 1996)		

Notes: [a] Applied to the weight of this category in 1995 annual nominal personal consumption expenditures, 2.13 percent, as contrasted to the December 1995 CPI relative importance of 0.8 percent.

[b]See text.

Has quality change bias increased or decreased? Table 2 provides some insights to that issue. To take the specific example of 1980, we can aggregate the rates of bias given in Table 2 and come up with an upward CPI bias due to quality change and new products of 0.488 percent per year, compared to 0.613 for 1996. The main differences come from the reversal of the previous downward bias for apparel and the increased upward bias in the appliance/radio/ TV component due to the growing role of personal computers. Partially offsetting these sources of increased upward bias are reductions in the extent of upward bias in used cars, airline fares, and prescription drugs.

VI. Estimates of Biases by Type and in Total

The CPI is not a cost of living index, but rather a fixed weight index, implemented by means of a modified Laspeyres formula. This creates an immediate conflict between the objectives of the CPI and many of the purposes for which it is intended. For example, the CPI is used to index private contracts, tax brackets, and government transfer programs, such as Social Security, in order to compensate beneficiaries for changes in the cost of living. A fixed weight index exaggerates the effect of price changes on the cost of living, because it fails to allow for substitutions that enable consumers to avoid the full impact.

The assessment of biases in the CPI requires a cost of living index as a point of reference. An approximation to a cost of living index can be generated by combining the results of research on different types of biases in the CPI. The purpose of this section is to summarize this research and assess the importance of these biases in the CPI. Our estimates depend primarily on studies produced prior to the convening of our Commission, many of them by the BLS.

Our Interim Report of September 15, 1995, presented initial estimates of biases in the CPI. We estimated that the overall bias had been 1.5 percentage points per annum in recent years, but changes in the CPI methodology then in prospect from BLS would eliminate as much as 0.5 percentage point per annum of this bias, reducing the bias going forward to 1.0 percentage point per annum. We have now revised our estimates to reflect changes in the CPI announced by BLS on March 29, 1996, and new estimates of the impact of biases due to the introduction of new products and changes in the quality of existing products. The BLS has eliminated some of this bias totaling 0.24 percentage point per year, raising our estimate of the bias going forward by one-quarter of one percentage point. In addition, we have revised our estimates of new products/quality change bias upward by 0.10 percentage point per year.[58]

In assessing biases in the CPI it is essential to separate two types of substitution bias. First, BLS uses a fixed weight index based on the modified Laspeyres formula to combine price indexes for 207 items for 44 areas into a national CPI. The weights are derived from the Consumer Expenditure Survey (CES) and reflect surveys of individual households. We refer to the substitution bias at this level as Upper Level Substitution Bias. This bias is measured as the difference between the modified Laspeyres formula used by BLS and a Tornqvist index, which is (approximately) free of substitution bias.[59] Most estimates cluster around 0.2 to 0.25, including numerous estimates from BLS. The latest estimates available to the Commission reflecting just produced unpublished corrections of previous research by BLS show an average bias over the period 1988-1995 of about 0.15 percentage point per year. While we have not had time to analyze these new results, to be conservative, we adopt this figure.

The second type of substitution bias results from combining price observations for approximately 71,000 goods and services and information on prices for housing components of the CPI into indexes for the 207 items and 44 areas. We refer to the substitution bias at this level as Lower Level Substitution Bias. The prices to be collected are selected by probability sampling. The probabilities are derived from the CES and the Point-of-Purchase Survey (POPS) of retail establishments and are intended to reflect the share of items and areas in consumer expenditures in the base period.

Beginning in 1978 BLS introduced a sample rotation procedure in the estimation of price indexes within each item and area category. At the same time prices were combined in a way that reflected the modified Laspeyres index formula.[60] These two changes had the effect of introducing considerable Lower Level Substitution Bias, a fact discovered by Reinsdorf (1993) after a lapse of fifteen years.[61] This issue has been intensively studied by BLS and steps have been taken to deal with it, beginning in January 1995.[62]

For data from the CPI covering the thirty-month period from June 1992 to December 1994, Moulton and Smedley (1995) have estimated that the difference between the modified Laspeyres formula used at the lower level of aggregation by BLS and a weighted geometric mean formula for non-shelter components of the CPI to be 0.49 percentage point per annum. This difference is an estimate of the bias of the Laspeyres formula, since Shapiro and Wilcox (1996) have shown that the geometric mean provides an unbiased estimate of the underlying cost of living index. Armknecht, Moulton, and Stewart (1995) have estimated the bias for owners' equivalent rent to be 0.50 percentage point per annum.[63] BLS is currently testing the feasibility of producing indexes based on this methodology for price data beginning in 1990. Substitution of the weighted geometric mean formula for the modified Laspeyres formula at the lower level of aggregation is an important step in the direction of a cost of living index.

In January 1995 the BLS introduced an improved method for the imputation of price changes for food at home, owners' equivalent rent, and prescription drugs. These changes are described by Armknecht, Moulton, and Stewart (1995). For food at home items the changes included the introduction of a procedure called "seasoning." The seasoning period is the time to obtain the data needed to weight each new sample observation before introducing it into the index. This period was lengthened to three months for food at home items, breaking the link between the weights for these items and prices eventually used in the CPI.

On March 29, 1996, the BLS announced that the seasoning procedure would be extended to all non-shelter items, effective with the CPI for June 1996.[64] The announcement pointed out that residential rent and owners' equivalent rent were no longer subject to the bias associated with sample rotation procedures, as a consequence of the changes introduced in January 1995. In addition, the BLS stated that (with rare exceptions) the weight for a substitution item would be kept constant throughout the life of the item. BLS estimated the reduction in bias due to the January 1995 changes to be 0.14 percentage point per annum, while the 1996 changes for the non-shelter items reduced the bias by a further 0.10 percentage point per year. This reduces the Moulton-Smedley estimate of the remaining Lower Level Substitution Bias to 0.25 percentage point per annum. On July 16, 1996, BLS introduced changes in the classification and definition of the hospital and related services component of the CPI.[65] These were intended to improve the measurement of this important component of the CPI, but were not accompanied by an estimate of bias reduction. Thus, our point estimate of Lower Level Substitution Bias is 0.25 percentage point per annum.

The goal of BLS is to measure goods and services of constant quality; however, the disappearance of products from the marketplace necessitates the substitution of other products. Armknecht and Weyback (1989) summarized the methods used by BLS to adjust the CPI for quality change.[66] Elimination of new goods bias and quality change bias are essential steps in measuring the cost of living. Important empirical research on new goods bias has been done for breakfast cereals by Hausman (1996), prescription drugs by Griliches and Cockburn (1994), new cars by Pakes, Berry, and Levinsohn (1993), and many others as described above in Section V.[67] We have estimated the total bias due to new products and quality change of existing products to be 0.6 percentage point per year.

Reinsdorf (1993) has provided the principal empirical evidence on New Outlet Substitution Bias. This is based on comparisons between prices for certain food and fuel items for outlets rotating into the sample covered by the CPI and outlets rotating out. He estimated the bias to be 0.25 percentage point per annum. Lebow, Roberts, and Stockton (1994) have extrapolated this estimate to the CPI as a whole by identifying components of the index that would be affected by outlet substitution bias. These amount to 40% of the CPI, so that Outlet Substitution Bias is 0.1 percentage point per annum.

These separate biases are approximately additive and likely to be independent of modest swings in the true inflation rate. Thus, a bias of 1 percentage point implies that when changes in the CPI show inflation rising from 3% to 5%, it is likely actually to be rising from 2% to 4%. Note the bias primarily affects the level, not the change, in the inflation rate. At very high rates of inflation, the bias may increase (one might assume greater outlet and commodity substitution), but we currently have no evidence regarding this issue.

Table 3 summarizes our evaluation of biases in the CPI. This includes point estimates based on the best available evidence as well as a plausible range for the overall bias. The average of our estimates of the overall bias in the CPI is 1.1 percentage point per annum with a range of 0.8 to 1.6 percentage point.

TABLE 3
Estimates of Biases in the CPI-Based Measure of the Cost of Living (Percentage Points Per Annum)

Sources of Bias	Estimate
Upper Level Substitution	0.15
Lower Level Substitution	0.25
New Products/Quality Change	0.60
New Outlets	0.10
Total	1.10
Plausible Range	(0.80-1.60)

The BLS is preparing for a benchmark revision in January 1998, when the CPI will incorporate new expenditure weights from the 1993-1995 Consumer Expenditure Surveys. However, BLS will retain the modified Laspeyres formula, so that our estimates of bias will carry over to the revised CPI. In addition, BLS has continued to introduce important modifications in the CPI in order to improve measurements and remedy deficiencies that have come to light. However, these revisions, like the forthcoming benchmark revision, employ the modified Laspeyres framework, so that important differences between the CPI and a cost of living index will remain.

The Upper Level Substitution Bias in the CPI will persist after the forthcoming benchmark revision of the CPI, since BLS plans to retain the modified Laspeyres formula. Second, BLS has reduced so-called formula bias, the part of Lower Level Substitution Bias resulting in substantial measure from the introduction of sample rotation procedures and the modified Laspeyres index at the Lower Level of aggregation in 1978. However, the objective of the changes in January 1995 and those announced in March 1996 was to improve the implementation of the modified Laspeyres formula, not to eliminate the Lower Level Substitution Bias quantified by Moulton and Smedley (1995). Finally, New Item, New Outlet, and Quality Change Biases are unaffected by the changes already announced by BLS or the benchmark revision.[68]

To summarize we have revised the estimates presented in our Interim Report to reflect BLS revisions of the CPI and the accumulation of new findings on the magnitude of biases. Our main conclusion is that the limitations imposed by the modified Laspeyres formula make the CPI unsuitable for cost of living measurement. By combining a Tornqvist formula at the Upper Level of aggregation and a weighted geometric formula at the Lower Level, BLS could eliminate both types of Substitution Bias. However, these changes alone would fail to encompass adjustments for New Item, New Outlet, and Quality Change Biases. Adjustments for these biases are essential for measurement of the cost of living.

Figure 2 illustrates the compounding effect of a 1.1 percentage point per annum bias on CBO projections of the CPI-U through 2006. While 1.1 percentage point may seem to be a small amount in any given year, cumulatively year after year it adds up to a sizable difference, 14% over a dozen years.

FIGURE 2
Effect of a 1.1 Percentage Point Upward Bias
in the CPI-U Through 2006

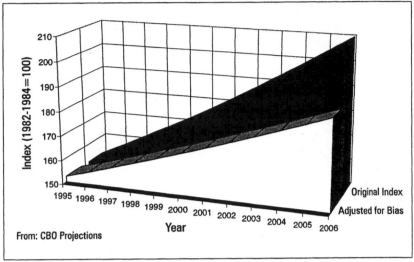

From: CBO Projections

VII. Other Issues

A. A SEPARATE PRICE INDEX FOR THE ELDERLY?

In principle, if not practice, a separate cost of living index could be developed for each and every household based upon their actual consumption basket and prices paid. As noted above, the aggregate indexes use data reflecting representative consumers. Some have suggested that different groups in the population are likely to have faster or slower growth in their cost of living than recorded by changes in the CPI. We find no compelling evidence of this to date, and in fact two studies suggest that disaggregating by population group, for example by region or by age, would have little effect on measured changes in the cost of living.[69] Further, work on this subject remains to be done. In particular, the prices actually paid, not just expenditure shares, may differ.[70]

Beyond the different consumption baskets, it is important to understand our analyses of the sources of bias are applied to representative or average consumers. Some consumers will substitute more than others, and the substitution bias may be larger for some, smaller for others. Likewise, some are more likely to take advantage of discount outlets; others less so. Perhaps most importantly, the benefits of quality change and the introduction of new products may diffuse unevenly throughout the population. Some will quickly gain the benefits of cellular telephones, for example, while others may wait many years or decades or never use them. This is yet another reason why we have been very cautious in our point estimates for these particular sources of bias.

B. BROADER CONSIDERATIONS ON THE QUALITY OF LIFE

Not all change is positive and not all change is positive for everyone. In making the case for the importance of quality change, we have also to look at the other side of the ledger. There are at least three types of change to consider here: 1. New goods may drive out older goods which are still valued by a subgroup of the population, or what is equivalent, the loss of economies of scale may drive up their price significantly. To the extent that it is measured, it does not represent a new problem of the price index construction. 2. An existing good or service may deteriorate in its quality. That is a less frequent phenomenon, in spite of the mantra that "they don't make them the way they used to." The most significant recent example is probably the HMO-induced tightening-up of the rules of access to medical care which is likely to be perceived as a significant deterioration in the expected services that had been contracted for by the purchase of medical insurance. It is unlikely, however, to have outweighed the medical advances of recent years. Few would trade today's restricted access to medical care, for a more free access to the technologies of yesteryear, foregoing the improvements in bypass operations, ulcer treatments, or cataract surgeries. 3. The largest effect may come from change in our physical, social, and economic environment which impose on us higher expenditures necessary to keep up with our previously achieved utility levels.

It is not clear, however, whether events such as a colder winter, the appearance of AIDS, or a rise in the crime rate should be included in the definition of a price index. A change in expenditures due to an unanticipated change in weather should raise the price index only to the extent that energy prices go up, not quantities consumed. The latter, if the event persists, will ultimately affect the commodity weights in the index, but that is a different matter. The rise in AIDS would drive up the price index of health, if we define it as the expenditure necessary to achieve an equivalent base-period health level. But while this component represents a real rise in the "cost-of-living," it may not be an appropriate component in an indexing formula, since there are no "gains" among the young which could be called to "compensate" the retirees for such price increases.

The appearance of AIDS did raise the cost of living. Counting subsequent improvements in its treatment as a positive quality change will be inappropriate, if the original deterioration in the environment was not taken into account in the measurement framework in the first place. Similarly, counting quality improvements in locks and other security devices, may overestimate the "gains" from such defensive consumer investments.

While it is impossible to provide a full and accurate accounting for such changes, it is extremely unlikely that the rise of such "bads" out-balances the "good" that is contained in the developments alluded to above. In the major areas of concern and poor measurement, environment, health, and crime, there have been gains in the first two and we have come close, in recent years, to holding steady on the last one. Thus, while we do recommend extending measurement efforts beyond the current concept of what constitutes the consumption "basket," we see no strong reason to temper our conclusions about the measurement issues in the areas we did examine: the more traditional components of consumption as defined in the current content of the CPI. The following presents some brief background for our view.

The industrial revolution caused widespread air and water pollution, and this was indeed a negative factor up until the 1950s and 1960s. However, since then a shift from coal to natural gas as the dominant energy source for home heating, cleaner fuels and cars and environmental regulation have caused a major decline in the presence of many types of contaminants in the air and water. The shift in heating fuels also brought about a major increase in cleanliness and convenience around the house, as the coal scuttle was replaced by the silent and automatic transmission of natural gas. The CPI implicitly values the improvement in air quality made possible by mandated anti-pollution devices in automobiles, since it treats the cost of mandated anti-pollution devices as an improvement in quality rather than an increase in price. We have recommended that the CPI treat changes in price due to additional anti-pollution devices as a price rather than quality increase. But that concept, incorporated in our quality change bias estimates in this report, leaves the improvement in air quality unmeasured. This is a source of understatement in our final estimate of CPI bias. Further, the CPI is inconsistent, since a portion of the higher cost of electricity, steel, paper, and other products is also due to environmental regulation, and the benefits of higher air and water quality made possible by regulation of products other than automobiles is not taken into account.[71]

Crime is another type of externality. The rate of crime victimization increased in the past, e.g., from 0.096 incidents per capita in 1970 to 0.098 incidents in 1981. Since then, however, the victimization rate has fallen to 0.074 incidents in 1992 (the latest year available).[72] The share of violent crimes increased from 0.025 in 1970 to 0.028 in 1981 and decreased slightly to 0.026 in 1992. Since 1992 there has been widespread attention to a sharp decline in homicide rates in many major American cities.

Looking further for negative factors, perhaps the most important are such social issues as divorce, illegitimacy, and the reduced role of the nuclear family. The divorce rate increased by 50 percent between 1970 and 1980 but since then has been stable.[73] The suicide rate was stable between 1980 and 1992 but the age-adjusted death rate declined by 14 percent, while the infant mortality rate fell by 58 percent between 1970 and 1992. Perhaps most importantly, life expectancy at birth increased from 70.8 in 1970 to 75.5 in 1993. The major negative has been that births to unmarried women have increased, from 18.4 percent to 30.1 percent. There may be other intangible negatives, such as perceived increased job insecurity, possible increased inequality, and the decreased job opportunities for workers with only a high school education.

On the positive side, there is no question that goods have improved in ways that our discussion of quality change cannot fully incorporate. Gordon (1990, p. 38) notes a number of dimensions of quality which his measures did not capture, some of which are the faster speed and reduced vibration of jet planes, improved reliability of appliances and automobiles, improved sound quality of audio equipment in homes and automobiles, improved safety devices on home power tools and power lawn mowers, reduction in the noise, weight, and installation cost of room air conditioners, and "immeasurably better picture quality of color TV sets."

Many aspects of the change in the American standard of living from the rural horse-drawn economy of 1870 to today's modern economy occurred many decades ago and are not current sources of CPI bias. The elimination of animal waste was a major contribution of the motor car, in addition to its speed and flexibility, but this achievement was largely accomplished before World War II. The achievement of electrical appliances in reducing household drudgery was largely accomplished by the 1960s. But some improvements have been continuous. There has been a steady transition in the quality and variety of home entertainment options, from the player piano, to the radio, to black-white and then color TV, to the VCR, and now cable TV, satellite TV, and the World Wide Web and the other features available with personal computers. Further, the rapid spread of central air conditioning has made possible a substantial movement of households to the southern and southwestern states. Millions have chosen to take this option, voting with their feet to enjoy milder winters with artificially cooled summers.

Overall, we find that the presumed negatives (pollution, crime, suicide, divorce), the worsening of which may have increasingly detracted from the quality of life at one time, have reached a plateau and in the case of pollution and crime seem actually to have reversed direction, thus recently improving the quality of life. The remaining negatives are important but seem to us to have been more than offset by increased quality and variety of goods, services, and choice of outlets along dimensions that are partly but not entirely captured by our measures of bias, but most importantly by the major increase in longevity which perhaps swamps everything else. Accordingly, our estimate of the current bias in the CPI is, if anything, probably understated.

VIII. The Commission's Recommendations

INTRODUCTION

Our recommendations are directed at three different audiences: 1. Our elected officials (the President and the U.S. Congress), who are the providers of funds, the supervisors, and also major consumers of the information contained in the CPI; 2. The BLS, which is the producer of the CPI; and 3. The community of professional economists and statisticians, who ultimately provide both the manpower and the knowledge base required for a successful operation of this major measurement and observational tool for our economy. The role of the BLS in this can be viewed as running one of our major National (Economic) Observatories, producing both timely information about the state of our economy and providing the inputs for advancing our knowledge of and understanding about how it functions and the interrelationships among its various components.

RECOMMENDATIONS

1. **The BLS should establish a cost of living index as its objective in measuring consumer prices.**

    All of our specific recommendations are aimed toward this goal.

2. **We recommend the development and publication of two indexes:**

    One which is published monthly on a timely basis and is designed to maintain the spirit of the cost of living index yet accommodate the inconsistent timing schedules of the required information; and a second index which is published and updated annually and revised historically to introduce improvements arising from new information and new research results. The purpose of having two indexes is to accommodate the complex issues that must be addressed and the time delay in obtaining all of the necessary data.

    The recommendations to the BLS are divided into three parts: 1. Short run: those we think can be implemented immediately, with little additional resources or new data collection initiatives. These center on changing the current CPI computation, primarily to make it more current, and second, on computing an annually updated and subsequently revised COL index; 2. Intermediate run: Reforms that are feasible within the current state-of-the-arts, but would require new data collection, reorganization of activities, and changes in the detail of the various sub-indexes produced by the CPI; and 3. Longer-run recommendations, emphasizing topics and areas that need additional research and attention.

Short Run

3. **The timely, monthly index should continue to be called the CPI and should move toward a COLI concept by adopting a "superlative" index formula to account for changing market baskets, abandoning the pretense of sustaining the Laspeyres formula.**

    To accommodate the delay in obtaining information on quantities needed to combine the price changes of items in the lowest groupings, BLS should move away from the assumption that consumers do not respond at all to price changes in close substitutes. We thus recommend BLS move to a "trailing Tornqvist" Index (weighted geometric mean of price relatives), at the stratum and ELI level, and also, concurrently, to geometric means of price relatives at the elementary aggregation level. Both of these moves would alleviate the problem of the growing irrelevancy of "baskets" based on decade-old consumption patterns, reduce significantly the substitution and formula bias, and facilitate the speedier introduction of new goods and services into the index.[74]

    a. Because of the lag in collecting up-to-date information on consumer spending patterns, the weights will have to be based on a trailing two- or three-year average of past expenditures, e.g., 1993-4 weights for the 1996 price changes. They should be changed every year.[75] This implies that

    b. The BLS should organize itself for "permanent" rather than decadal revisions in the CPI. Both the weights and the priced commodity and services assortment need more frequent updating. Also,

    c. Wherever possible, scanner data and other "outside" data should be used both to reduce the cost of data collection and (primarily) to expand the assortment of goods and services priced concurrently, to provide current item weights, and to introduce new items as quickly as they enter the market. Whether this will result in a net reduction in the cost of data collection is an open question.

    d. As subsequent data become available, the weights are updated, and new goods are introduced and their history extended backward, the information incorporated in the published CPI should undergo retroactive revision, as far back as the new information warrants, in the form of a new annual COL index, using a compatible "superlative-index" formula. This "revised" COL index would be published annually, with a lag of a year or two, and would be subject to additional revisions after new information emerges and new methodology is introduced. The published versions of this index need never be "final."

4. **The BLS should move to geometric means at the elementary aggregates level.**

We believe it to be the closest approximation to a full implementation of the COLI concept, which could be ultimately implemented also at this level, as scanner data become available for most of the currently sampled commodities. Changing to geometric means will not only solve the "formula bias" problem, much of which has been recently eliminated by a switch to "pre-seasoning," but will also alleviate the below-stratum-level substitution bias. It will not solve, however, the "outlet bias." To aid in updating the required weights, the BLS should be able to acquire the detailed commodity-level shipments data currently collected by the Census but not accessible to the BLS.

Intermediate Run

5. **The BLS should study the behavior of the individual components of the index to ascertain which components provide most information on the future longer-term movements in the index and which items have fluctuations which are largely unrelated to the total and emphasize the former in its data collection activities.**

    This could result in the down-weighting or even elimination of data collection for certain cities and a revision of the commodity structure of the index which would consider some goods as having a national market, sampling a larger number of items but with less regard to geography, focusing on geographical differences only for more "local" commodities, such as fuel costs, rent, personal services, and fresh produce.

    Currently, the BLS collects a large number of price quotes on bananas, because they are inexpensive to collect and their prices are quite variable, even though these variations are not related systematically to the underlying trend-movements in the CPI. At the same time, less attention is paid to less variable but more likely to change (disappear or be redesigned) and harder to measure commodities, such as surgical treatments, consumer electronics, and communication services.

6. **The BLS should change the CPI sampling procedures to de-emphasize geography, starting first with sampling the universe of commodities to be priced and then deciding, commodity by commodity, what is the most efficient way to collect a representative sample of prices from which outlets, and only later turn to geographically clustered samples for the economy of data collection.**

    The current city-level price indexes are useless for geographical comparisons of levels and misleading as measures of rates of change, since they are not based on any clearly defined levels. To do an adequate job of describing the geography of price levels in the U.S. will require the collection of prices for the same commodities and services in different cities. To study differential changes in the price levels across cities, arising from different competitive and population trends, it may prove adequate to sample the "national" commodities in specific cities only once a year or so, on a rotating basis. More generally, one could design a model consisting of an underlying "national" trend level of the CPI, which would be the primary focus of monthly estimation, and more slowly changing city differentials, which would be based on less frequently collected data.

This would allow the CPI to concentrate resources on expanding the sample and analysis in rapidly changing areas of the commodity and services spectrum, such as health services, communication services, and food away from home, where quality change and commodity turnover is endemic.

Moving to a notion of a new "basket" each year will allow for a faster introduction of new items and new outlets. Moving to a national sample for most of such items would allow expansion of the number of specific items (models, varieties, types) sampled within a particular ELI and reduce thereby the number of forced substitutions. Also, this would allow for the use of new sources of data, such as scanner data on prices, and industry-wide information on sales of specific items (for more detailed weights), leading to a quicker identification of new goods and their faster incorporation into the index. This is also the level at which more extensive quality adjustments and "comparable" substitutions could be made, recognizing the appearance of new outlets and new versions of services which provide consumers, effectively, with cheaper sources for the same or similar items consumed previously.

7. **The BLS should investigate the impact of classification, that is item group definition, on the price indexes, to improve the ability of the index to fully capture item substitution.**

In addition, a classification rule should be implemented for new products that groups them within the same low-level group (stratum) as those for which consumers are most likely to substitute for them. On-line news services which compete with newspapers, automobile purchases with leases, and drugs with the surgical procedures they replace, are examples of products for which direct comparisons are needed so that the full substitution effect can be accounted for.

8. **There are a number of additional conceptual issues that require attention. The price of durables, such as cars, should be converted to a price of annual services, along the same lines as the current treatment of the price of owner-occupied housing. Also, the treatment of "insurance" should move to an ex-ante consumer price measure rather than the currently used ex-post insurance profits based measure.**

9. **The BLS needs a more permanent mechanism for bringing outside information, expertise, and research results to it.**

This Commission did not have the resources or the time to investigate all the various aspects of the CPI in adequate depth. Nor would a subsequent similar group if it were again assembled ad hoc. A more permanent body should be created, at the request of the BLS, organized by an independent public professional entity, such as the American Economic Association, the NRC-NAS or NBER, with a significant resource commitment. Such a group could pursue more fundamental research in cooperation with the BLS and provide a framework for experimentation with various alternative data collection and estimation approaches. It would also provide the BLS with a more permanent channel for access to a range of professional and business opinions on the statistical, economic, and current market issues arising in the normal process of data collection, on index number construction, and on the implementation of some of the reforms suggested here.

Longer Run

10. **The BLS should develop a research program to look beyond its current "market basket" framework for the CPI.**

In the longer run, the big issues are new commodities and new services and the changing economic, social, and environmental climate within which the consumer is operating. This program should explore measuring the value of time saved by new medical procedures and communication devices, the value of life extended and its associated quality, the losses experienced, in terms of longer distances to new shopping centers by the closing of some neighborhood stores, and the "consumption" increases forced on consumers, by rising crime, new diseases, or changes in taxation.

11. **BLS should investigate the ramifications of the embedded assumption of price equilibrium.**

This assumption, which means that prices or quantities adjust immediately to quality changes or the introduction of substitutes is fundamental to many elements of the methodology and its failure to hold sometimes is at the heart of many of the issues discussed in this report. We recommend that BLS identify the methodological changes required to relax this major assumption as research warrants.

12. **The BLS should develop a number of new data collection initiatives to make some progress along these lines.**

First and foremost, BLS or a companion agency will need to collect data on detailed time use from a large sample of consumers. We would also need to extend the current health status survey to include more information on various "quality of life" issues. Progress should also be made (perhaps jointly with the BEA, which is already doing work in this area such as environmental satellite accounts) on incorporating data from victimization surveys and from various measures of the status of our physical environment into an experimental set of national satellite social-economics accounts, accounts that value not only the market consumption basket, but also the resulting leisure and quality of life experienced by the average individual. Such accounts could also provide information on the distribution of these measures across different age and social groups. It will be difficult to integrate these into the main cost of living framework, but over time, progress on these fronts should provide useful supplemenatary information to policy makers and the public.

Suggestions for Congress

13. **Congress should enact the legislation necessary for the Departments of Commerce and Labor to share information in the interest of improving accuracy and timeliness of economic statistics and to reduce the resources consumed in their development and production.**

14. **Congress should provide the additional resources necessary to expand the CES sample and the detail collected, to make the POPS survey more frequent, and to acquire additional commodity detail from alternative national sources, such as industry surveys and scanner data.**

    While the Commission has identified some potential areas of cost savings, and it sympathizes with the recent trend to use private business sector methods to make the federal government more efficient, it notes the overwhelming trend for private businesses to be investing heavily on information technology, from tangible capital such as hardware to intangibles such as increasingly important software, to human capital.

15. **Congress should establish a permanent (rotating) independent committee or commission of experts to review progress in this area every three years or so and advise it on the appropriate interpretation of the then current statistics.**

    This would be useful in its own right, but especially so to smooth the transition to a new index.

16. **Congress and the President must decide whether they wish to continue the widespread overindexing of various federal spending programs and features of the tax code. If the purpose of indexing is fully and accurately to insulate the groups receiving transfer payments and paying taxes, no more and no less, they should pass legislation adjusting indexing provisions accordingly.**

This could be done in the context of subtracting an amount partly or wholly reflecting the overindexing from the current CPI-based indexing. Alternatively, a smaller amount could be subtracted from the new revised annual index if and when it is developed and published regularly, to more closely approximate a true cost of living index.

We hasten to add that the indexed programs have many other features and raise many other issues beyond the narrow scope of a more accurate cost of living index. We also wish to express our view that these findings and their implications need to be digested and understood by the BLS, the Congress, the Executive Branch, and the public.

To the Economists and Statisticians

These professions should treat training in data collection, data analysis, and interpretation more seriously and give it more space and attention in the standard curriculum. There should be more emphasis on measurement and sampling issues in the training of economists and statisticians. Effort should also be put into improving the ties between professionals in government and their academic and business colleagues. The academic world needs to be cognizant of the important work done by its colleagues in government who provide them with much of the "raw material" for their subsequent analyses and show more appreciation of their efforts and understanding of the constraints under which they are laboring.

IX. Conclusion

While the CPI is the best measure currently available, it is not a true cost of living index. It suffers from a variety of conceptual and practical problems as the vehicle for measuring changes in the cost of living. Despite important BLS updates and improvements in the Consumer Price Index, it is likely that changes in the CPI have substantially overstated the actual rate of price inflation. Moreover, revisions have not been carried out in a way that can provide an internally consistent series on the cost of living over an extended span of time. More importantly, **changes in the Consumer Price Index are likely to continue to overstate the change in the true cost of living for the foreseeable future.** This overstatement will have important unintended consequences, including overindexing government outlays and tax brackets and increasing the federal deficit and debt. If the intent of such indexing is to insulate recipients and taxpayers from changes in the cost of living, use of the Consumer Price Index has in the past, and will in the future, substantially overcompensate (on average) for changes in the true cost of living.

This report has laid out a variety of issues to be addressed in developing a more accurate measure of the cost of living. It has also presented a series of recommendations to the agency responsible for the nation's price statistics and to the elected officials who are funders, supervisors, and consumers of those statistics. We have no doubt that implementation of our recommendations would greatly improve the accuracy of the nation's price statistics. This in turn would lead to more accurate measurement of everything from cost-of-living adjustments in private contracts and public programs to information for the Federal Reserve to improved inputs to the nation's national income and product accounts. These improvements in turn would better enable citizens and policy makers alike to measure economic progress over time, among groups, and across countries.

While the Commission's best estimate of the overstatement of changes in the cost of living based on changes in the consumer price index is a little over one percent, our broader point is that even small differences compound over time and matter a lot. This was evidenced in Section II when the improvement in the treatment of owner-occupied housing was introduced early in the 1980s. The same is true of the recently corrected formula bias issues which added an additional bias of about 0.24 percent per year for 1979-95. The cumulative ramifications are substantial.

While subsequent analysis, research, and economic events may result in a slight change in these estimates — at least as likely to be up as down in our opinion — some care in their use is warranted. While the analysis in this report represents our best judgment, this Commission did not have the substantial resources that the previous major effort to examine the nation's price statistics, the so-called Stigler Commission, had in 1961. The Stigler Commission was able to commission and produce substantial original research, while this Commission did not have the time or resources to do so. Nevertheless, this report incorporates new information from a wide variety of sources, both within the government and from outside the government. We are gratified by the tremendous outpouring of suggestions, advice, and assessment of individual issues that have arisen in the course of the committee's investigation.

The readers of this report need some time to digest and understand the results, analysis, and recommendations. This includes the BLS, the Congress, the Executive Branch, the private sector, and academe. We very much hope that careful and thoughtful consideration will be given to the findings presented in this report in the spirit in which they are offered: an attempt to provide some guidelines on how to improve the production and use of the nation's price statistics and the continuous process of improving them in a complex, dynamic economy.

Endnotes

1.   We would like to thank the staffs of the Bureau of Labor Statistics, Congressional Research Service, Congressional Budget Office, Senate Finance Committee, and other individuals in academe and the private sector, too numerous to mention here for valuable assistance and advice during the Commission's work.

2.   The two most commonly used are the CPI-U and CPI-W. The former is for all urban consumers, roughly 80% of the population; the latter is for urban wage and clerical workers, about 32% of the population. Note that the expenditure shares may be quite different than the average for any particular household, and also on average for subgroups of the population. Also, the prices paid for some products may differ for some households from the prices actually sampled. In principle, if not practice, a separate cost of living index could be developed for each and every household based on its actual consumption basket and prices paid. The overall index is used to approximate this with the data reflecting representative consumers. Whether this is itself sufficiently misleading as to warrant separate price indexes for different population subgroups is discussed below.

3.   See Congressional Budget Office (1994).

4.   See Gillingham and Lane (1982).

5.   See Duggan, Gillingham, and Greenlees (1995).

6.   See Congressional Budget Office (1995).

7.   See O'Neill (1995). These CBO budget estimates are relative to CBO's January 1995 baseline and do not include the small adjust assumed in the out-years of the budget resolution.

8.   These estimates are relative to the CBO's May 1996 Baseline. See CBO (1996).

9.   Chapter 19 of BLS Handbook of Methods. We are especially grateful to John Greenlees and Brent Moulton of BLS for clarifying several of these issues for the Commission.

10.   Prices are actually collected in 88 locations, called primary sampling units, or PSUs. In eight PSUs (the five largest urban areas), prices are collected for all items every month. In other areas, prices are collected monthly for food, fuels, and a few other items, and bimonthly for all other items. Of the 44 areas which go into the index every month, 32 are self-representing because of their size and 12 are composites constructed from 56 PSUs which provide representation for smaller and mid-size cities across the country.

11.   The housing component properly captures the multiple period consumption accrued subsequent to the purchase of a house. This same approach is warranted but not used in measuring durable goods such as automobiles and refrigerators.

12.   Only 184 of the item groups are actually priced. The other 23 strata account for less than 2 percent of the weight of the overall index. Price indexes for these groups are moved with changes in the indexes for the item groups which are priced.

13.   This example is current and real, provided by BLS. The names of the brand and store are withheld to adhere to confidentiality requirements.

14.   There are other reasons that may result in the disappearance of a specific item from a specific outlet. When the reason is loss of competitive market share, the BLS replacement procedures are likely to result in upward bias.

15.   This procedure is based on the assumption that the marketplace adjusts fully and instantaneously to price differences among competing products. This can happen in two ways: prices of substitutes change immediately to make them equal (quality-adjusted), or quantities of what would be higher priced products fall to zero, making them disappear from the market.

16.   The market basket has been updated once per decade historically and introduced with a several year lag. For current data, it represents an average derived from surveys for 1982-1984. The next revision of the index is scheduled for introduction in 1998 at which time the base period will be updated to 1993-1995.

17.   Only seasonal factors are revised historically.

18.   Sometimes a new product is introduced with sample rotation. An example might be a new variety of apples.

19.   The ability of the CPI to fully capture price impacts such as these depends on the degree to which the classification structure is consumption-based. That is, items which are the closest substitutes for each other in terms of how they are used, must be in the same item group, the lowest level at which indexes are constructed. The item structure is updated with the decadal revisions of the CPI. The new item structure which will be introduced with the 1998 revision will make some improvements toward placing close substitutes together. Much more is needed.

20.   Another way to state this is that the elasticity of substitution among items within the lowest grouping, say, types of apples, is assumed to be zero.

21.   Each method has come to be named for its inventor. See below.

22.   This index is called the Laspeyres index.

23.   This index is called the Paasche index.

24.   See Fisher (1922).

25.   See Diewert (1976).

26.   See Tornqvist (1936).

27.   See Moulton and Smedley (1995).

28.   See Diewert (1995).

29.   See Shapiro and Wilcox (1996b).

30.   See Carruthers, Sellwood, and Ward (1980), Schultz (1994), Dahlen (1994), and Woolford (1994).

31.   For detailed discussion of Lower Level Substitution Bias, see Moulton (1996).

32.   See Moulton and Smedley (1995).

33. This undoubtedly arose both to save overtime pay and to accommodate retailers who prefer BLS price-takers to be in their establishments when they are less crowded.

34. See Jorgensen and Slesnick (1983).

35. See Fisher and Griliches (1995).

36. There is no presumption that the magnitude of upward quality bias has declined over time. One consideration is that the growing importance of such hard-to-measure categories as consumer electronics and medical services may have increased the significance of quality change bias in the past decade. Another problem is suggested by a "thought experiment" recently conducted by Nordhaus (1996), who extrapolated backward substantial upward bias in the CPI over a long period of 190 years and arrived at implausibly low estimates of the standard of living of the average U.S. citizen in the year 1800. The implausibility of continuous upward bias in earlier decades at the rate suggested for recent decades in this report implies that in some earlier era the upward bias in the CPI was substantially less. This, of course, is natural. Long ago more was more important than better, e.g., enough to eat was more important than variety. As incomes rise beyond some point it is natural to expect increased demand for quality in many goods and services. We return to this issue below in our discussion of housing prices.

37. *Consumer Reports* since 1959 has based its quotation for the average price of a particular model on an average of prices obtained in a market survey, typically of 13-20 price quotations obtained across the country. Thus a shift to discount stores would show up in the *Consumer Reports* price quotations and account for part of the difference between Gordon's indexes and the CPI index for the same category.

38. As a further example of the difficulty of disentangling quality change from other sources of bias, one important fact to be assessed is the relatively large recent difference between the growth rates of the CPI and deflator for Personal Consumption Expenditures (hereafter PCE deflator). The PCE deflator is part of the National Income and Product Accounts, which is the responsibility of the Bureau of Economic Analysis, a division of the Department of Commerce. Over the 12 months ending in August, 1996, the CPI rose at 2.9 percent per year, while in the four quarters ending in 1996: Q3, the implicit PCE deflator rose at 2.0 percent per year. An alternative PCE deflator excluding expenditures on personal computers and medical care increased at 2.7 percent per year, suggesting that much of the difference between the PCE deflator and CPI over this period may involve their differing treatments of computers and medical care. This calculation was made by Bob Arnold of the CBO by subtracting nominal and real expenditures on medical care and consumer purchases of computers from total personal consumption expenditures. But that is not just an issue of differing treatment of quality change, but also substitution bias, since consumer expenditures on both personal computers and medical care have increased greatly since the 1982-84 base year of the CPI.

39. The number of cellular phone subscribers is taken from *Business Week*, December 2, 1996, p. 104.

40. All annual growth rates calculated in this report are logarithmic.

41. Brown's (1994) compilation of annual rent paid by a working class household yields $5160 for 1988 (Table 7.9a) and $1803 for 1973 (Table 6.9a), for a ratio of 2.86. The ratio of the CPI unadjusted rent index for the two years is 2.43.

42. All citations regarding housing quality in this section refer to the *U. S. Census of Housing, 1970* and the U. S. Census Bureau, *American Housing Survey, 1993*.

43. Data from *Statistical Abstract of the United States*. 1978 issue, Tables 1371 and 1373. 1995 issue, Tables 1214 and 1230.

44. The 1918 and 1950 data are for annual rental expenditures of working class households, from Brown (1994), Tables 3.6A and 5.10.

45. Brown (1994), p. 63.

46. This estimate of 1.0 percent per year multiplies an estimate of 1.5 percent per year for telephone service by its weight in this category of roughly two-thirds.

47. *The U. S. Consumer Electronics Industry In Review 1995*, Electronic Industries Association, p. 13.

48. Data provided by the BEA. Audio-video equipment includes VCRs, camcorders, and videotapes but excludes "audio media," i.e., cassettes and CDs. By 1996, Q3 computers accounted for 0.43 percent of nominal PCE and 1.34 percent of real PCE in 1992 dollars.

49. While the CPI incorporates a matched-model index that records a decline in computer prices of 10-20 percent per year, this is applied to a negligible weight (based currently on 1982-84 weights) and so has no practical importance for assessing the magnitude of the quality change bias in the personal computer category. Berndt, Griliches, and Rappaport (1995) have estimated an annual difference between 'matched model' indexes for personal computers (of the type used by the CPI) and hedonic indexes (used by the BEA) of roughly 15 percent per year.

50. Recent changes in the CPI treatment of apparel are discussed in Liegey (1990, 1994).

51. A total of 1,769 matched price comparisons were made for 1914-47 and 4,640 for 1965-93.

52. Recall from footnote 49 that the CPI treatment of apparel changed in 1985.

53. The 1967-93 annual rates of growth for the 'raw' price of new cars 6.65 percent, the safety-pollution adjustment -2.03 percent, the fuel economy adjustment -1.10 percent (totaling 3.52 percent), and the new car CPI 4.42 percent.

54. The growth for trucks are similar. Data for 1970 and 1983 come from Statistical Abstract, 1990, Table 1027, and for 1993 from *Statistical Abstract*, 1995, Table 1025.

55. In 1987 the BLS began to adjust for quality changes in used cars in a parallel manner to its adjustment for new cars.

56. The 1982 Census of Retailing reports that the number of gas pumps in the United States declined 28 percent between 1972 and 1982, and that the fraction of self-service pumps (which was not reported in 1972) had reached 54 percent by 1982.

57. The BLS is moving to price and reprice a hospital bill every month, a potential improvement, although not something which per se gets at quality change.

58. In addition to the comprehensive bias estimates presented in our Interim Report, estimates have been made by Erwin Diewert (1996), Shapiro and Wilcox (1996), and others. An especially valuable earlier survey was presented by Lebow, Roberts, and Stockton (1994).

59. Aizcorbe and Jackman (1993) have estimated Upper Level Substitution Bias, but these estimates have been updated and revised by BLS.

60. For details, see Gillingham (1974).

61. See Reinsdorf (1993), pp. 227-254.

62. The results of BLS research on Lower Level Substitution Bias are summarized in Moulton (1996).

63. See Armknecht, Moulton, and Stewart (1995).

64. See Division of Consumer Prices and Price Indexes (1996b).

65. See Division of Consumer Prices and Price Indexes (1996a).

66. See Armknecht and Weyback (1989).

67. See Hausman (1996), Griliches and Cockburn (1994), and Pakes, Berry and Levinsohn (1993).

68. Although the BLS is continuously attempting to improve the price measures, for example moving to price and reprice hospital bills.

69. See Boskin and Hurd (1985); Jorgensen and Slesnick (1983). However, very preliminary unpublished work suggests that for the period 1982-91 the larger fraction of expenditures on out-of-pocket healthcare by the elderly combined with the more rapid rise in healthcare prices than overall prices for this period might lead to a slightly faster rise in a price index for the elderly. The rate of healthcare price inflation has slowed substantially of late, so it is unlikely this result will be reproduced in the mid-1990s. Also, as noted above in Section V, healthcare inflation is seriously overstated because of the substantial uncounted quality change.

70. Seniors get special discounts, for example, and their geographic distribution, and other factors might cause the prices they pay to differ from those recorded in the CPI.

71. Detailed case studies in Repetto et al. (1996) demonstrate substantial understatement of output and productivity growth, and hence an overstatement of price growth, in the electricity, pulp-paper, and agricultural industries.

72. All data in the paragraph come from the *Statistical Abstract*, 1995, Table 317.

73. Data in this paragraph come from the *Statistical Abstract*, 1995, Tables 114, 124, 136, and 141.

74. A parallel trailing chained-link Laspeyres formula, with revisions producing a comparable Fisher Ideal Index with a 4-year lag might be useful as well. Even so, we will still recommend the move to geometric means at the elementary aggregates level.

75. What needs more rapid changing are the commodity strata weights and the assortment of items priced. City weights could be held constant and changed much less frequently. Here decades would do. See Shapiro and Wilcox (1996a) for additional discussion of the mechanics of such revisions.

References

Advisory Commission To Study The Consumer Price Index. 1995. "Toward a More Accurate Measure of the Cost of Living, Interim Report," September 15, 1995.

Aizcorbe, Ana M. and Patrick C. Jackman. 1993. "The Commodity Substitution Effect in CPI Data, 1982-1991," *Monthly Labor Review*, Vol. 116, pp. 25-33 (December 1993).

Armknecht, Paul A. 1996. "Improving the Efficiency of the U.S. CPI in the Future," paper presented at NBER Productivity Workshop, April 19, 1996.

Armknecht, Paul A. and Donald Weyback. 1989. "Adjustments for Quality Change in the U.S. Consumer Price Index," *Journal of Official Statistics*, Vol. 5, No. 2, pp. 107-123 (1989).

Armknecht, Paul A., Brent R. Moulton, and Kenneth J. Stewart. 1995. "Improvements to the Food at Home, Shelter, and Prescription Drug Indexes in the U.S. Consumer Price Index," Working Paper 263, Bureau of Labor Statistics (1995).

Berndt, Ernst and Zvi Griliches. 1993. "Price Indexes for Microcomputers: An Exploratory Study," in *Price Measurements and Their Uses*, edited by M. Foss, M. Manser, and A. Young; NBER Studies in Income and Wealth vol. 57. Univ of Chicago Press, 1993, pp. 63-99.

Berndt, Ernst R., Iain Cockburn, and Zvi Griliches. 1996. "Pharmaceutical innovations and market dynamics: Tracking effects on price indexes for anti-depressant drugs," Brookings Papers on Economic Activity, 1996.

Berndt, Ernst R., Zvi Griliches, and Joshua G. Rosett. 1993. "Auditing the Producer Price Index: Micro Evidence from Prescription Pharmaceutical Preparations," *Journal of Business and Economic Statistics*, 1993 11(3), 251-264.

Berndt, Ernst R., Zvi Griliches, and Neal Rappaport. 1995. "Econometric estimates of price indexes for personal computers in the 1990's," *Journal of Econometrics*, 68 (1995) 243-68.

Berry, Steven, Samuel Kortum, and Ariel Pakes. 1996. "Environmental Change and Hedonic Cost Functions for Automobiles," NBER working paper 5746, September 1996, forthcoming in Proceedings of the National Academy of Sciences, 1996.

Boskin, M. and M. Hurd. 1985. "Indexing Social Security Benefits: A Separate Price Index for the Elderly," *Public Finance Quarterly*, Volume 13, Number 4, pp. 436-449 (October 1985).

Brown, Claire. 1994. *American Standards of Living*, Oxford, UK: Basil Blackwell Ltd., 1994.

Carruthers, A. G., D. J. Sellwood, and P. W. Ward. 1980. "Recent Developments in the Retail Price Index," *The Statistician*, Vol 29 (1980), pp. 1-32.

Congressional Budget Office. 1994. "Is the Growth of the CPI a Biased Measure of Changes in the Cost of Living?" CBO Papers, Washington. Congress of the United States, October, p. 32.

Congressional Budget Office. 1995. "The Economic and Budget Outlook: Fiscal Years 1996-2000," Report to the Senate and House Committees on the Budget, Washington, Congress of the United States, January 1995, Table 2-8, p. 43.

Cutler, David and Mark McClellan. 1996. "The determinants of technological change in heart attack treatment," NBER working paper #5751, Cambridge, MA, Sept. 1996.

Cutler, David M., Mark McClellan, Joseph P. Newhouse, and Dahlia Remler. 1996. "Are Medical Prices Declining?" NBER working paper 5750, September 1996.

Dahlen, J. 1994. "Sensitivity Analysis for Harmonising European Consumer Price Indices," paper presented at the International Conference on Price Indices (October 31-November 2, 1994), Ottawa, Statistics Canada.

Diewert, Erwin. 1976. "Exact and Superlative Index Numbers," *Journal of Econometrics*, Vol. 4, No. 2, pp. 115-145 (1976).

Diewert, Erwin. 1996. "Comment on CPI Biases," *Business Economics,* Vol. 31, No. 2, pp. 30-35 (April 1996).

Diewert, W. Erwin. 1995. "Axiomatic and Economic Approaches to Elementary Price Indexes," Working Paper No. 5104, Cambridge, National Bureau of Economic Research, Inc. (May 1995).

Division of Consumer Prices and Price Indexes. 1996a. "Changing the Hospital and Related Services Component of the Consumer Price Index," Bureau of Labor Statistics, Press Release (July 16, 1996).

Division of Consumer Prices and Price Indexes. 1996b. "Extending the Improvements in the CPI Sample Rotation Procedures and Improving the Procedures for Substitute Items," Bureau of Labor Statistics, Press Release, March 29, 1996.

Duggan, James, Robert Gillingham, and John Greenlees. 1995. "Housing Bias in the CPI and its Effect on the Budget Deficit and the Social Security Trust Fund," Office of Economic Policy, U.S. Department of the Treasury, June 30, 1995, p. 6.

Fisher, F.M. and Zvi Griliches. 1995. "Aggregate Price Indices, New Goods, and Generics," *Quarterly Journal of Econometrics* (1995).

Fisher, Irving. 1922. *The Making of Index Numbers*, Boston, Houghton-Mifflin, 1922.

Gillingham, Robert and Walter Lane. 1982. "Changing the Treatment of Shelter Costs for Homeowners in the CPI," *Monthly Labor Review*, June 1982, p. 9.

Gillingham, Robert. 1974. "A Conceptual Framework for the Consumer Price Index," Proceedings of the Business and Economics Section, American Statistical Association, pp. 246-252 (1974).

Gordon, Robert J. 1990. *The Measurement of Durable Goods Prices*. University of Chicago Press for NBER, 1990.

Gordon, Robert J. 1996. "The Sears Catalog Revisited: Apparel and Durable Goods," mimeo, Northwestern University, April 1996, revised August 1996.

Griliches, Zvi and Iain Cockburn. 1994. "Generics and New Goods in Pharmaceutical Price Indexes," *American Economic Review,* 1994, 84(5), 1213-1232.

Griliches, Zvi and Iain Cockburn. 1996. "Generics and the Producer Price Index for Pharmaceuticals," in *Competitive Strategies in the Pharmaceutical Industry*, edited by Robert Helms, Washington, DC: AEI Press, 1996, pp. 19-34.

Hausman, Jerry A. 1966. "Valuation of New Goods under Perfect and Imperfect Competition," in Timothy Bresnahan and Robert J. Gordon, eds., *The Economics of New Goods*, Chicago, University of Chicago Press (1966).

Hausman, Jerry. 1996. "Valuation of New Goods Under Perfect and Imperfect Competition," in T. Bresnahan and R. J. Gordon, *The Economics of New Goods, Studies in Income and Wealth* (University of Chicago Press for NBER, 1996).

Jorgenson, Dale W. and Daniel T. Slesnick. 1983. "Individual and Social Cost-of-Living Indexes," *Price Level Measurement*, W.E. Diewert and C. Montmarquette (eds.), Ottawa, Statistics Canada, pp. 241-336 (1983).

Lebow, David E., John M. Roberts, and David J. Stockton. 1994. "Monetary Policy and 'The Price Level,' " Washington, D.C., Board of Governors of the Federal Reserve System (1994).

Lebow, David E., John M. Roberts, and David J. Stockton. (no date) "Monetary Policy and 'The Price Level,'" mimeo, Federal Reserve Board, Washington, D.C.

Liegey, Paul F., Jr. 1990. "Adjusting Apparel Indexes in the Consumer Price Index for Quality Differences," in Murray F. Foss, Marilyn E. Manser, and Allan H. Young (eds.), *Price Measurements and Their Uses*. Chicago: University of Chicago Press for NBER.

Liegey, Paul F., Jr. 1994. "Apparel Price Indexes: Effects of Hedonic Adjustment," *Monthly Labor Review* (May), pp. 38-45.

Moulton, Brent R. 1996. "Estimation of Elementary Indexes of the Consumer Price Index," Bureau of Labor Statistics (May 1996).

Moulton, Brent R. and Karin E. Smedley. 1995. "A Comparison of Estimators for Elementary Aggregates of the CPI," Bureau of Labor Statistics, (June 1995).

Nordhaus, William D. 1996. "Do Real-Output and Real-Wage Measures Capture Reality? The History of Light Suggests Not," in T. Bresnahan and R. J. Gordon, *The Economics of New Goods, Studies in Income and Wealth* (University of Chicago Press for NBER, 1996).

O'Neill, June. 1995. "Prepared Statement," Consumer Price Index, Hearings before the Committee on Finance, U.S. Senate, 194th Congress, First Session, Washington, U.S.G.P.O., Table 1, p. 146.

Pakes, Ariel, Steven Berry, and James A. Levinsohn. 1993. "Applications and Limitations of Some Recent Advances in Empirical Industrial Organization: Price Indexes and the Analysis of Environmental Change," *American Economic Review*, Vol. 83, No. 2, pp. 241-246 (May 1993).

Randolph, William C. 1988. "Housing Depreciation and Aging Bias in the Consumer Price Index," *Journal of Business and Economic Statistics* (July 1988), vol. 6, no. 3, pp. 359-71.

Reinsdorf, Marshall B. 1993. "The Effect of Output Price Differentials on the U.S. Consumer Price Index," in Murray F. Foss, Marilyn E. Manser, and Allan H. Young, eds., *Price Measurements and Their Uses: Studies in Income and Wealth*, vol. 57, Chicago, University of Chicago Press for NBER.

Repetto, Robert, et al. 1990. "Has Environmental Protection Really Reduced Productivity Growth?" World Resources Institute, 1990.

Schultz, B. J. 1994. "Choice of Price Index Formula at the Micro-Aggregation Level: The Canadian Empirical Evidence," paper presented at the International Conference on Price Indices (October 31-November 2, 1994), Ottawa, Statistics Canada.

Shapiro, M. D. and D. W. Wilcox. 1996a. "Alternative Strategies for Aggregating Prices in the CPI," paper prepared for the conference on Measuring Inflation and Real Growth, Federal Reserve Bank of St. Louis, October, 1996.

Shapiro, Matthew D. and David W. Wilcox. 1996b. "Mismeasurement in the Consumer Price Index: An Evaluation," Working Paper No. 5590, Cambridge, National Bureau of Economic Research, Inc. (May 1996).

Shapiro, Matthew D., and David W. Wilcox. 1996c. "Mismeasurement in the Consumer Price Index: An Evaluation." NBER Macroeconomics Annual 1996.

Slifman, L., and C. Corrado. 1996. "Decomposition of Productivity and Unit Costs," mimeo, Federal Reserve Board of Governors, November 1996.

Statistical Abstract of the United States. 1978.

Statistical Abstract of the United States. 1990.

Statistical Abstract of the United States. 1995.

The U. S. Consumer Electronics Industry In Review 1995, Electronic Industries Association, p. 13.

Tornqvist, Leo. 1936. "The Bank of Finland's Consumption Price Index," Bank Of Finland Monthly Bulletin, Vol. 10, pp. 1-8 (1936).

Trajtenberg, Manuel. 1990. "Product Innovations, Price Indices, and the (Mis) Measurement of Economic Performance," NBER Working Paper no. 3261, February 1990.

Triplett, Jack. 1990. "The Theory of Industrial and Occupational Classifications and Related Phenomena," Proceedings of the Bureau of the Census 1990 Annual Research Conference, August 1990.

U. S. Census Bureau. 1993. American Housing Survey, 1993.

U. S. Census of Housing, 1970.

Woolford, K. 1994. "A Pragmatic Approach to the Selection of Appropriate Index Formulae," paper presented at the International Conference on Price Indices (October 31-November 2, 1994), Ottawa, Statistics Canada.

Appendix: Figures

FIGURE A-1

Effect of Correcting a 1.1 Percentage Point Overstatement in the CPI on Annual Federal Deficits

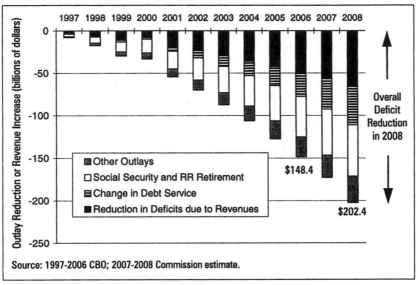

Source: 1997-2006 CBO; 2007-2008 Commission estimate.

FIGURE A-2

Effect of Correcting a 1.1 Percentage Point Overstatement in the CPI on Future Federal Debt

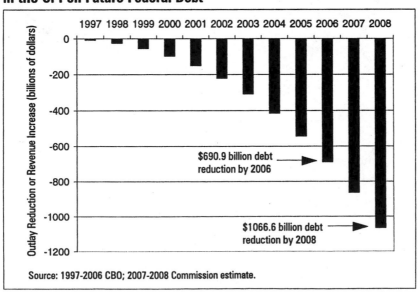

Source: 1997-2006 CBO; 2007-2008 Commission estimate.

Members of the Advisory Commission to Study the Consumer Price Index

Michael J. Boskin, Ph.D., Chairman
Tully M. Friedman Professor of Economics
& Senior Fellow, Hoover Institution
Stanford University
Stanford, California

Ellen R. Dulberger, Ph.D.,
Director of Marketing Strategy
IBM Personal Computer Company
Somers, New York

Robert J. Gordon, Ph.D.
Chairman, Department of Economics
& Stanley G. Harris Professor in the Social Sciences
Northwestern University
Evanston, Illinois

Zvi Griliches, Ph.D.
Paul M. Warburg Professor of Economics
Harvard University
Cambridge, Massachusetts

Dale Jorgenson, Ph.D.
Chairman, Department of Economics
& Frederic Eaton Abbe Professor of Economics
Harvard University
Cambridge, Massachusetts

PART *2*

Does the CPI Overstate Inflation?

An Analysis of the Boskin Commission Report

by Dean Baker

In December 1996, the Advisory Commission to Study the Consumer Price Index, generally referred to as the Boskin Commission, issued its report on the accuracy of the consumer price index (CPI) as a measure of the cost of living. The commission concluded that the CPI overstated the true increase in the cost of living by between 0.8 and 1.6 percentage points a year, with its best estimate as 1.1 percentage points. The commission's report has drawn considerable interest, since it could provide a rationale for lowering the cost-of-living adjustment for Social Security and other benefits and for reducing the indexation of tax brackets. These moves could raise tax revenues and lower federal spending by several hundred billion dollars over the next seven years, going a long way toward bringing the federal budget into balance.

To many, raising taxes and cutting Social Security by way of a technical fix is attractive politically, although the costs to taxpayers and benefit recipients will be substantial. But politics aside, it is important to determine whether the commission's assessment of the CPI is accurate.

The CPI is perhaps the most important piece of economic data produced by the government's statistical agencies. It is used in calculating the size and growth of gross domestic product, real wages and income, and just about every economic measure that is used to make comparisons across time. We should make every effort to address problems in the construction of the CPI, but, at the same time, the index should not be altered for political convenience.

Unfortunately, the process followed in setting up the Boskin Commission does not foster confidence in its conclusions. The Senate Finance Committee established the commission to determine not whether but how much the CPI overstated inflation; the committee explicitly sought a finding that the CPI overstated inflation in the hope of facilitating tax increases and spending cuts. Of the economists who make up the commission, each had already testified that he or she believed the CPI substantially overstated inflation. In fact, of the six highest estimates that economists put forward in testimony regarding the size of the overstatement in the CPI, five came from the five members of the commission (Popkin 1995).[1] Prominent economists who questioned whether the CPI was overstated, such as Janet Norwood, former commissioner of the Bureau of Labor Statistics, and Jack Triplett, the former chief economist at the Commerce Department, were not invited to serve on the commission.

Unlike the Price Statistics Review Commission, appointed in 1959 and chaired by Nobel Prize-winning economist George Stigler, the Boskin panel commissioned no original research; it relied instead on a limited and often quite dated body of existing research. In another departure from the Stigler Commission and standard research practices, it held no public sessions in which its findings could be debated or subjected to professional scrutiny. Therefore, the commission's conclusions must be regarded as tentative findings until they are evaluated by the economics profession. At this point, they do not represent a consensus within the discipline.

The analysis that follows examines the commission's argument that the CPI substantially overstates inflation. The first part looks at the wide-ranging and unavoidable implications of the commission's findings for economic research and public policy issues. The second section, which is somewhat more technical than the other parts of this analysis, is a review of the evidence put forward by the commission. The third section looks at whether inflation rates differ across demographic groups, and it puts forward some suggestions for improving the CPI. The fourth section briefly examines the concept of the cost of living and contrasts it with the notion of a price index, which the CPI is intended to be.

I. The Implications of the Boskin Commission's Conclusions

The consumer price index plays a direct or indirect role in the construction of a large portion of the statistics that concern economists and policy makers. Therefore, the finding that the CPI overstates the true rate of consumer inflation would have significant implications for economic research and public policy. In fact, there are few areas of economic research where this finding would not require a re-evaluation of large amounts of empirical work as well as the theories this work supports. In the case of public policy, these implications go well beyond changing the indexation formula used for tax brackets and government benefits; rather, they call into question the entire national policy agenda.

THE CPI IN ECONOMICS

The most common use of the CPI in economics is as a deflator to allow comparisons of real wages, consumption, and income over time. Thus, if the Boskin Commission's conclusion about the bias of the CPI is correct, then any economic research that involves such comparisons would have to be adjusted to remove the effect of the bias in the CPI. Such an adjustment would mean that real wages, consumption, and income have risen approximately 1.1% a year more rapidly than current measures indicate. For example, if nominal wages rose 4.0% in 1996, and the inflation rate, as measured by the CPI, was 3.0%, then the real wage increase in 1996 was 1.0%. However, if the true rate of inflation, adjusting for the presumed overstatement, was only 1.9%, then real wages actually rose 2.1% in 1996. Real measures of income and consumption growth would have to be adjusted upward in exactly the same manner.

Moreover, Baker (1996a) shows that the CPI was higher relative to the true rate of inflation in the past than it is at present. Problems with the CPI were more severe in the past, primarily because the ability of the Bureau of Labor Statistics to measure quality improvements and to pick up new goods has improved in recent years.[2] Therefore, if the CPI is currently overstated, then it was overstated by even more in the recent past, and acceptance of the Boskin Commission's midpoint estimate of 1.1% as the size of the current bias implies an even larger bias in the 1950s and 1960s, possibly as large as 2% a year (see **Figure 1**).

From the standpoint of economic research, adjusting the CPI for this overstatement of inflation implies much more rapid wage and income growth both through individual lifetimes and for the nation as a whole. Instead of having risen at the rate of about 0.7% a year since 1973, average hourly wages under the Boskin scenario would have risen about 1.8% per year. Of course, the

FIGURE 1: Annual Inflation Rates (Adjusted and Unadjusted)

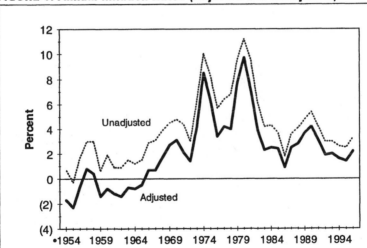

Evidence from commission member Robert Gordon and other sources indicates that any CPI overstatement would have been considerably larger in the past than it is at present. If the size of the current annual overstatement is 1.1 percentage points, then the annual overstatement may have exceeded 2.0 percentage points in past years, meaning that, at many times when there was public concern about inflation, the economy was actually experiencing deflation. For example, extrapolating the commission's adjustment backward implies that, throughout the 1950s and into the mid-1960s, prices were actually falling. This was a period when the president appointed a council to set wage-price guidelines to keep inflation in check, and many of the nation's top economists struggled to develop policies that would allow low unemployment while keeping inflation under control.

Source: *Economic Report of the President* and Baker 1996a.

commission's adjustment does not eliminate the *slowdown* of wage growth since 1973. Using BLS methodology, the CPI indicates average wage growth of 2.8% annually for the previous 22-year period (1951-1973). Since BLS methods for measuring quality and incorporating new goods improved so much between these two periods, the commission's adjustment implies that the annual rate of real wage growth may have been as much as 4.8% during this earlier period.

The finding of more rapid wage, income, and consumption growth through individual lifetimes implies a very different pattern for these variables than appears in current research. It will be necessary to examine how such theories as the lifetime income hypothesis stand up when measures of real income and consumption are adjusted in accordance with the Boskin Commission's conclusions.[3] The commission's adjustment also implies that real interest rates are currently 1.1% higher than is generally believed, meaning that the rate at which individuals discount future income is much greater as well.

A direct implication of the finding that incomes have been growing faster than is currently believed is that the levels from which they grew must have been lower than we thought.[4] For individuals and for the nation as a whole, the commission's adjustment implies that Americans had to have been quite poor in the recent past. Under the Boskin scenario, median family income (the income of a family at the midpoint in the income distribution) did not cross the poverty level until about 1960 (see **Figure 2**) (Baker 1996a and 1996b). Thus, the lower inflation estimate implies that most people who are currently in their seventies or older have lived much of their lives in poverty. The *average* hourly wage in 1960 would have been less than $5.50 an hour, measured in today's dollars, compared to over $16.00 an hour at present.

The commission's adjustment also has implications for other measures. Most of the price data used by Bureau of Economic Analysis (BEA) to construct the consumption component of the deflator for gross domestic product (the personal consumption expenditure deflator, or PCE), comes from the BLS measures in the CPI. While the aggregation method used by BEA avoids approximately 0.15% of the bias identified by the Boskin Commission, most of the other sources of bias would be the same in the PCE as in the CPI.[5] In addition, Gordon (1990) presents at least as much evidence that quality improvements are inadequately captured in investment goods as in consumption goods. Therefore, the overstatement of inflation, and the resulting understatement in real output growth, is probably as large for investment goods as it is for consumption. Thus, it is reasonable to assume that the understatement of GDP growth is approximately equal to any overstatement of the CPI.[6]

An understatement of real GDP growth implies an understatement of the same magnitude in productivity growth (see **Figure 3**). Productivity growth measures the increase in real final output in the private business sector (con-

FIGURE 2: Real Median Family Income (1995 Dollars)

This graph shows the path of the typical or median family's income through the postwar period using both the current measure of inflation and a measure that incorporates the commission's estimate of bias in the CPI. If inflation has been less rapid than is generally believed, then incomes have been growing in real terms by more than has been generally recognized. This means that the levels from which they grew were far lower than we thought. If the commission's estimate is applied backward, then the typical family had to have been living at a poverty-level income as recently as 1960. The median family income in 1953 would have been only about 70% of the current poverty level.

Source: *Economic Report of the President* and Baker 1996a.

sumption, investment, and net exports) for each hour worked. If the Boskin Commission is correct in its claim that the CPI has been overstating inflation by 1.1% a year, then productivity measures have also been understating productivity growth by 1.1% a year. (Productivity growth can be understated only if the growth of a category or categories of real final output have been understated.) Again, it is important to note that the Boskin Commission's conclusion cannot help explain the productivity slowdown since the earlier postwar period. Because the CPI was higher relative to the true inflation rate in the 1950s and 1960s than it is at present, the magnitude of the productivity slowdown would be greater, not smaller, under a Boskin Commission scenario.[7]

The commission's adjustment would necessitate reconstructing series for real GDP growth that would then be used in macroeconomic analysis and studies of long-term growth and productivity. This reconstructing may lead to different conclusions about the importance of factors such as capital, labor, and technology to growth. It may also lead to different conclusions about the

FIGURE 3: Annual Productivity Growth (Adjusted and Unadjusted)

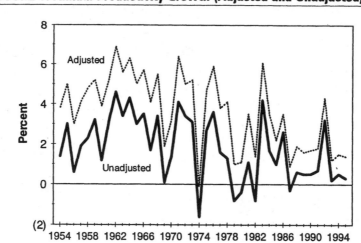

This chart shows (1) the annual rate of productivity growth in the nonfarm business sector as indicated by current data and (2) the rate of productivity growth implied by using the commission's adjustment. The commission's adjustment implies that inflation in consumer goods and services has been significantly less than is indicated by current data, which implies that the growth in real consumption has been far greater than current data show. In addition, the research of commission member Robert Gordon indicates that the error in measuring the rate of inflation in investment goods is at least as large. This means that annual output growth in the business sector and, therefore, productivity growth have been understated by roughly the same amount as the CPI has been overstated.

Source: *Economic Report of the President* and author's calculations.

impact of inflation on growth. While a significant portion of economists currently believe that even relatively moderate levels of inflation have a negative impact on growth, the studies that provide the basis for this belief, if the Boskin Commission is right, were all based on overstated measures of inflation. Some of the periods of low inflation and high growth would actually turn out to be periods of deflation. A link between modest deflation and growth would require a new theoretical explanation.

It is also important to remember in this context that the size of the bias has not been constant through time. In addition to Gordon's work showing a substantial decline in the size of the quality bias from the 1950s to the 1980s, Bryan and Cecchetti (1993) find that the substitution bias was far larger during the 1970s then it has been in the 1980s and 1990s.[8] This finding means that it is not possible to correct current series for inflation or real output growth by simply subtracting or adding the same number for all years. The Boskin

Commission's conclusions imply not only a significant upward bias in inflation and downward bias in output, but also a bias that varies considerably over the postwar period. This fact will seriously complicate any effort to reconstruct the macroeconomic history of the recent past.

The impact of real interest rates on investment and output may also turn out to be somewhat different than indicated by current research. The commission's conclusion implies that the real interest rate has been substantially higher than current data indicate through the whole postwar period, but the necessary correction will be somewhat larger for earlier years than it is at present. (For example, the commission's adjustment implies that the real federal funds rate is now about 3.75% — the nominal rate of 5.25% minus commission-adjusted inflation of 1.5%.) If the Boskin Commission is correct, economists will have to redo studies of the impact of interest rates on investment and growth using the corrected measures of the real interest rate, investment, and GDP (see **Figure 4**).

FIGURE 4: Real Interest Rates (Adjusted and Unadjusted)

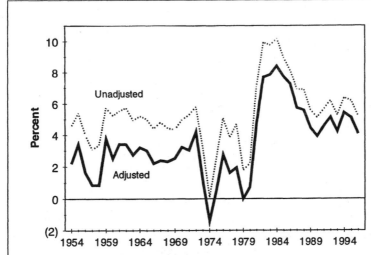

This chart shows the real interest rate on 10-year government bonds since 1953, before and after applying the commission's adjustment. The real interest rate is defined as the nominal interest rate minus the inflation rate. If inflation has been overstated throughout this period, then the real interest rate has been considerably higher than current data indicate, meaning both that the real returns individuals and corporations have received on their assets have been far higher than had been believed, and that the rate at which individuals discount future benefits (or costs) is much greater than current research indicates.

Source: *Economic Report of the President* and author's calculations.

Another area in which the Boskin Commission's conclusions would require a substantial reexamination of current economic theory is international finance. The real foreign exchange rate is constructed using the CPI as a deflator. Current theories of exchange rates assert that the purchasing power of different currencies should not diverge much over long periods of time. This theory means, for example, that if inflation in the United States has been on average 10% higher than the rates of inflation experienced by our trading partners, then the value of the dollar should decline by approximately 10% against their currencies, leaving the real value of the dollar unchanged. Using the current CPI, the real value of the dollar declined 16.5% from 1973 to 1995 (*Economic Report of the President, 1996*, Table B106). However, if the CPI overstates inflation, then the real value of the dollar has fallen far more than this measure indicates: projecting back a 1.1% overstatement means that the real value of the dollar relative to other currencies has declined by nearly 40% since 1973 (see **Figure 5**). The commission's adjustment would also require a new analysis of short-term movements in currency values, since it implies that real interest rates in the United States (which are believed to be a major short-term determinant of exchange rates) have been much higher relative to real interest rates in other countries.

Alternatively, it is possible that the price indexes of our trading partners overstate inflation by approximately the same amount as the CPI. This would remove the problem of the huge decline in the real value of the dollar, but it still leaves other problems for economic analysis. It is unlikely that all price indexes overstate inflation to exactly the same extent, and even relatively small differences (e.g., 0.5% annually) can compound to relatively large magnitudes over time. If the overstatement in the U.S. index approaches the magnitudes suggested by the Boskin Commission, then the amount of variance in the overstatements across indexes is likely to add a large degree of uncertainty to all international comparisons of variables such as real interest rates, productivity, and output growth. The amount of uncertainty may be large relative to the size of the variables. For example, differences in measured productivity growth across countries are likely to be small enough to be within the range that could be explained by measurement error in price indexes. A sustained 1.0% difference in productivity growth between nations is quite large; however, the Boskin Commission's conclusion would suggest that a difference of this magnitude could be attributable completely to measurement error (see **Figure 6**).

The implications of a significant overstatement of foreign price indexes would be the same as they are for the United States. In other words, the growth of real wages, income, and output would have been far more rapid across the world than current data indicate. The commission's adjustment implies that it might be necessary to add 2 percentage points or more to the already high

FIGURE 5: The Real Value of the Dollar (Adjusted and Unadjusted)

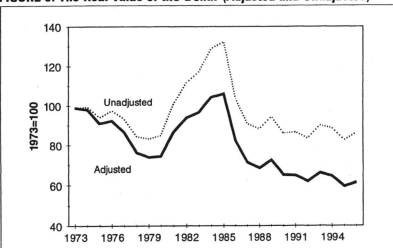

This chart shows the real exchange rate using both current inflation data and the commission's adjustment. The real exchange rate measures the value of the dollar against the value of the currencies of our trading partners, when both the dollar and the foreign currencies are adjusted for rates of inflation in each country. According to economic theory, the *real* value of currencies should not change very much when measured against each other. A country that experiences more rapid inflation rate than its trading partners should see a fall in the *nominal* value of its currency measured against other currencies, keeping its real value approximately the same. The dollar has experienced a large nominal decline that could be explained by a more rapid rate of inflation in the U.S. than in other nations over this period. However, the commission's adjustment implies that the inflation rate in the U.S. was not significantly more rapid than the inflation rate in other nations, meaning that the real value of the dollar declined by nearly 40% since 1974, an enormous change in its value.

Source: *Economic Report of the President* and author's calculations.

growth rates experienced by Japan and Europe in the 1950s and 1960s (see **Figure 7**). This is not impossible, but it does present a different picture of how quickly world output has grown, as well as a different picture of how poor the developed economies must have been in the recent past.

Application of the commission's adjustment to foreign price indexes would also imply that many European nations are currently enduring painful disinflation for no reason. The Maastricht accord requires nations to maintain an annual inflation rate below 3.0% in order to join the currency union in 1999. If the price indexes of the European nations also overstate inflation by 1.0% to -1.5% annually, this target will be far easier to reach. It would even be possible that some nations have already satisfied the Maastricht requirement and are needlessly restraining economic growth in an effort to push inflation down further.

FIGURE 6: Comparative Productivity Growth (Adjusted and Unadjusted)

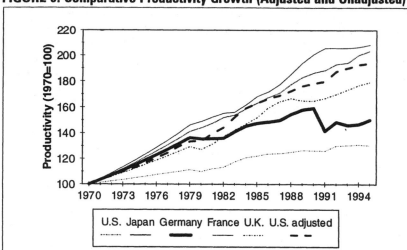

The possibility that inflation measures, and therefore measures of real output, may be in error by 1.1 percentage points or more adds an enormous component of uncertainty to our efforts to understand the economy. This graph compares U.S. productivity growth, using current data, with that of Japan, Germany, France, and the United Kingdom. As can be seen, the current measures indicate that productivity growth in the U.S. has lagged significantly behind the growth in these four nations over the last 25 years. However, when productivity growth is corrected for the commission's adjustment, the U.S. jumps from a distant fifth to third place, close behind Japan and France, the two leaders. Although it is possible that these countries have similar errors in their own measures of inflation, the fact that the errors are so large relative to the numbers we are trying to measure (e.g., productivity growth ranges between 1.0-2.5 percentage points annually) makes any sort of international comparisons of growth extremely problematic. Our findings are at least as likely to be attributable to erroneous measurements as actual differences in performance.

Source: *OECD Economic Outlook* and author's calculations.

The commission's adjustment will also require a reexamination of studies that analyze sectoral demand and output through time. The amount of bias found by the commission is not the same across sectors. For example, it finds that quality improvements in consumer electronics were understated by 3.6 percentage points a year (SFC 1996, 61). But if price increases were overstated, then the increase in real output was understated by the same amount. In most other areas of the index, the understatement of quality improvements was not found to be anywhere near as large, meaning that the price of consumer electronics has been falling far more relative to the price of other goods than is indicated by current data. If the commission's assessment of the problems in measuring quality is correct, then it will be necessary to adjust the

FIGURE 7: Per Capita GDP (Japan and Germany, Adjusted)

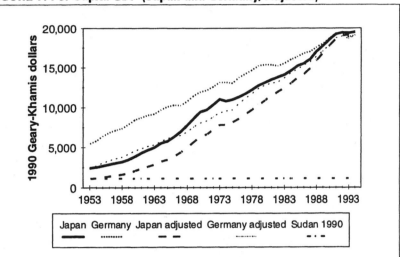

This chart compares the rise in real per capita income (in 1990 dollars) in Japan and Germany using current inflation measures, with the rise that would be indicated if their price measures were subject to the same overstatement as the Boskin Commission attributes to the CPI. The current measure of per capita GDP in Sudan, one of the poorest countries in the world, is included to provide a basis of comparison. By any measure, Japan and Germany experienced enormous growth over this period. However, if the commission's adjustment is correct, Japan was at an income level comparable or below Sudan's at the start of this period, and Germany was not too far above that level.

Source: Maddison 1995 and author's calculations.

current data on relative price movements for all goods to account for the varying degrees of measurement error across categories.

The Boskin Commission's findings also mean that studies that use an aggregate CPI to construct a counterfactual are seriously flawed. For example, studies that examine the impact of deregulation in industries such as air travel, trucking, or communication typically construct a counterfactual scenario that assumes that prices will rise at the same rate as the overall CPI. If the prices in the industry being examined are correctly measured, then the Boskin Commission's findings imply that a counterfactual based on the CPI overstates the rate at which prices should have been expected to rise. Therefore, previous studies must have significantly overstated the true gains from deregulation (see **Figure 8**) (e.g., Crandall and Ellig 1996).

If the CPI contains a substantial bias, then there are few areas in economics where large portions of the currently accepted theory and empirical work will not have to be reexamined, if not discarded altogether. At present, while

FIGURE 8: The Gains From Airline Deregulation (Adjusted and Unadjusted)

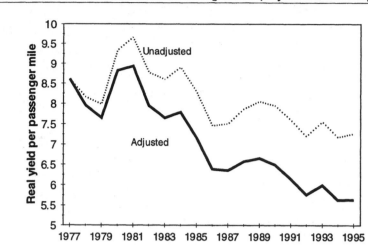

This chart compares estimates of real airline fares in the period since airline deregulation using the current CPI and a commission-adjusted CPI. The measure using the current CPI shows a real decline in airfares of more than 30%, indicating substantial gains from airline deregulation. The fare decline using the commission-adjusted CPI is only about 15%. A gain of this magnitude could easily be offset by more restrictive ticketing practices or other declines in service quality that have accompanied airline deregulation. In this case, and in many others, economists' assessments of the impact of economic policies will have to be reexamined if the commission's conclusions are accepted.

Source: Crandall and Ellig 1996 and author's calculations.

conducting their research, virtually no economists, including members of the commission, take into account the possibility that the CPI substantially over-states inflation (see Appendix A). The fact that the Boskin Commission's con-clusions may invalidate vast amounts of economic research conducted over the last 40 years is not a reason to reject them, but it should raise serious doubts, at least enough to subject the commission's arguments to critical scrutiny.

THE CPI IN ECONOMIC POLICY

As noted above, the Boskin Commission's conclusions imply a different eco-nomic history than the one found in current economic data. Projecting a 1.1% overstatement of inflation back through time implies both much more rapid income growth over the postwar period and much lower levels of real house-hold income in the recent past than we have believed until now to be the case. Such a dramatic change in our understanding of recent history has significant implications for public policy.

One major implication is a stunning success for the war on poverty. When President Johnson initiated the series of programs in 1965, the poverty rate, based on the 1965 poverty line, was approximately 17%. Under our current measures of poverty today, the percentage of people living below the poverty line is only slightly lower — about 14.5% in 1994. However, if the Boskin Commission's conclusions are correct, then we have been overstating the poverty rate by an increasing amount each year, since we have raised the poverty line in accordance with the CPI. The commission's adjustment implies that the correct poverty line for a family of four in 1995 should have been $9,450, instead of the Census Bureau's $15,570 (Baker 1997, 430), implying a poverty rate of approximately 7.5%. While poverty would still exist, a 50% reduction would have to be seen as substantial progress.

Another major policy implication of the Boskin Commission's conclusions is that the concern over government deficits is completely misplaced. The economic rationale for reducing the deficit is that deficits raise interest rates and crowd out investment. Lower investment in turn slows productivity growth and will therefore make future generations worse off. However, if the Boskin Commission's conclusions are correct, then investment and growth are proceeding at a healthy pace. Future generations will be extremely prosperous even if we do nothing to reduce current deficit levels.

If the Boskin Commission's adjusted measure of inflation is applied to the current projections used by the trustees of the Social Security trust fund, the so-called intermediate scenario (the standard basis for policy analysis) shows an incredibly bright future. The average annual wage in 2030 will be approximately $56,000 in today's dollars, compared to $25,000 at present. By 2050 it will be almost $90,000 *in today's dollars*. If real median family income grows at the same rate, it will be $96,000 in 2030 and $140,000 in 2050, compared to $40,000 in 1995.

Using the commission's adjustment affects projections of future incomes by a magnitude more than *20 times* larger than the impact of deficit reduction. The Congressional Budget Office estimates that maintaining a balanced budget over the next 33 years will add approximately $770 per year to the average wage in the year 2030.[9] By comparison, the commission's adjustment adds $17,440 to the average wage projected for 2030. This means that, if the Boskin Commission is correct, projections for the future are already far brighter than anything that we can hope to accomplish by reducing the deficit (see **Figure 9**). Furthermore, the Boskin Commission's conclusions radically alter the generational issues facing the nation. While future generations will be far richer than we had expected, the commission's conclusions imply that the current elderly were poor through much of their lives. For example, in 1960, when a current 70-year-old would have been in his early thirties, the median family

FIGURE 9: Deficit Reduction vs. Commission Adjustment

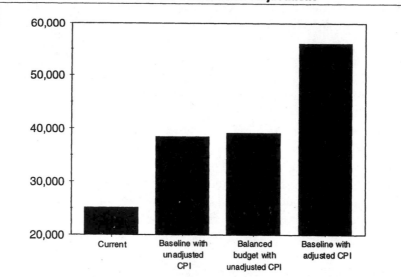

This chart compares the impact on projections of future living standards of balancing the budget with the impact of adjusting projections of real wage growth in accordance with the Boskin Commission's conclusion. The chart indicates that the average annual wage is projected to rise from about $25,000 at present to about $38,400 by 2030 (in today's dollars) if the government continues to run significant deficits over this period. If the government balances the budget throughout this period, the Congressional Budget Office projects that wages will increase slightly more, to $39,120 by 2030 (also in today's dollars). However, if the baseline projections are adjusted in accordance with the Boskin Commission's conclusion, then the average wage will be nearly $56,000 by 2030 (in today's dollars). Thus, the impact of the Boskin Commission's conclusions on projections of future living standards dwarfs any gains that could be accomplished by deficit reduction or almost any other policy imaginable. If the commission is correct, then the future looks far brighter than our current projections indicated was ever possible.

Source: CBO, Social Security Trustees Report, and author's calculations.

income would have been approximately $16,500 in today's dollars (Baker 1996a). The average wage in 1960 would have been about $5.50 an hour (in today's dollars), compared to over $16.00 at present and $38.70 in the commission-adjusted projection for 2030 (see **Figure 10**). These numbers would seem to undermine any arguments for cutting benefits for the elderly in order to improve prospects for our children. Since the Boskin Commission's adjustment implies that the elderly were poor most of their lives — and are not very well off right now (their median family income is just over $20,000) — it seems hard to justify cutting their benefits to help future generations.

FIGURE 10: Average Real Hourly Wage

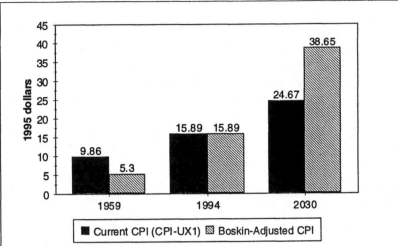

This chart shows average real hourly wages in 1959 and 1994 and projections for 2030 (in 1995 dollars), using the current CPI as well as a measure that is adjusted in accordance with the commission's estimate of bias. Applying the commission's adjustment backward implies that the average real hourly wage was only $5.30 in 1959, only slightly above the current minimum wage. When the commission's adjustment is applied forward to projections of future wage growth, it implies that real wages will more than double by the year 2030. These projections suggest that today's retirees were much poorer throughout their working lives than has been recognized, and that today's youth face a prosperous future.

Sources: *Economic Report of the President, Social Security Trustees Report*, and Baker 1996a.

II. The Evidence for an Overstated CPI

The Boskin Commission constructed its estimate of bias in the CPI by summing estimates of four distinct types of bias. The first source of bias in the index is attributable to consumers substituting goods that rise less rapidly in price for goods that rise more rapidly. The commission estimated this bias at 0.4 percentage points annually. The second type is retail outlet substitution bias, which results from consumers switching from traditional retail outlets to discount stores. The commission estimated this bias at 0.1 percentage points annually. The third type is quality bias, which results from the CPI failing to accurately measure the improvement in quality in goods and services. The fourth type is called new goods bias, which is attributable to the failure of new goods and services to enter the CPI when they first appear on the market. The commission pegged the combined size of these latter two sources of bias at 0.6 percentage points annually.

To clarify the subsequent discussion, it is worth noting a fifth source of bias that has been largely eliminated. This bias is sometimes referred to as "formulaic" or "sample rotation" bias, because it resulted from a sample rotation procedure that BLS introduced in 1980. Under this rotation procedure, which was intended to allow the CPI to follow current buying patterns more closely, one-fifth of the stores and items priced in the CPI were changed each year to reflect new buying patterns. This procedure was helpful in keeping track of new products and stores, but, because of a methodological error (discovered by BLS), it led to an overstatement in the measure of inflation of approximately 0.24 percentage points annually (Moulton 1996). In January 1995 and June and July 1996, BLS adopted new procedures that should have largely eliminated this source of bias. But although formulaic bias should no longer be present in the index, its use in the past may affect some of the estimates of bias mentioned in the subsequent discussion.

SUBSTITUTION BIAS

Traditional substitution bias is the most well-researched and least disputed source of bias in the index. As it is currently designed, the index uses a fixed market basket of goods and services constructed from consumer expenditure data averaged over a three-year base period — the current base period is 1982-84. The base will be updated to expenditure patterns derived from 1993-95 data beginning in 1998.

The substitution bias results when consumers change their consumption patterns in response to changes in relative prices. They will purchase fewer of the goods that rise in price and more of the goods that fall in price. The CPI as currently constructed measures the rate of inflation as if consumption patterns did not respond at all to changes in relative prices.

The BLS has done extensive research on the impact of this source of bias. It has calculated its average size over the period from 1988 to 1995 as 0.14 percentage points (Aizcorbe and Jackman 1993; 1997 update).[10]

The commission reduced its estimate of the size of this bias from 0.2% a year in its interim report to 0.15% in its final report, rounding it up slightly from the 0.14-percentage-point average annual bias found by the BLS research. However, this average was driven up by the higher inflation years of the late 1980s, and especially by the Gulf War-related surge in oil prices in 1990. (The size of the substitution bias increases when there are large differences in the rate of inflation across types of goods.) BLS has found this bias to average just 0.1 percentage point in the environment of low and even inflation that the economy has experienced in recent years.

The commission has also included an estimate of bias of 0.25 percentage points for what it terms "lower-level" substitution bias. (They refer to the traditional substitution bias discussed above as "upper-level" substitution bias.) Traditional substitution bias refers to substitutions between broad categories of goods, such as apples and oranges or beef and chicken, while lower-level substitution bias refers to switches within more narrow categories, such as between Macintosh apples and Granny Smith apples or between round steak and chuck steak. The impact of this sort of substitution is much less researched and far more poorly understood.

Research on this source of bias was initiated by BLS earlier in the decade (see Moulton 1993; 1996). Problems arise in attempting to determine the impact of lower-level substitution primarily because BLS does not have data on consumption patterns at this low a level of aggregation. As a result, switches in consumption in response to relative price changes are not directly measured (as is the case with higher-level substitution bias) but instead have to be inferred.

One method that BLS has used to examine the size of this bias is to compare its current measure of inflation to one that aggregates inflation rates at the lower level using geometric means. While the current method of aggregating inflation rates assumes that the quantity consumed of each good remains constant (arithmetic means), geometric means implicitly assume that consumers respond to relative price changes among types of goods by keeping the share of their spending on each good constant. For example, if Granny Smith apples rise in price by 10% relative to the price of other apples, then consumers will purchase 10% fewer Granny Smith apples, thereby keeping their expenditure share constant. This procedure contrasts with the current method, in which BLS assumes no change at all in the purchase of Granny Smith apples. Moulton (1993) and subsequent work (Moulton and Smedley 1995; Moulton 1996) have estimated that this assumption leads to a reduction of about 0.25 percentage points in the measured rate of inflation. The Boskin Commission took this number as its measure of lower-level substitution bias and added its 0.15% estimate of upper-level substitution bias to get an estimate of overall substitution bias of 0.4 percentage points.

There are three problems with this estimate. First, the method BLS uses to measure lower-level substitution bias employs an assumption about consumption behavior that is not plausible in many cases. For example, clothes washers and clothes dryers are in the same CPI category; it is not reasonable to assume that consumers substitute from washers to dryers in response to a price rise in washers. Assuming this sort of substitution behavior leads to an overstatement of the true size of lower-level substitution bias.[11]

The second problem with the commission's estimate is that the research on lower-level substitution bias has not been carried out over a long enough period to determine whether the size of the bias is constant or diminishing. Lower-level substitution leads to a persistent bias in the index only if goods continually diverge in price through time. If Granny Smith apples rise in price relative to other apples in one year and fall the next, then no bias results from the current methodology. The research into this source of bias has not been carried through long enough to determine how much of it persists through time.

The third problem with the commission's estimate is that simply adding upper- and lower-level substitution biases to obtain an overall measure of substitution bias incorporates some amount of double-counting of substitution bias. The categories of goods in which lower-level substitution is likely to be most important will also be places where it can be expected that there is significant substitution at the upper level. For example, suppose apples rise by 10% in price this year, largely because Granny Smith apples jump 25%. Taking account of the lower-level substitution from Granny Smith to Macintosh apples may lower the measured increase in the price of apples to 5%. The difference between the 10% price increase and 5% price increase would represent the impact of lower-level substitution in apples.

However, the size of the upper-level substitution bias, as consumers switched from apples to oranges, would have been measured using a 10% reported price rise for apples. If the correctly measured price rise for apples was only 5%, then the BLS measure of the upper-level substitution bias will overstate its amount. In other words, just adding together upper and lower substitution will overstate the true size of the substitution bias.

Given the limited research on the size of lower-level substitution bias, any estimate of the full size of the substitution bias must be considered tentative. As an alternative to the commission's assumption that the geometric mean provides an accurate measure of the impact of lower-level substitution, this analysis assumes that half of the 0.25 percentage points of bias calculated through this approach can be attributed to lower-level substitution bias. This makes the total size of the substitution bias 0.28 percentage points annually (0.15 plus 0.125 percentage points).

The BLS is currently carrying through additional research that will allow it to better estimate the size of the substitution bias and to reduce its impact on the index. The agency will attempt to determine how much of the lower-level bias is attributable to categories in which the assumed substitutions are implausible. In areas of the index in which it is reasonable to assume that substantial substitution occurs within product categories, BLS will begin to aggregate using geometric means. This change should reduce or eliminate lower-level substitution bias from the index in the near future.

BLS also plans to formalize the presentation of its data on the size of upper-level bias by constructing an experimental index that incorporates substitution. This index will appear with a considerable lag, however, since actual expenditure data do not become available until about nine months after the end of the year.

RETAIL OUTLET SUBSTITUTION BIAS

The emerging consensus about retail outlet substitution bias is that, if it exists at all, it is very small. The Boskin Commission estimated its size at 0.1 percentage points, down from 0.2 percentage points in its interim report. The basis of this bias is the price reduction that consumers obtain from shifting from higher-cost retail stores to lower-cost outlets. The CPI does not capture this change because it monitors only the change in prices within the same stores. This shortcoming would not be a problem if markets were in equilibrium, since any differences in price are presumably reflecting differences in the quality of services provided. If some consumers continue to shop at both traditional retail stores and at discount stores, then at the margin consumers must view the lower price and lower quality of service to be roughly offsetting.

But if markets are not in equilibrium, and consumers are increasingly switching to discount stores (as has been the case), then it is possible that there is a gain to consumers that is not being picked up by the CPI and that would give it an upward bias. It is relatively easy to generate an estimate of the magnitude of the possible bias generated by retail outlet substitution.

Approximately 30% of the CPI consists of goods such as food (consumed at home), household appliances, and apparel that can be sold in discount stores (see **Figure 11**). Each year consumers switch their buying so that the share of discount stores in this portion of the index increases by approximately 0.7 percentage points (MacDonald and Nelson 1991, cited in Moulton 1997). This translates into approximately 0.21% of the index (0.7% times 30%) consisting of goods that switched from traditional retail outlets to discount stores in a given year. If the savings on these goods after adjusting for differences in service quality is 10%, then the upward bias in the CPI would total 0.021% annually.

This assumed difference of 10% is actually quite large. It means that consumers weigh the price differences between stores against any extra distance traveling to a discount store, any reductions in the quality of customer services or return policy, or any other inconvenience associated with the discount store, and find the discount store on net 10% better. Yet, other consumers are still choosing to shop at traditional retail stores. In effect, the assumption of a 10% pure difference in price is saying that some consumers, seeing

FIGURE 11: Retail Outlet Substitution Bias: What's the Impact?

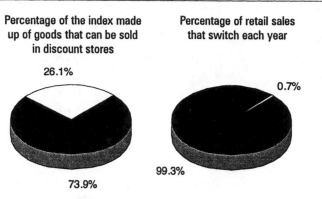

The left chart shows the percentage of the CPI that is made up of goods that can in principle be sold at discount stores. The major components that fall into this category are food at home, household appliances, household supplies, apparel, tobacco, toys, and sporting goods. Of these items, only about 0.7% of sales switch in a given year from traditional retail outlets to discount stores. This amount is equal to approximately 0.2% of the total CPI (0.7% * 26.2%). Retail outlet substitution bias could potentially apply to these goods.

Source: Author's calculations.

identical stores right next to each other, are choosing to shop at the one that charges 10% more. This would fall on the high side of plausibility, implying that the substitution bias is even less than 0.021% a year.

It is also possible that the switch to discount stores is evidence of an effect that causes the CPI to understate inflation. Because of declining real incomes, consumers may perceive themselves as being forced to shop at discount stores, particularly if they feel they have to sacrifice some of the service quality of traditional retail stores in order to take advantage of the lower prices available at discount stores. A reduction in service quality by traditional retail stores trying to remain competitive in price would not be picked up in the CPI, leading to an understatement in the true rate of inflation.[12]

It is also worth noting that the commission identifies both the movement from diverse retail outlets to homogeneous discounters, and the opposite movement to an increasing variety of speciality shops (SFC 1996, 42), as sources of unmeasured gain to consumers. While this is not impossible, change does not necessarily imply improvement.[13] In any case, any bias in the CPI attributable to retail outlet substitution is extremely small. Determining the exact size and direction of bias that factors in changes in service quality will require further research.[14]

NEW GOODS BIAS AND QUALITY BIAS

The most controversial of the commission's conclusions is its estimate of the size of the quality and new goods bias in the index. The commission estimated that the combined effects of these biases was an overstatement of inflation of 0.6 percentage points annually. Little research has been conducted on the extent and direction of quality bias in the CPI, and the commission was forced to base its estimates either on quite dated research or on simple speculation. Thus, one may reasonably feel considerable uncertainty about the accuracy of the commission's estimates.

In attempting to assess the commission's estimate, it is important to remember that BLS already makes extensive adjustments for quality in the CPI. The debate, then, is not about whether the quality of goods and services are getting better but rather about the rate at which they are getting better. BLS has not kept consistent data on the amount of quality improvements it has attributed to various areas of the CPI, but in categories of goods that make up roughly 70% of the index (virtually all of the nonshelter portion), BLS imputed quality improvements of 1.76 percentage points in 1995 (Smedley and Moulton 1996, Table 2). These quality imputations lowered the measured rate of inflation in these areas from 3.92% to 2.16%. Applying the Boskin Commission's estimate of quality and new goods bias to the 1995 data would make the true rate of improvement in the quality of these goods and services for that year *2.36%* (1.76% plus 0.6%).

Table A gives breakdowns for the rate of quality improvement in the various categories of the index for 1995. Column 1 presents the rate that is already assumed in the CPI; column 2 presents the rate that would be implied by the Boskin Commission's estimates of bias; and column 3 presents an alternative set of estimates, which will be developed later in this section. As can be seen, current BLS procedures led to substantial adjustments for quality improvements in all areas of the index. However, the Boskin Commission argues that goods and services are improving at an even more rapid rate, and that therefore the CPI overstates the true rate of inflation.

Before examining the evidence for the commission's claim, it is worth noting the size of the quality imputations in 1995 compared with previous years. BLS does not have a consistent series showing the size of the quality imputations year by year, but it does have data for 1983 and 1984. The quality imputations for these years, over roughly the same categories of items, were 1.11% and 1.23%, respectively. By 1995, the magnitude of the quality imputations was *0.59 percentage points* larger than the average for the two earlier years (1.76% minus 1.17%). If 1995 is a representative year, then this difference implies either that the rate of improvement in the quality of goods and services has increased 50% in the last 12 years (from 1.17% to 1.76%) or that

TABLE A: Estimates of Annual Rates of Quality Improvement

Major and selected minor components	Current (1995) quality imputations	Commission's estimate	Alternative estimate
1. Food and beverage	1.39	1.69	0.53
2. Housing	1.57*		
3. Apparel and upkeep	3.37	4.37	2.8
4. Transportation	1.13	1.4	0.93
5. Entertainment	4.79	5.7	4.53
6. Other goods and services	0.6	0.87	0.59
7. Medical care**	2.51	5.14	2.51
Total	1.76	2.36	1.32

*   BLS data excludes shelter.
** BLS data excludes many medical procedures.

Source: BLS, SFC 1996, and author's calculations (see text).

the changes in methodology have led the CPI to record 0.59 percentage points more quality improvement. Some combination of these effects is possible as well (see **Figure 12**).

While research is needed to determine why imputed quality improvements are so much larger than in the recent past, there are some logical implications of this trend in measured quality improvement. If the actual rate of quality improvement has not changed over the last 12 years, the data for 1995 imply that the current CPI is approximately 0.6% lower relative to the true rate of inflation that it was in 1983-84. This would mean that, if the CPI understated quality improvement by 0.6% annually in the earlier period, as argued by the Boskin Commission, then it is currently measuring quality improvement correctly.

In addition to being quite large, the basis of many of the current quality adjustments in the CPI also raises the possibility that quality is being overstated and inflation is being understated. The CPI has several different methods for assessing quality improvements. For the vast majority of its price quotes, BLS is able to price the exact same product and therefore does not need to make any quality adjustment. For about 4.0% of its price quotes, the agency has to find a substitute product because the original is no longer available. In most of these cases, it is possible to find another product that is almost identical to the earlier one, and no quality adjustment is necessary. The cases for

FIGURE 12: A Changing Quality Bias Through Time?
Quality Improvements Imputed in the CPI

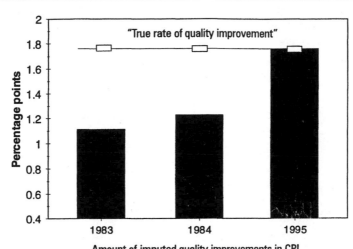

Amount of imputed quality improvements in CPI

This chart shows the rate of quality improvement in the CPI that BLS attributed to the 70% of the index for which it has data. The bars show that the size of the quality improvements attributed in the CPI increased by nearly 0.6 percentage points over this period. The line shows a hypothetical "true" rate of quality improvement that assumes that Boskin Commission's estimate of a 0.6 percentage point annual bias through the 1980s is correct, and therefore that the true rate of quality improvement through this period was 1.77 percentage points annually. If the true rate of quality improvement has not changed, then BLS measured the rate of quality improvement almost perfectly in 1995, falling just 0.01 percentage point below the rate that would be applied by assuming that the Boskin Commission's estimate of quality bias was correct for the 1980s.

Source: Smedley and Moulton 1996 and author's calculations.

which it is necessary to make some sort of quality adjustment typically amount to only about 1.3% of all the price quotes in the CPI for a given year.

In some of these cases, BLS attempts to measure quality improvements in new products directly by using hedonic regressions, or by attempting to establish the market price of the quality improvement. (Hedonic regressions measure quality by calculating prices of specific characteristics, such as additional memory in computers.) An example of the latter would be treating the price of an airbag, which is now standard equipment in new cars, as a quality improvement and not as an increase in the price of the car.

However, because it is often not possible to directly compare the quality of a new product and the product it replaced, it is sometimes necessary to impute the amount of quality improvement. The BLS makes such imputations through a "link pricing" method, which assumes that the price change for the new product in the index is the same as the price change for other products in the same category of goods. The remaining difference in price between the new and old product is viewed as a change in quality.

Hulten (1996) shows that far more quality improvement is attributed to new items in the sample for which quality could not be directly measured than it is for products for which BLS actually attempts to measure quality. In 1995, BLS made direct quality adjustments to 0.46% of its price quotes (Smedley and Moulton 1996, Table 2). The total amount of quality improvements attributed to these products led to an increase in quality for the portion of the index for which BLS has data of 0.11 percentage points. BLS used link pricing in 0.57% of its price quotes; by contrast, these quotes accounted for quality improvements of 0.99 percentage points. If the rate of quality improvement in the goods that were linked in was no greater than the rate for items in which it was measured directly, then the linked goods would have added only 0.14 percentage points of quality improvement to the index (0.11% divided by 0.46%, then multiplied by 0.57%). In this case, the quality improvements attributed to the linked goods would have been too high and would have led to an overstatement of quality of 0.85 percentage points.[15] A similar calculation would have led to an overstatement of quality improvements in 1983 and 1984 as well, although the size of the overstatement would be considerably smaller.

The commission seems to have paid little attention to the existing evidence on the size of the quality imputations that already appear in the CPI. The large absolute amount of the imputation, as well as the large increase in the size from the early 1980s to 1995, might raise suspicion that the rate of quality improvement has been overstated. Hulten's observation — that most of this quality improvement is imputed from items for which there has been no direct effort to measure quality — should also provide a basis for suspicion. The limited amount of available evidence leaves a large realm of uncertainty, and more research is needed to determine exactly how and where BLS is imputing quality improvements.

The Boskin Commission's estimate of 0.612 percentage points as the size of the annual quality and new goods bias in the CPI is the sum of a series of estimates of bias in various categories in the index. As noted before, since there has been little effort to evaluate the direction and extent of quality and new goods bias in the CPI, the commission was forced to rely on a limited, and often dated, body of research. Thus, its estimates of bias cannot be rigorously derived from empirical research.

There are six distinct problems that can be identified in the commission's estimates of quality and new goods bias:

1. Many of the estimates depend exclusively on introspection — thought experiments in which the commission members speculate on the amount of bias in the index. The commissioners use introspection to make estimates of bias that cover 58.33% of the index and account for 0.171 of the 0.612-percentage-point estimate of quality and new goods bias.

2. In a set of estimates, the commission has misinterpreted the findings of earlier research. This problem arises in estimates of bias in items that make up 10.37% of the index and account for 0.242 percentage points of the commission's estimate of bias.

3. In some estimates, the commission has made dubious extrapolations from research. Estimates that cover 6.47% of the index and account for 0.038 percentage points of bias fall into this category.

4. In another set of estimates, BLS has implemented a procedural change that has not been taken into account. These estimates cover 5.73% of the index and account for 0.172 percentage points of bias.

5. In the commission's treatment of personal financial services, a category that covers 0.4% of the index and accounts for 0.009 percentage points of bias, the source of bias identified (if accurate) should apply to the measure of personal income in the national income and product accounts, not to the consumer price index.

6. One of the commission's estimates (for nonprescription drugs and medical supplies) has no support whatsoever. This estimate covers 0.39% of the CPI and accounts for 0.004 percentage points of bias.

Each of these first five problems will be examined in turn.

First, however, it is worth noting another problem that arises with many of these estimates, and that is double-counting. In many cases it appears that the commission's estimates of quality and new goods bias also incorporate the impact of other sources of bias in the index. The commission explicitly notes this problem in the report:

> Evidence on quality change bias developed in other studies, for instance Gordon (1990), is based on an attempt to measure prices directly from sources independent of BLS price quotations, using such sources as mail order catalogues and *Consumer Reports*. However, any differences between these independent indexes and the CPI for the same goods may reflect not just quality change and new product bias, but also traditional substitution bias (since the mix of products and models shifts faster in the alternative source than the CPI), outlet substitution bias (since alternative price quotes are often an average of market prices which adjusts for the changing mix of discount stores), and formula bias (since the alternative indexes are free from the formula bias problems discussed previously). (SFC 1996, 33)

However, the commission seems largely to have ignored this observation in its subsequent examination of quality and new goods bias. This problem of double-counting will be noted at several points in the subsequent discussion.

Introspection.

Nearly a third of the Boskin Commission's estimate of quality and new goods bias is based on introspection. In these estimates the commission members used their judgment to speculate on how much the CPI understates quality improvements in various categories of expenditures. While their judgment is not necessarily wrong, economists ordinarily do not view this sort of specula-tion as a substitute for evidence. Instead, they usually try to find evidence that exists independently of the opinions of the particular economist or econo-mists who are carrying through the research. The absence of any such evi-dence for many of the commission's estimates means that the estimates can-not be evaluated critically by normal economic procedures.

The commission's estimate of the quality bias in the category of foods and beverages provides an example of the way in which the commission used introspection. The commission estimated that bias in this category amounted to 0.3 percentage points annually. The only research cited to support this esti-mate was a study of the importance of new breakfast cereals (Hausman 1996), which concluded that the increased variety of breakfast cereals led to an un-measured gain to consumers in this area of 0.25% annually. The main support for the commission's estimate is the following exercise in introspection:

> How much would a consumer pay to have the privilege of choosing from the variety of items available in today's supermarket instead of being constrained to the much more limited variety available 30 years ago? A conservative estimate of the extra variety and convenience might be 10% for food con-sumed at home other than produce, 20% for produce where the increased variety in winter (as well as summer farmers' markets) has been so notable, and 5% for alcoholic beverages where imported beer, microbreweries, and greatly improved distribution of imported wines from all over the world have improved the standard of living. (SFC 1996, 41-2)

It is difficult to evaluate the accuracy of this kind of exercise. In the case of food and beverages, however, BLS already makes substantial adjustments for quality. In 1995, BLS attributed 1.39 percentage points of quality improve-ment to this category (Smedley and Moulton 1996, Table 2), implying that the quality of the food and beverages consumers purchased in 1995 was 1.69% better than it was in 1994. The current BLS measure therefore imputes an extremely rapid rate of quality improvement in this category (see **Figure 13**). There is no indication from the commission's discussion of its introspection that the quality improvements already in the CPI were factored into its esti-

FIGURE 13: How Good Is the Food?
Estimated Quality Improvement 1994-95

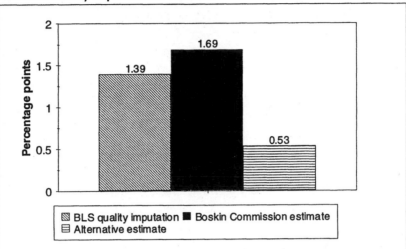

This chart shows the implied rate of improvement in the quality of food and beverages between 1994 and 1995 according to the CPI, the Boskin Commission, and an alternative estimate developed in this section. The CPI imputed a rate of quality improvement in this category of 1.39% in 1995. The Boskin Commission estimated that the CPI still undercounted quality improvements in this category by 0.3 percentage points, implying a 1.69% rate of quality improvement in 1995. The alternative estimate assumes that the quality of food and beverages actually improved at a 0.53% rate; this is the average rate of quality improvement that BLS attributed in this category in 1983 and 1984.

Source: Smedley and Moulton 1996 and author's calculations.

mates.[16] If they were, the commission's estimate of the true amount of quality improvement in this category for 1995 would have to be 1.69 percentage points, not 0.3 percentage points. This is not impossible, but it is a strong claim to rest exclusively on a thought experiment.

The commission used a similar exercise in introspection to obtain an estimate of 0.25 percentage points as the size of the annual bias in the shelter component, which makes up 28.3% of the index. The commission derived this estimate by an extrapolation from a comparison with its own index of rental prices, which is based on data from the U.S. Census Bureau's Current Housing Reports. The commission's index showed average rental prices increasing approximately 1.0% per year more rapidly than the BLS rental index. The commission then claimed that the average size of rental units had increased by approximately 1.0% per year as well.[17] Since the average size of a rental unit had increased by 1% a year, and the average rent paid in the commission's index increased at a rate that was 1% greater than the CPI index, the commission concluded that the CPI rental index had accurately tracked the price per square foot in rental housing but had failed to pick up the improvements in quality. The commission then uses introspection to estimate the size of the unmeasured quality improvement: "A conservative estimate is that the total increase in quality per square foot, including the rental value of all appliances, central air conditioning, and improved bathroom plumbing, and other amenities, amounts to 10 percent over the past 40 years, or 0.25 percent a year" (SFC 1996, 46).

This estimate presents the same problem as the estimate of bias in the food and beverage component: it is hard to evaluate a number obtained through introspection. However, it is worth noting three problems that arise in the construction of the commission's alternative index, which formed the basis for this exercise in introspection.

First, and most importantly, the commission's index takes no account of the location of housing. The Housing Survey conducted by the Census Bureau simply gives average rents for the nation as a whole. Over the last 20 years there has been a significant shift of population from the relatively high-cost Northeast to the relatively low-cost South. According to the Consumer Expenditure Survey, 27.3% of all renters lived in the Northeast in 1973, compared with just 22.3% in 1992; the share of renters living in the South rose from 28.9% to 33.0% over this period. There has also been a shift in population from cities and nearby suburbs to distant suburbs where land, and therefore housing, tends to be cheaper. Both these population shifts would have the effect of lowering the Census measure of rental costs relative to a location-specific measure like the CPI. The persistence of substantial price differentials indicates that consumers place considerable value on housing location.[18] Therefore, there seems little justification for the commission's decision to ignore location in its assessment of housing quality.

A second reason for questioning the commission's assessment is that it assumes that the price per square foot of housing is constant as the size of units increase. This assumption would imply that a 4,000 square foot house typically sells for twice the price of a 2,000 square foot house. This seems unlikely if for no other reason that the cost of housing construction is less than proportionate to the square footage.[19]

A third reason why the commission's index might understate the true increase in costs is that a smaller portion of the population was renting at the end of the period it examined than at the beginning. According to the Consumer Expenditure Survey, 41.2% of households were renters in 1973; by 1993 the percentage had fallen to 37.0%. If the rental population on average has a lower income than the homeowner population, then the average renter in 1993 was at a lower point in the income distribution than the average renter in 1973. This means that the commission's index is calculating the average rent paid by a relatively poorer segment of the population in 1993 than in 1973. This would lead its index to rise less rapidly than one that had followed rent for the same segment of the population.

All three of these factors would tend to cause the per foot rental index the commission constructed from the Housing Census to rise less rapidly than the rental index in the CPI. It would not be easy to quantify each of these effects, but it is plausible that their sum exceeds the commission's 0.25% estimate of the size of the annual quality improvement in rental housing. Therefore, the commission's exercise in introspection gives little reason to believe there is a high-side bias in the BLS measure of shelter prices.

The commission also used introspection to derive an estimate of 1.0 percentage point annually in measuring the quality of household utilities, 0.33 percentage points for the category "other housefurnishings," and 0.25 percentage points for motor fuel. In the case of utilities the commission noted a "continuous improvement in the quality of telephone service (e.g., reduction of static and improvement in clarity), improved convenience (credit card pay phones, itemized billing), and a great increase in picture quality and consumer choice achieved by cable television viewed as a new product (SFC 1996, 48). In the case of the "other housefurnishings" category, the commission cites the availability of new products and fabrics that are less susceptible to stains and children's accidents (SFC 1996, 50). The basis for the quality bias estimate in motor fuels is the increased availability of automatic credit-card readers built into gas pumps (SFC 1996, 56).

In none of these cases does the commission cite any evidence of how much consumers actually value the improvements noted. More importantly, the commission presents no evidence that it has taken into account the amount of quality improvement that BLS has already attributed in these areas. (The discussion in the report implies that the commission assumed that BLS imputed no quality improvement for these factors.) There is no hard evidence on either of these points, but the large quality adjustments that are already incorporated into the CPI make it unlikely that the improvements noted by the commission were completely missed by BLS. Determining whether the CPI actually understated or overstated inflation in these areas will require something more than introspection.

Misinterpreted research findings.
While the commission lacked any research to support many of its conclusions, some of the estimates in which it does cite research misinterpret its

findings. In particular, using a study of durable goods prices by commission member Robert Gordon (1990), the commission makes estimates of the size of annual quality bias of 2.83 percentage points for household appliances, 4.69 percentage points for television sets, 2.0 percentage points for entertainment commodities, and 0.9 percentage points for personal care commodities. It also estimates a 1.0-percentage-point annual bias in apparel based on a study of apparel prices by Gordon (1996). Evidence in both these studies indicates that the CPI was actually overstating quality improvements and *understating* inflation for these goods in the periods examined. The commission cites evidence from two studies co-authored by commission member Zvi Griliches (Berndt, Cockburn, and Griliches 1996; Griliches and Cockburn, 1994) to argue that the CPI overstates the rate of inflation in prescription drugs by 2.0% annually. These studies also provide evidence that the current BLS procedures may actually overstate quality improvement in prescription drugs and therefore understate the true rate of inflation.

Gordon's 1990 study constructed alternative indexes based on Sears catalogs and issues of *Consumer Reports* for a series of durable goods. The study focused mostly on the producer price index and investment goods, but it also includes comparisons for several household appliances with the CPI. Unfortunately, the study is somewhat dated (its endpoint is 1983), and it conflates different sources of bias, which results in double-counting.

The commission, using a comparison between Gordon's "energy and repair cost adjusted" *Consumer Reports* index and the CPI, finds a 2.83-percentage-point CPI overstatement of inflation for household appliances and a 4.69-percentage-point overstatement for television sets for the period from 1974 to 1983. This measure leads to several types of double-counting (as noted in the earlier quote from the commission's report).

A better measure of quality bias can be obtained by comparing Gordon's Sears index for these products with the CPI (see **Figure 14**). This measure removes some of the double-counting, since it involves no substitution between retail outlets. This index actually rose *more rapidly* than the CPI for this period, suggesting that the CPI overstated quality improvement and *understated* inflation for these goods. On average, Gordon's Sears index for these goods showed a 0.77% higher annual rate of inflation for these goods than did the CPI (Baker 1996a, Table 10). The actual degree of understatement of inflation for these products implied by Gordon's study is even larger, since the CPI included an upward formula bias for the last three years attributable to sample rotation bias. Factoring in the impact of this additional source of bias gives an estimate of 0.85% as the size of the overstatement of quality improvement implied by Gordon's study.[20]

Gordon's recent study of apparel prices, in which he used Sears catalogs

FIGURE 14: Competing Price Indices:
CPI, Sears, and *Consumer Reports*-Adjusted

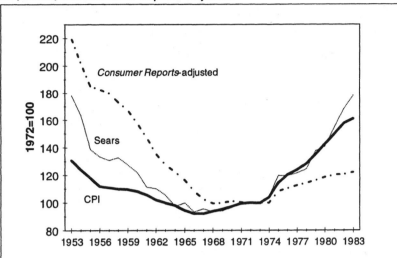

This chart shows the rate of inflation for a series of major household appliances as measured by the CPI, an index constructed by Robert Gordon based on Sears catalogs, and an "energy and repair cost adjusted" index he constructed from *Consumer Reports* magazine. The CPI and Sears index follow reasonably closely over the whole period, with the CPI showing a somewhat higher rate of inflation until the mid-sixties and then a lower rate in later years. The *Consumer Reports* index falls rapidly relative to both indices throughout the period. Since the Sears index already includes factors that take energy usage and repairs at least partly into account, the divergence is probably attributable to the fact that Gordon attached too large a premium to these savings when he added them into his *Consumer Reports* index.

Source: Gordon 1990 and author's calculations.

to construct apparel indexes for the periods 1914-47 and 1965-93, suffers from the same problems as his earlier work. The commission broke the latter period into two subperiods, and found an upward quality bias (and therefore an understatement of inflation) in the CPI apparel index in 1965-85 and a downward quality bias in the CPI in 1985-93. Based on the latter, the commission estimated the size of the annual quality bias in the CPI apparel index as 1.0%.

A careful reading of the Gordon study shows that it conflates different sources of bias and therefore cannot be used to support this estimate. Specifically, the comparison of the CPI apparel index with the Sears catalog index will measure not only the effect of quality bias but also sample rotation bias, which was largely eliminated from apparel when BLS introduced a seasoning method for new items in apparel in October 1989. The CPI apparel index has actually increased 0.57% less than Gordon's Sears index in the years since BLS changed its methodology (a 2.38% annual increase in the CPI apparel index compared with 2.95% increase in the Sears index) (see **Figure 15**). As with the Gordon studies, both of the studies that form the basis of the estimated bias in prescription drug prices conflate different sources of bias (Cockburn and Griliches 1994; Berndt et al. 1996). The estimates of bias in these studies include not only the impact of new goods, but also the impact of changing the weights of the drugs in the sample. This is a form of lower-level substitution bias, not quality or new goods bias (SFC 1996, 57).[21] Apart from this issue, both of these studies provide evidence that the current BLS procedure might understate inflation in prescription drugs.

These studies construct several different price indexes and examine the

FIGURE 15: Inflation in Apparel: CPI and Sears

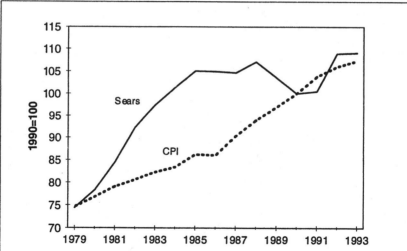

This chart compares the rate of inflation in apparel products as measured by the CPI and an index based on Sears catalog prices constructed by Robert Gordon. The Sears index generally rises more rapidly except for the period between 1985 and 1990. In 1985 BLS changed its procedure for goods that were closed out, at a sale price, at the last point they were included in the sample; this procedure would have led to a higher measured rate of inflation. In 1989 BLS changed the way new apparel items were brought into the sample, and this change seems to have led to a lower measured rate of inflation in apparel. In the three years for which Gordon has data following this change in procedure, his Sears measure showed on average a 0.57 percentage point higher rate of inflation.

Source: Gordon 1996 and author's calculations.

difference between these indexes and ones they modeled on BLS procedures. The Cockburn and Griliches study models the CPI methodology that was in place prior to 1995, while the Berndt et al. study models the BLS procedure used in the producer price index. One of the main issues these studies examine is the impact of the introduction of generic drugs on drug prices. Prior to 1995, BLS treated generic drugs as a distinct product from the equivalent branded drug, and therefore the lower price of the generic drug was not recorded as a price decline. The Berndt et al. study was more extensive, since it also estimated the quality gain associated with the introduction of new branded drugs.

An alternative approach for generic drugs, suggested in both articles, treats half the difference between the price of a branded drug and a generic as a price decline and half as a decline in quality. While the various indexes the articles constructed that embodied this approach all declined relative to the indexes modeled on BLS procedures, the indexes rose significantly more rapidly than an average price index, which the authors also calculated. This index treated the generic the same as the branded drug and simply tracked the average price paid in the market based on the relative market shares of the branded and generic drugs. For the two drugs examined in the Cockburn and Griliches study, the average price index fell an average of 7.00% a year more rapidly than the index they favored.[22]

A comparable average price index in the Berndt et al. study also rose significantly less rapidly than the authors' preferred index. The difference between these indexes was larger than the estimated quality gain associated with the introduction of new drugs. The difference between the annual rate of price change shown by the average price index and the preferred measure in the study was 3.94%, while the average estimated quality gain associated with the introduction of new drugs was just 0.4%.[23] This difference implies that for this category of drugs, the average price index would have overstated quality improvements and understated inflation by 3.54 percentage points annually.

The new methodology adopted by BLS in 1995 effectively applies the methodology used to construct the average cost indexes in these two studies. As noted before, this procedure treats generic and branded drugs the same, and so there is no quality loss associated with the shift to the generic version. Yet even though the active agent in branded and generic drugs is the same, real differences exist in quality control and the inert substances used that can have significant consequences for many patients. In any case, many doctors and patients believe there is a difference in quality between branded and generic drugs, and only by violating standard economic procedure can this perception be ignored.[24] Therefore, following standard economic practice, and the results of these two studies, it can be inferred that the current methodology would lead to a substantial understatement of inflation when generic drugs become available.

In all the cases discussed above, the Boskin Commission made estimates of a high-side bias in the CPI that rely on research indicating that the CPI may actually understate inflation in these categories. While these studies cannot be taken as conclusive evidence of an understatement of inflation, they certainly cannot be used to support the estimates of bias in the Boskin Commission report.

Questionable extrapolations.

Two of the Boskin Commission's estimates of quality and new goods bias — those for new and used cars and for computers — rest on dubious extrapolations from research findings. The commission estimated an annual bias of 0.59 percentage points in the measure of new and used car prices. (The bias estimate for used cars actually appears as 1.59 percentage points in the table, but it is described as 0.59 percentage points in the text.) This estimate is also loosely derived from Gordon (1990), and therefore suffers from the same problem of double-counting as the earlier estimates. The commission estimated an annual bias of 15.0 percentage points in the CPI measure of computer prices; this estimate relies on a study by Berndt, Griliches, and Rappaport (1995).

Although the Gordon study concluded that the CPI index of new car prices rose at approximately the same rate as the alternative index constructed in the study over the period 1958-83 (Gordon 1990, 367), the commission inferred a bias of 0.59% based on the increased durability of automobiles. Its estimate of increased durability is based on an increase in the average age of automobiles in use. As the commission notes (p. 55), this increase may be at least partially attributable to factors other than durability, such as a rise in the relative price of new cars or an increase in the number of households with a second or third car. The validity of adding an adjustment for durability also requires that durability not be correlated with any of the variables in Gordon's hedonic regressions. Otherwise, increased durability would already have been factored into his index.

It is also worth noting that BLS actually makes extensive quality adjustments for factors that increase the durability of cars. Appendix B gives a list of some of the quality adjustments related to durability that BLS has made since 1992.

The issue of double-counting that arises with Gordon's new car index stems from the formulaic bias that resulted from the introduction of the sample rotation system in 1980. As with appliances, this bias would have led to a higher measured rate of inflation in the CPI new car index in the last three years of the Gordon study.

However, this problem of double-counting is small compared to the fact that the CPI new car index rose *1.73% less* per year than Gordon's alternative index over the last four years studied (a 6.84% annual rise in the Gordon alternative index compared with 5.11% in the CPI). Gordon attributes this difference to the inclusion in the CPI of imported cars; his own index included only domestic cars. The sharp rise in the dollar during this period should have led to a relative decline in the price of foreign cars (Gordon 1990, 367).

Imported cars may explain part of the difference between the two indexes, although they constituted only about 15% of the domestic market at the time. To explain the full difference, the decline in the relative price of foreign cars would have to have been about 11.5% annually over these four years, for a cumulative (and implausible) fall in relative price of approximately 50%. Therefore, Gordon's index should be taken to indicate some understatement of inflation in the CPI new car index in the final years of his study (see **Figure 16**).

Any assessment of the quality bias in the new car index should also take into account the nature of the procedure BLS uses to make quality adjustments for new cars. Each year BLS receives information from the auto manufacturers detailing all the price increases they claim were attributable to qual-

FIGURE 16: Car Prices: CPI and Commission

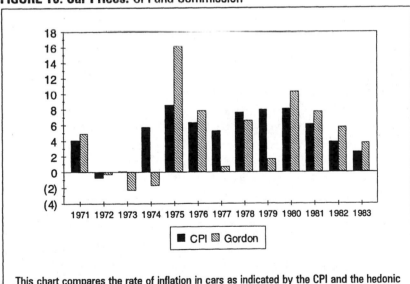

This chart compares the rate of inflation in cars as indicated by the CPI and the hedonic index Gordon constructed in his 1990 study. The two follow each other reasonably closely on average, but Gordon's new car index rises considerably more rapidly than the CPI in the last four years of his study.

Source: Gordon 1990 and author's calculations.

ity improvements. The cost of these improvements is then deducted from the actual increase in car prices to generate the increases that appear in the CPI new car index. Although BLS independently evaluates the manufacturers' claims before accepting a cost increase as a quality improvement, this does not seem like a process that is likely to lead to an undercounting of quality and an overstatement of price increases for new cars. (A similar process is now applied in constructing the used car index as well.) In total, the quality adjustments that BLS applied over the period 1967-94 reduced the average annual rate of inflation in the new car category from 5.40% to 3.78% (Abraham 1995).

The commission's extrapolation from the Berndt, Griliches, and Rappaport study to generate an estimate of 15% as the size of the annual bias in the CPI's measure of computer prices suffers from three serious problems. First, many of the computers examined were clearly for business use and therefore not relevant to the CPI measure of inflation. Second, if different computer users value features differently (e.g., some users place a premium on additional RAM while others consider additional memory of little or no value), then the study does not give an accurate measure of the rate of price decline in computers. Third, in a rapidly changing industry, it cannot be assumed that price patterns observed in the period 1989-92 would still be applicable in 1997 and later.

As to the first problem, the study examined all desktop and portable computers without distinguishing between those used for business purposes or consumption. The average price for the computers examined over the period 1989-92 was $4,066; $22,655 was the highest price (Berndt et al., Table 3). Over the three-year period examined, the average price (not adjusted for quality) fell 26.2%, from $4,616 in 1989 to $3,378 in 1992 (Berndt et al., Table 1). The relatively high prices of the computers in this study would suggest that a large portion of the models being examined were purchased primarily for business use. Therefore, the price declines in these models are not relevant to the CPI, which tracks prices for goods used in personal consumption.

The second problem seems unavoidable, since consumers use computers for different purposes. While some users have been willing to pay a large premium for additional RAM or speed, many users assign these characteristics relatively little value. For these users, the measured decline in price would considerably overstate the true gain. This possibility is also suggested by the finding of the Berndt et al. study that the values placed on various characteristics in the hedonic regressions for desktop computers were not stable over the period examined. It is possible that the rate of price decline in this category already recorded in the CPI (an average of 8.3% over the last seven years) overstates the gains for many consumers.

The third problem is that it is questionable whether it is possible, in this case, to extrapolate to the present and future findings that are based on a study that used data from the period 1989-92. One of the main purposes of the Berndt et al. study was the examination of products in an industry experiencing extraordinarily rapid technological change. It may be the case that the pace of technological progress in computers is unchanged, but it certainly cannot be assumed that computers are still improving at the same rate and will continue to do so in the future.

Certainly the implications of this assumption seem questionable. Adding the commission's 15% estimate of the size of the annual bias in the computer index to the 8.3% rate of price decline recorded in the CPI gives an annual rate of price decline of 23.3%. If this rate is assumed to continue through 1997, the quality-adjusted price of a computer this year would be just 12% of its 1989 price. By the year 2000, the quality-adjusted price will have fallen to 3.2% of its 1989 level. This extrapolation is not necessarily wrong, but it suggests that extraordinary rates of technological change cannot be assumed to continue indefinitely. [25]

It is also worth noting the low price elasticity of computers that would be implied by the commission's estimate. If the commission's estimate is correct, the average decline in the nominal price of computers over the period 1989-96 was 23.3%. The average increase in the CPI over this period was 3.4%. Even if a commission-adjusted CPI is used (3.4% - 1.1% = 2.3%), the average real price decline for computers was over 25% annually. Computer sales rose by 186% over this period, from 8,469,600 in 1989 to 24,200,000 in 1996,[26] implying an annual rate of growth of 16.2%. Real GDP grew by roughly 2.0% a year over this period (3.0% using a commission-adjusted measure), which means that if computers are a normal good the demand for which can be assumed to grow at least as fast as overall income, then the expected rate of growth in computer demand should have been 2% a year in the absence of any decline in the relative price of computers. This means that a growth rate of approximately 14.2% in the demand for computers can be attributed to their relative price decline. If the commission's estimate of bias is correct, the implied price elasticity of demand for computers is just 0.53 (14.2/26.6 = 0.53), meaning that the demand for computers is extremely inelastic (see **Figure 17**). Again, this conclusion is not impossible, but it may cause one to question the commission's use of the Berndt, Griliches, and Rappaport study.

The consequence of a bias in measuring computer prices would not be large in any case: the weight of computers in the CPI is currently just 0.1%. The commission presented evidence suggesting that it should perhaps be as high as 0.4%. Even if this weight is correct, and the bias in the CPI measure is as much as 10 percentage points annually, the resulting bias in the index as a whole would be just 0.04 percentage points.

FIGURE 17: The Decline in Computer Prices: CPI and Commission

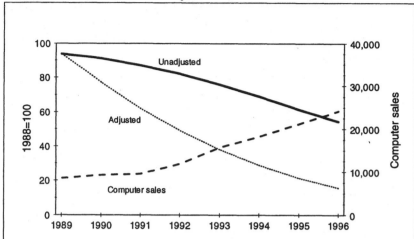

This chart shows the decline in computer prices by using the BLS measure and an index that incorporates the bias that the commission attributes to computer pricing. It shows that computer prices would have fallen to less than 20% of their 1989 level by the commission's measure. The chart also shows the increase in computer sales over this period. Sales did not quite triple over this seven-year period. If the commission's judgment of the true rate of price decline is accurate, then demand for computers has been extremely inelastic.

Source: BLS and SFC 1996.

Ignoring changes in BLS procedures.

The commission's report presents estimates of what the commission believed the bias in various categories to have been in the recent past, but it seems to have intended these estimates to apply to the present and near future as well. However, in two areas where the commission found evidence of bias — hospital services and professional medical services — BLS has changed its procedures, and so the estimates of past bias cannot be applied to the future.

The commission, using two studies, one examining the price of cataract surgery (Wilcox and Shapiro 1996) and the other examining the cost of treatment for heart attacks (Cutler et al. 1996), estimated the size of the annual bias in hospital services and professional medical services as 3.0 percentage points. These studies raise two sets of issues, one of which is likely to be addressed by the recent change in CPI methodology, while the other will not. The reason for the finding of a large CPI bias in measuring the price of cataract surgery in the Wilcox and Shapiro study was the reduced duration of the hospital stay associated with this procedure. The authors note that the average hospital stay associated with cataract surgery was seven nights in the 1950s, while currently the operation is usually performed on an out-patient basis. The methodology used by BLS prior to 1997 would have missed the reduction in cost associated with this change, since it priced specific procedures.[27] However, the methodology implemented in January 1997, which will attempt to follow the hospital bills associated with specific medical problems, should pick up the large cost savings noted in the Wilcox and Shapiro study and therefore eliminate this source of bias.[28]

The issues raised by the Cutler et al. study are more complex. This study attempts to set a price on a given outcome, measured in terms of increased life expectancy following heart attacks. Focusing on outcomes, however, inevitably raises questions that are difficult for economists to address. For example, it is not easy to determine how much value should be attached to reduced recovery time or an increase in mobility after knee surgery. Nor is it clear how the need for additional future expenditures, such as necessary medication or physical therapy, ought to be counted. This set of questions will be addressed more fully in the section discussing the distinction between a price index and a cost-of-living index.

Misidentifying the composition of the CPI.

The commission estimated a 0.2-percentage-point annual bias in the personal and educational services category based on an assumed annual bias in the financial services category. It attributed this bias to unmeasured gains from cash management accounts and automated teller machines (ATMs). The problem with this estimate is that the unmeasured gains the commission refers to should be included in the national income and product accounts under income, not in the CPI. One of the categories of personal income in these accounts is the value of imputed interest payments by financial intermediaries (U.S. Department of Commerce 1991, M-7). This amount includes the value of services such as free checking provided to customers who maintain funds in accounts that pay either no interest or less than the market rate of interest. A determination of whether there has been any undercounting of the gains from innovations such as cash management accounts or ATM machines would require an examination of the methodology used for determining the real value of these imputations. However, these gains would not affect the CPI, which is intended to be a deflator for cash income only. Therefore, regardless of the accuracy of the commission's assessment of the unmeasured quality gain resulting from these innovations, it should not be included in a measure of quality bias in the CPI.

Summing up: Is there evidence for quality and new goods bias?

On close analysis, the commission's estimates of unmeasured gains from quality improvements and new goods has little support. Exercises in introspection
can be informative, but they cannot substitute for actual evidence. In some
cases the commission used research that presented evidence of overadjusting
for quality to support its claim that quality was being undercounted. In some
cases it made extrapolations from research that were altogether unwarranted,
and it ignored, in making two of its estimates, an important change in BLS
procedures. In one case, it noted a problem that is irrelevant to the construction of the CPI, and in another it presented no justification whatsoever for its
estimate. In short, the commission's estimate of the size of the quality and
new goods bias in the CPI can at best be seen as speculative. It does not rest on
a solid foundation of empirical research.

Suppose the categories in the CPI were examined in this same speculative way but with an eye toward finding a CPI *understatement* of inflation
rather than an overstatement. The following exercise generates an alternative
set of estimates with as solid a foundation as those propounded by the commission. (They are summed up in Table B below.)

The estimates that rely exclusively on the commission's introspection
provide a good starting point. In the food and beverage category, the commission developed an estimate based on how much better it thought various products had become over the last 30 years, without any obvious reference to the
quality adjustments already included in the CPI. As an alternative, it is possible to derive an estimate based on the size of these adjustments. In 1995
BLS imputed quality improvements of 1.39% in the food and beverage category; in 1983 and 1984 it attributed rates of quality improvement of 0.31%
and 0.75%, respectively. Suppose that the BLS imputations for quality improvement in these earlier years were accurate, and that the rate of quality
improvement in this category had not changed from the early 1980s. Based on
that assumption, it could be estimated that the true rate of quality improvement in 1995 was just 0.53% (the average of the 1983 and 1984 numbers),
implying an overstatement of quality improvement in this category of 0.86
percentage points.

In the shelter component of housing, the commission noted that average
rents had risen about 1.0 percentage points a year *faster* on average than the
BLS shelter index. It concluded that this was not fast enough to account for
what it believed the rate of quality improvement to be. It is possible to develop
a crude market-based measure of quality improvement in this area. Comparing the sale price of new homes to the sale price of existing homes allows a
determination of how much more new homes are valued than existing homes.
Multiplying this ratio by the ratio of new homes to the existing housing stock

gives a crude measure of how rapidly new construction is improving the existing housing stock. Over the period from 1976 to 1993, this ratio averages just 0.24% a year.[29] If this amount is doubled to 0.48% to include the impact of additions and improvements on existing housing and the removal of inferior units from the housing stock, it still gives a rate of quality improvement that is 0.52 percentage points less than the gap between the average rent index used by the commission and the shelter index in the CPI. We might thus enter this 0.52% figure as the alternative measure of the rate of overstatement of quality improvement in the CPI shelter index.

While the commission noted quality improvements in utilities that it claimed were unmeasured in the CPI, it is also possible to identify some important quality declines in this category. The breakup of AT&T's monopoly on telephone service has created many new options for consumers, but it has also led to a considerable amount of search costs as consumers seek out the best deals. An additional 1.5 hours per year per household spent looking at telephone advertisements or comparing offerings would be equal to a 5.0-percentage-point unmeasured deterioration in the quality of telephone service.[30]

Such search costs would affect other utilities as well. In most areas, garbage collection used to be a city service or performed by a private contractor with a monopoly in a given area. Now, it is increasingly common for households to arrange their own garbage collection. This arrangement may allow many to obtain lower-cost service, which should be picked up in the CPI, but the additional time spent searching will not be counted.

A last form of quality deterioration that can be included in this category results directly from the growth of cable television, which the commission views as an unmeasured quality improvement. While cable television offers new options to consumers, it also has affected the quality of broadcast television. It can be argued that the quality of broadcast television has deteriorated as more "event" programming (sports, concerts) becomes available exclusively on cable or other forms of pay television. The most obvious example of such a deterioration is a gradual migration of sporting events from free television to cable. For example, Andrew Zimbalist calculated that the number of baseball games available on free television declined by 7% from 1987 to 1992 (1992, 157). Insofar as a deterioration in the quality of free television is a factor, the decision to pay for cable television must be seen as an increase in the cost of living rather than an unmeasured quality improvement. Households now have to pay upwards of $30 a month for broadcasts that they used to get free.

For an alternative estimate, apply the 5.0 percentage points of unmeasured quality decline that was speculated to have occurred in telephone services to the whole category. Over a 20-year period, this comes to 0.25 percentage points a year, which we will use as the alternative measure of the rate of overstatement of quality improvement in the CPI "other utilities" index.

In motor fuels, one of the other areas in which the commission relied on introspection, there is also an important source of unmeasured quality decline. The number of gas stations and pumps has declined significantly in recent years.[31] An addition of just three minutes a week in the time an average household spends traveling to gas stations or waiting to use a pump would lead to an unmeasured cost to consumers of $52 per year (based on average hourly compensation of about $20 per hour), or about 5.0% of average annual expenditures on gasoline and motor fuel.[32] Averaged over a 20-year period, this unmeasured decline in quality comes to 0.25 percentage points annually. We'll use this as the alternative estimate for motor fuel.

In the cases where the basis of the commission's estimates were misinterpreted research findings, we enter the actual research findings as our alternative estimate. As noted earlier, Gordon's study (1990) provides evidence that the CPI was overstating quality improvements in household appliances by 0.85 percentage points annually in the last period he examined. The commission also used the Gordon research to generate estimates of bias for the entertainment commodities and personal care categories; we therefore apply an alternative quality overstatement of 0.59 percentage points to the entertainment commodities category to account for the two-thirds weight in this category attributable to goods that might be subject to the same bias.[33] We also apply the estimate from Gordon's research to 10% of the weight in the personal care category of other goods and services, which includes products such as hair dryers.[34]

For apparel, we enter as the alternative estimate the 0.57-percentage-point annual overstatement of quality improvement derived from Gordon 1996. The Berndt et al. (1996) study, which found that an average price index that approximates the current CPI methodology understated inflation by 3.54 percentage points annually, even after accounting for the quality gains associated with new drugs,[35] provides a basis for our alternative estimate for prescription drugs.

In the case of new and used cars, the alternative estimate assumes that one-third of the difference (0.58 percentage points of 1.73 percentage points) between Gordon's index and the CPI in the last four years of his study actually reflects an understatement of inflation in the CPI. The other two-thirds can be attributed to the impact of Japanese cars on the CPI and random factors. Since sample rotation bias would have raised the CPI relative to Gordon's index by approximately 0.3 percentage points annually, this amount must be added in to yield an understatement of inflation of 0.88 percentage points. We offer no alternative estimates of bias for the other areas of the index where the commission claimed to have evidence of bias.

Table B sums up our alternative estimates of quality bias. The table also

Table B: Estimates of Quality Bias in the CPI

Major and Selected Minor Components	Relative Importance	Current (1995) Quality Imputations	Commission's Estimate of Bias	Source of Estimate	Alternative Estimate of Bias	Source of Alternative Estimate
1. Food and Beverage	17.33	1.39			-0.86	Smedley & Moulton 1997, see text
Food at home other than produce	8.54		0.3	Introspection		
Fresh fruits and vegetables	1.34		0.6	Introspection		
Food away from home	5.89		0.3	Introspection		
Alcoholic beverages	1.57		0.15	Introspection		
2. Housing	41.35					
Shelter	28.29		0.25	Introspection	-0.52	see text
Other utilities, incl. telephone	3.22		1	Introspection	-0.25	see text
Appliances, incl. electronic	0.81		5.6	Gordon 1990	-0.85	Gordon 1990
Other house furnishings	2.64		0.3	Introspection		
3. Apparel and Upkeep	5.52	3.37	1	Gordon 1996	-0.57	Gordon 1996
4. Transportation	16.95	1.13				
New vehicles	5.03		0.59	Gordon 1990	-0.58	Gordon 1990
Used vehicles	1.34		0.59	Gordon 1990	-0.58	Gordon 1990
Motor fuel	2.91		0.25	Introspection	-0.25	see text
5. Entertainment	4.37	4.79				
Commodities	1.98		2	Gordon 1990	-0.88	Gordon 1990
6. Other Goods and Services	7.12	0.6				
Personal care	1.17		0.9	Gordon 1990	-0.09	Gordon 1990
Personal and education expenses	4.34		0.2	Introspection		
7. Medical Care	7.36	2.51		Berndt et al. Griliches & Cockburn		Berndt et al.
Prescription drugs	0.89		2	none	-3.54	see text
Nonprescription drugs and med. sup.	0.39		1	Cutler et al. and		
Professional medical services	3.47		3	Shapiro & Wilcox		
Hospital and related services	2.26		3			
Total	100	1.76	0.612		-0.437	

lists each of the commission's estimates and the evidential basis for each estimate. In contrast to the commission's estimate of an annual understatement of quality improvements of 0.612 percentage points, this alternative estimate shows that the CPI overstates the amount of quality improvements by 0.437 percentage points annually. This estimate implies that the true rate of quality improvement in 1995 was 1.32 percentage points rather than the 1.76 percentage points attributed by BLS.

The alternative estimates developed in this section do not rest on a solid body of empirical evidence, but they are at least as plausible and consistent with the evidence produced by the commission. In the absence of compelling evidence on the magnitude and direction of bias in most areas of the index, it is possible to speculate that the CPI is biased in either direction. While such speculation may provide direction to subsequent research, it is not a substitute for research. At present, the research does not exist to support the claim that there is an overstatement in the CPI due to quality or new goods bias. Unless and until such evidence is produced, it is reasonable to assume that the BLS numbers are accurate.

THE FINAL SCORE ON THE ACCURACY OF THE CPI

Table C provides the alternative set of estimates of bias in the CPI.

The size of the substitution bias is estimated at 0.28 percentage points. As discussed earlier, this estimate accepts the Boskin Commission's 0.15-percentage-point estimate for upper-level substitution bias and accepts half of its 0.25-percentage-point estimate for lower-level substitution bias. The size of this latter bias should move toward zero over the next few years as BLS changes its procedures in accordance with further research.

The size of the retail outlet substitution bias is estimated at 0.02 percentage points annually, compared with the commission's estimate of 0.1 percentage points. As was noted earlier, this bias could apply only to the percentage of total consumption that switches each year from traditional retail outlets to discount stores. Since this consumption accounts for only about 0.2% of the whole index, the estimate of 0.02 percentage points implies a bias of 10% on this small category of items. Our estimate ignores the considerable evidence of an unmeasured decline in the service quality at retail stores, which may be far more than offsetting.

The size of the bias attributable to new goods and quality is estimated at -0.44 percentage points, the sum of the estimates of bias developed in the previous section. The estimate is quite speculative, but it is constructed from the same sort of evidential foundation as the Boskin Commission's estimates in this area.

The sum in the final row is a negative net bias of 0.14 percentage points,

TABLE C: Sources of Bias in the Consumer Price Index

Type	Percent
Substitution bias*	0.28
Retail outlet substitution bias	0.02
New goods and quality bias	-0.44
Total	-0.14

* Will be falling to 0.15 due to planned changes in methodology.

Source: Author's calculations, see text.

implying that the CPI *understates* inflation each year by this amount. Given the limited evidence for the estimates of quality bias, it would not be appropriate to alter economic research or public policy based on this figure. However, it at least raises the possibility that the CPI understates inflation.

We will never derive an exactly accurate CPI — even if we all agree on exactly what we want the CPI to measure. We can, however, work towards one that is approximately accurate for the purposes for which it is used. The estimate presented here, and the evidence on which it is based, support the argument that the CPI meets this standard.

III. Is Inflation the Same for Everyone?

An important issue, given the uses of the CPI, is whether all segments of the population experience the same rate of inflation. It is possible that there is a bias in the overall CPI that may be partially or completely offset by differences in inflation rates experienced by specific segments of the population. Therefore, it is important to determine whether it is appropriate to use the same measure of inflation for all demographic groups within society.

THE ELDERLY

The commission argued on the basis of two studies that were more than a decade old (and which used even older data) that there are not significant differences in the inflation rates experienced by different demographic groups.[36] In reaching this assessment, the commission largely dismissed the findings of an experimental index for the elderly, computed by BLS since 1982, that showed that the elderly experience a rate of inflation that is 0.3-0.4% higher than the rate for the population as a whole (BLS 1996) (see **Figure 18**). The commission noted that the finding of a higher rate of inflation for the elderly was primarily driven by the large increases in health care costs over this period, and it argued that these increases appear to have slowed, and that health care inflation is significantly overstated in any case (SFC 1996, 71 fn).

In this regard, much hinges on which health care expenditures are measured in the CPI. Current budget plans call for increases in Medicare premiums that could be as much as $500 per person per year by 2002, an amount equal to approximately 5% of the current median income of a woman over age 65 living alone. The current CPI would not pick up this increase in Medicare premiums; it would be viewed as a reduction in a government subsidy, not an increase in the price of health care. (The methodology for treating health care expenditures will be discussed in more detail in the next section.)

The question of whether the elderly or other segments of the population

FIGURE 18: Do Costs Rise More for the Elderly?

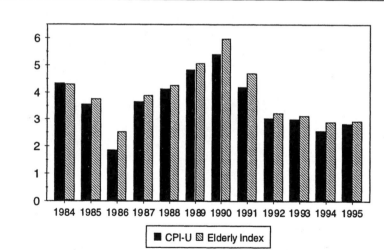

This chart compares the rate of inflation calculated each year using the overall CPI (CPI-U) with the rate of inflation shown by the experimental elderly index designed by BLS. On average, the elderly index has risen about 0.3 percentage points a year more rapidly than the overall CPI. Social Security payments are currently indexed to the CPI-W, which has risen about 0.1 percentage point a year less rapidly than the CPI-U. Counting in this difference means that the elderly index has actually risen about 0.4 percentage points a year more rapidly than the Social Security cost-of-living adjustments.

experience different rates of inflation requires more research, as the commission notes (SFC 1996, 71). Providing BLS with the resources that it would need to perfect its elderly index would probably go a long way toward answering this question.[37] Specifically, it will need the resources to monitor the actual buying habits of the elderly.

It is possible that the current index might accurately measure the rate of inflation experienced by the elderly and might contain an overall bias but still not be biased as a measure of the rate of inflation experienced by the elderly. This would be the case if the rate of inflation experienced by the elderly was not affected by the sources of bias identified by the commission. (For example, perhaps the elderly aren't big purchasers of computers or cellular phones, or, because they are less mobile, they don't change their purchasing habits in response to changes in prices.) The commission presented no evidence whatsoever showing that any bias in the index would apply equally across groups.

THE WEALTHY

In fact, the commission presents a brief discussion of the product cycle (SFC 1996, 34-5) that seems to suggest that any problem in the incorporation of new goods in the CPI would primarily lead to an understatement of the gains experienced by the wealthy, rather than gains to the population as a whole. The commission gives the example of the VCR, which was introduced in the late 1970s at a price of $1,000. In the first years after VCRs were introduced, their price fell rapidly while the quality improved enormously. However, this period of rapid price decline was largely missed in the CPI, since it did not include VCRs when they first appeared on the market. Of course, most people did not buy VCRs when they cost $1,000 – for the most part, only relatively affluent people would have been willing to make such a purchase, and these are the people who benefited from the large price decline. The bulk of the population, which didn't buy VCRs until their price had fallen (and they had been incorporated into the CPI), experienced no gain from this price decline. Therefore, no unmeasured gain accrued to the typical consumer.

The same pattern could apply to most new products. When they first appear on the market they are expensive, and only the wealthiest segment of the population can afford to buy them. Then they fall rapidly in price and become accessible to the population as a whole. Insofar as the CPI misses this large price decline, it is missing a gain experienced almost exclusively by the wealthy. According to economic theory, the price at which a consumer is first willing to purchase a product tells us exactly how much the consumer values it. Therefore, the consumer who is willing to buy a VCR at $300 experiences no gain as the price drops from $1,000 to $300. If the price drops further, this consumer will experience a gain. If new goods are important in total consumption, as the commission argues, then it is likely that the CPI significantly overstates the inflation rate experienced by the wealthy, *and* that the inflation rate experienced by the wealthy differs substantially from that experienced by the rest of the population.

This point suggests a possible improvement in the CPI. The current index is expenditure weighted: the weight assigned to each item is based simply on the sum of total consumer expenditures on that item. As a result, the buying habits of high-income individuals have a higher weight than the consumption patterns of moderate-income people. It would be relatively simple to switch to a person-weighted index in which the purchasing patterns of each person received equal weight. With this system, the weight assigned to an item in the CPI would be the average *share* of household expenditures that go to the item. Instead of averaging expenditures across households, expenditure *shares* would be averaged across households. In a person-weighted index, if 30% of a poor person's expenditures go to food, but only 1% of a wealthy person's expenditures go to food, their expenditure patterns would have the same impact in determining the overall weight for food in the CPI. The switch to a person-weighted index of this type has been considered by BLS at least as far back as 1978 (Layng 1978).

THE POOR

Over the last 30 years a considerable amount of research has been devoted to determining thresholds for poverty-level income. The official measure of the poverty threshold was established in 1963 and has moved upward each year by the change in the CPI. The official poverty line for a family of four in 1996 (two adults, two children) was approximately $15,900 in 1996 dollars. As noted in the first section, if the CPI substantially overstates inflation, then this figure must grossly overstate the true poverty level. Moving the 1963 poverty threshold by a commission-adjusted CPI would produce a 1996 poverty threshold of approximately $8,600 for a family of four.

In 1992 the National Research Council, acting at the request of the Joint Economic Committee of Congress, established a panel to examine the appropriateness of the current official poverty threshold. This panel consisted of many of the nation's leading experts on poverty. In carrying through its assessment, the panel reviewed a series of alternative methods used by various researchers to determine poverty thresholds. It also put forward its own method to establish a range for a poverty threshold (see **Figure 19**). All but one of the methods it examined, including the midpoint of the range produced by the panel, set a poverty threshold that is *higher* than the official measure, not lower (National Research Council 1995, 97–158).[38]

FIGURE 19: Poverty Thresholds

This chart shows a series of estimates of the poverty threshold for a two-adult two-child family in 1992 dollars. The official measure uses the original 1963 threshold set by the Census Bureau and moves it up by the inflation rate measured by the CPI. The commission-adjusted estimate takes the original 1963 threshold and moves it up by a commission-adjusted CPI. The other thresholds presented here are various efforts to reestimate the poverty threshold for years near 1992. These estimates were adjusted by the inflation rate measured by the CPI to convert them into 1992 dollars. The threshold shown for the National Research Council is actually the midpoint of the range given for a threshold. As can be seen, the commission-adjusted measure of a poverty threshold is far below the other measures, suggesting that either the commission's assessment of the CPI is wrong, that the poor experience much higher rates of inflation than the population as a whole, or that poverty is inherently a relative concept. The last possibility would undermine the theoretical basis for a cost-of-living index, and for conventional economics more generally.

Source: National Research Council (1995) and author's calculations.

The implication of this finding is that the CPI was actually *understating* the rate of inflation experienced by the poor. Either the poor experience a much higher rate of inflation than the population as a whole, or the CPI does not overstate the true rate of inflation.

There are several possible ways that the proponents of the view that the CPI overstates inflation could respond to the finding of the panel. First, they could question the accuracy of the work of the panel and the other researchers cited. Second, they could argue that the 1963 poverty threshold was set at far too low a level of income, and that the actual poverty level for that year should have been higher than the official measure. Third, they could maintain that poverty is inherently a relative concept: that social conceptions of poverty evolve through time, so that the standard of living viewed at the poverty level in 1963 might be very different from the standard of living viewed at the poverty level in 1995.

While all three of these explanations logically can reconcile the seeming inconsistency between the Boskin Commission's conclusion and the National Research Council's findings, there are problems with adopting each of them. The first explanation involves dismissing the work of the nation's leading researchers on poverty. There could be errors in their findings, but it is not reasonable to dismiss their research and their judgment out of hand.

The second explanation suffers from the same problem. The poverty researchers of the 1960s may have also erred in their judgments, but this has to be shown by evidence. In addition, applying the current poverty level backward using a commission-adjusted CPI would put close to half the population below the poverty line in 1963. It would be reasonable to demand more evidence of a CPI overstatement before accepting this radical change in our view of postwar economic history.

The third explanation, that standards of poverty are inherently relative, is on its face plausible. However, going this route undermines the conception of the "cost of living" on which the commission (and the whole economics discipline) bases its analysis. The commission has conducted its analysis as though it is possible to evaluate the improvements in various goods and services independently, without examining changes in the social and physical environment. If conceptions of poverty change as society evolves, then a person's well-being cannot be determined exclusively by the bundle of goods and services that they are able to consume. Instead, it is necessary to examine the set of needs that individuals are likely to incur in specific social contexts and then determine the extent to which households' incomes are capable of meeting these needs.

The set of issues raised by the possibility that conceptions of poverty are inherently relative go to the core of the distinction between a price index and a cost-of-living index. These issues will be discussed in detail in the next section.

IV. The CPI and a Cost-of-Living Index Compared

> As Denison (1971) and others have recognized, however, a single generally accepted index of welfare cannot be constructed. There is no straightforward way to measure the welfare cost of crime, congestion, and pollution of the air and water, or the welfare benefit of improved medical care and completely new products like the automobile, air conditioning, and home computers. (Gordon 1990, 41)

The distinction between a price index and a cost-of-living index is a topic that has surfaced repeatedly in the debate over the CPI. In some cases it has been suggested that the problem with the CPI is that it is a price index and that what we really want is a cost-of-living index. For example, Franklin Raines, director of the Office of Management and Budget, in suggesting the establishment of a commission to calculate a cost-of-living index, said that, "I think a smart group of people could get this done in a period of months instead of years."[39] But as Gordon notes in the citation above, the problems of producing a cost-of-living index, "a single generally accepted index of welfare," are immense.

BLS has always been careful to claim that the CPI is a price index, not a measure of the cost of living. The insistence on producing a price index, and not a cost-of-living index, is not attributable to laziness or stubbornness on the part of BLS; rather, it is due to the enormous complexity of the task involved in producing a genuine cost-of-living index. As BLS noted in a recent report to the House Budget Committee, a measure of the cost of living would have to move beyond a basket of market goods and services to an examination of "the level of public or government provided goods and services one enjoys; and the quality of the environment" (BLS 1995, 8).

The distinction between a price index and cost-of-living index is extremely important for the debate over the accuracy of the CPI. If the CPI is not a cost-of-living index, then there will always be factors that affect the cost of living that do not belong in the CPI. Some of these will lead to a higher cost of living and some will lead to a lower measure. One-sided efforts to incorporate only the factors that reduce the cost of living (e.g., new products like ATMs, cable television, and the Internet) will lead to a downward bias in the CPI. In a brief discussion of factors such as AIDS, crime, and congestion, which lead to a rise in the cost of living, the commission asserted emphatically that such factors do not belong in a price index like the CPI (SFC 1996, 72). The commission's argument, that a measure like the CPI should not move beyond the realm of pricing a market basket of goods and services, is reasonable. However, in the rest of the report the commission does not appear to accept the distinction between a cost-of-living index, which would try to incorporate all the factors that affect the quality of life, and a price index like the CPI.

The CPI is a price index that is intended to be used to deflate consumption expenditures out of money income. The fact that the CPI's target coverage is money income is important because individuals receive substantial amounts of income that are provided directly as services, not as money income. The health care benefits that millions of people receive from the government through Medicare or Medicaid and the health insurance that much of the workforce receives through employers are examples of income received in this form. Nearly two-thirds of health care expenditures come from these sources, rather than directly out of consumers' pockets, and are therefore excluded from the CPI. The commission suggested incorporating the payments made by the government and employers, a move that would raise the weight of medical care in total consumption from 7.3% to 16%.[40] Another example of non-money income is the financial services provided by banks in lieu of interest payments.

In both cases, these items are properly excluded from the CPI because the rate of price increase in these areas does not affect what households can purchase with their money income. A lower rate of inflation in the portion of health care covered by government expenditures or employer-paid insurance might mean that individuals are receiving more health care services for the same amount of the government's or their employer's money, but it does not mean they can buy more goods and services with the money income they have at their disposal. The same logic applies to financial services or any other noncash benefit received by consumers. Excluding these items from the CPI does not mean that they are unimportant, it simply means that they are irrelevant to the purchasing power of money income.

A second issue that has particular importance in the case of health care stems from the treatment of government-mandated subsidies. Most of the payments households make for hospital and professional medical services are actually routed through insurers.[41] At present, this practice often leads to situations in which the payer is subsidizing the care of others, since the vast majority of health expenditures go to provide care for a relatively small segment of the population.[42] In an unregulated market, insurers could often effectively discriminate among segments of the population by using factors like age, weight, career, and personal and family history to determine the likelihood that particular individuals will get sick and then adjusting their fees accordingly. While this sort of price discrimination could reduce the extent of subsidization across individuals, public policy usually tries to limit this process through mandatory community rating or restrictions on the consideration of preexisting conditions in granting insurance policies.

Although these restrictions on insurance companies further an important social end (providing the sick with health care), when combined with the current CPI procedures they create an accounting illusion. A rise in insurance premiums that results from the increasing ill health of a small group of individuals or from increased access to more expensive treatment would not appear as an increase in the cost of insurance in the CPI. In both cases, the increase in insurance premiums would be treated as an improvement in quality, since it is resulting from increased utilization. (This problem is particularly important in the case of Medicare, where the present approach does not treat the increase in premiums as a rise in health care costs. See **Figure 20**.)

This approach also leads to an important asymmetry from a policy standpoint. If the sick are provided with care through government programs or subsidies, the expenses are clear, and any resulting taxes will be readily measured as a reduction in disposable income. However, if the government institutes policies that require the healthy to subsidize the sick by regulating insurance practices, there is no recognition of this cost anywhere in the current system of accounts. This asymmetric treatment is neither accurate from an accounting standpoint nor desirable from a public policy standpoint.[43]

An alternative approach that avoids such problems would be to return to

FIGURE 20: Is This a Rise in the Cost of Living?
Medicare Premiums as a Share of Income

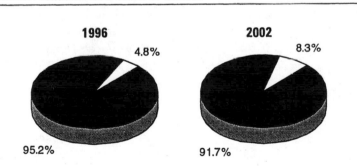

This figure shows the share of a typical single woman's income that goes to Medicare premiums in 1996 compared with the share that would go to Medicare premiums in 2002, if premiums rise by $50 per month. This increase is in the range that is currently being considered in legislation before Congress. Medicare premiums do not count at all in the CPI.

Source: 1994 median income from *Income of the Aged Chartbook, 1994*, Social Security Administration Office of Research, Evaluation, and Statistics, June 1996, p. 2. These numbers assume that median income will grow at the rate of inflation plus 1.0% per year from 1994 through 2002.

the procedure BLS had in place prior to 1964, when it priced the premiums for medical insurance directly. Under this system, premium increases attributable to increased utilization (more medical services being provided) were counted as price increases, not quality improvements, as would be the case under the current methodology. This approach effectively measures the change in what the average person pays out for health insurance premiums or copayments without trying to factor in the benefits he or she receives in return. Since the benefits received by any specific individual bear little relationship to what they have paid for their insurance, it is hard to see that any precision is lost in this approach.[44]

In considering this alternative, it is important to note that most health care expenditures are already effectively treated in the manner being suggested here. If households are taxed to support government-provided health care or wages are lowered to offset the employers' contributions to health care, these payments are treated simply as deductions from the disposable income available to households. In both cases, there are no adjustments made for any services that might be provided as a result of these payments. It is also worth noting that if the United States had adopted a national health care plan similar to Canada's, the current methodology would have resulted in the removal of virtually all health care expenditures from the index.

The alternative approach to measuring health costs suggested here does not imply that economists should not attempt to evaluate the benefits gained from health care expenditures. However, since the factors involved in such an assessment are inherently difficult to measure and subject to dispute, measures of the quality-adjusted price of health care might be best kept separate from the CPI. Giving health care special consideration also seems consistent with a general public attitude that health care is not simply another market good.

If this alternative approach were in effect, it would have had little net effect on the rate of growth of the health care component of the CPI. The annual rate of growth of per capita spending on health care, counting all individual payments (insurance and Medicare premiums, copayments and out-of-pocket spending), was almost identical with the rate of growth of the health care component of the CPI from 1970 to 1991 (8.12% for per capita spending compared to 8.17% for the CPI). However, the fact that the growth rates were almost identical in the past does not guarantee that they will continue to grow at the same rate. Households managed to reduce their share of total health care expenditures from 50.7% in 1970 to 34.1% in 1991 (Cowan and McDonnell 1993, 228), but it is unlikely that this trend will continue. In fact, it is likely to be reversed, as employers and the government increasingly try to shift costs back to consumers. The current methodology in the CPI will largely miss the impact that such cost shifting will have on living standards.

Apart from the accounting issue raised here, health care also poses other problems that go to the heart of the distinction between a price index and a cost-of-living index. The discussion of quality bias in the hospital and professional medical services category referred to a recent study examining the cost of treating heart attacks (Cutler et al., 1996). This study found that the rate of inflation was far lower than would be indicated by the CPI's methodology when the item being priced was defined as the years of life expectancy of heart-attack victims. The price index constructed in this manner actually showed a decline (i.e., the cost per year of extended life fell), while the index based on the CPI's methodology showed a substantial increase. This study is correct in arguing that the years of extended life attributable to improvements in treatment are of enormous value. However, incorporating these gains in a price index raises serious problems. First, gains in terms of life expectancy or quality of life outcomes do not affect the fact that medical care still has to be paid for with money. Second, measuring the outcome from treating an illness ignores the fact that the real determinant of well-being is health.

If a person can anticipate a quadrupling of his or her post-heart-attack life expectancy, but the price of treatment has doubled, the person will still have to find the money to pay for a procedure that has doubled in price, even though the price per year of post-heart-attack life expectancy has fallen by 50%. In the context of the CPI and its uses, the question is whether it would make sense to reduce a retiree's annual Social Security benefit based on this quality improvement. The rationale would be that, even though such people are getting less money each year — and will have to pay twice as much if they need to be treated for a heart attack — they are still as well off, because they can expect to live longer if they actually get a heart attack. To make the same point in an even more dramatic fashion, the discoveries of penicillin in the 1930s and the polio vaccine in the 1950s had enormous impacts on life expectancies and well-being. If a monetary value were assigned to the additional years of life or improved health associated with these developments, then a cost-of-living index probably would have shown large declines for the years over which these treatments became available.[45] It is not clear, however, that it would have been reasonable during these periods for wage contracts or benefits indexed to the CPI to have been reduced, in nominal terms. This sort of tradeoff between money income and health or longevity seems at least peculiar, if not wrong.[46]

The second problem with using the outcome of medical treatments as the item being priced is that the actual determinant of well-being is the health of the population. If the price of heart attack treatment were to double (measured by post-heart-attack life expectancy), but the incidence of heart attacks fell by

50%, then clearly the population is significantly better off. If health care pricing moves away from the cost of treating specific diseases or ailments and toward the cost of achieving a specific outcome, then it is hard to see why it should not move the additional step to pricing changes in the overall health status of the population. Such a measure might have relatively little to do with direct medical expenditures. Changes in diet and lifestyles may have at least as much impact on the overall health of the population as the medical treatment it receives. Other societal factors, such as stress or an unhealthy work environment, are also likely to have large impacts on health. Also, the onset of epidemics such as AIDS or polio would also have to be factored into any index of societal health. An accurate measure of the impact of these epidemics would have to factor in not only the direct health impact and the resulting expenditures, but also the loss of welfare resulting from changes in behavior induced by the spread of these diseases.

A move to such an index takes economists into realms where they are ill-equipped to travel. While it is possible to assign a price to anything, any effort to place a value on improved eyesight or the gain or loss of fertility will call for many subjective judgments. Such factors can have enormous impacts on people's lives, but they shouldn't necessarily be included in the CPI. It is reasonable to keep the measure of health care prices focused on the treatment of specific ailments, rather than a range of larger quality-of-life issues. This procedure will inevitably leave out some of the improvements and deteriorations in the provision of health care to the nation, but it may be preferable to a CPI that fluctuates with the weight of the population or the speed of assembly lines.

There are many other factors affecting the cost of living that are not counted in the CPI. A major one is crime. The costs associated with crime are enormous: a recent study estimated the total cost to society in 1991 at $667 billion (Anderson 1996, 16). This number includes some costs that are not borne by consumers directly, such as the cost of incarcerating prisoners and their lost productivity, and it also includes some questionable estimates of the emotional suffering associated with crime, but even if the estimate were cut in half, the cost of crime would have exceeded 8.0% of total consumer expenditures in that year. This estimate also made no effort to account for what may be the greatest cost of crime, the limits on personal behavior that are considered necessary because of fear of crime.[47] The commission correctly noted that crime rates have leveled off, and in recent years have even been trending downward (SFC 1996, 74-5), but a comprehensive measure of the impact of crime on the cost-of-living would have to examine all the ways in which crime or the fear of crime has affected people's lives. It is not necessarily a gain if there are fewer street crimes because fewer people are willing to venture out onto the streets at night.

Another factor that affects the cost of living is the financial and legal expenditures families must pay to maintain their economic security. If families consider their environment to be increasingly insecure, and therefore feel a need to insure against more contingencies or to more frequently consult lawyers, the increased demand for these services is itself an increase in the cost of living. This sort of increasing insecurity can result from factors such as the declining importance of family loyalties, increased job insecurity, greater litigiousness within society, or declining worker coverage by defined-benefit pension plans. All of these factors could require increased expenditures just to maintain the same level of personal security. Over the last 10 years, the share of the "personal business" category of expenditures in total consumer expenditures in the national income and product accounts has been rising at the rate of about 0.17 percentage points per year (from 6.0% in 1984 to 7.7% in 1994; see **Figure 21**).[48] While some of this increase in expenditures undoubtedly

FIGURE 21: The Cost of Living, the Cost of Lawyers:
Personal Business Expenditures/All Expenditures

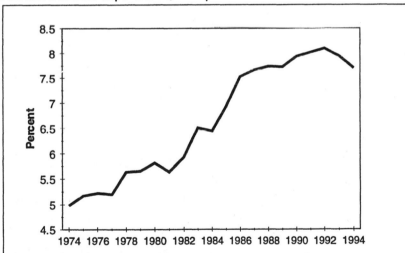

This chart shows the share of consumption expenditures that goes to the "personal business expenditure" category in the National Income and Product Accounts. This category includes expenditures for items such as insurance and legal fees that may enhance personal security but do not directly contribute to utility. These expenditures are arguably an increase in the cost of living insofar as they are caused by a growing sense of insecurity within society. These expenditures have grown as a share of total spending at the rate of roughly 0.17 percentage points annually from 1984 to 1994.

Source: National Income and Product Accounts and author's calculations.

measures a real improvement in services, at least part of it reflects an unmeasured increase in the cost of living. The size of this unmeasured increase could exceed 0.1% a year, implying that the CPI as a whole understates the increase in the cost of living by 0.1%.

Increased traffic congestion is also a factor that can lead to a rise in the true cost of living. A recent study calculated that the annual cost of congestion, measured in terms of additional fuel expenditures and time spent in traffic, rose from $230 per capita in 1986 to $380 in 1993 (both numbers are in current dollars) (Schrank and Lomax, 1996). These costs have risen as a share of consumption expenditures at the rate of 0.05 percentage points a year, from 1.9% of consumption expenditures in 1986 to 2.2% in 1993. A cost-of-living index would have to add such an estimate to the measured increase in the CPI.

Child care is another factor. Families with employed mothers spent over $17 billion on child care in 1993 (Census Bureau 1995). Insofar as these are expenditures made to allow women to go to work, then just measuring wages would overstate the gains to these women. The need to travel further to find open space for recreation, either because of a deterioration in the quality of public parks or increased congestion in urban areas, would be an increase in the cost of living. Similarly, if vacation spots became degraded as they become more populated, this change should be recorded as an increase in the cost of living.

Many factors affect the quality of life of the population, and therefore the cost of living, that would be difficult if not impossible for economists to measure. The commission at one point notes that these factors may not belong in the CPI: "It is not clear, however, whether events such as a colder winter, the appearance of AIDS, or a rise in the crime rate should be included in the definition of a *price* index" (SFC, 72, emphasis in original). In its recommendations the commission actually suggests collecting data on such factors for the construction of a broader cost-of-living index (SFC, 84).

The acknowledgment that such factors do not belong in the CPI, a price index, is a recognition of the fact that the CPI is not and should not be a cost-of-living index. This distinction is important, since much of the criticism of the CPI has been that BLS has not constructed a true cost-of-living index. The commission's acknowledgment is also important from a practical standpoint, because the necessary incompleteness of the CPI as a measure of the cost of living raises a clear potential for bias. As noted earlier, a determined effort to incorporate all the ways in which market goods and services *improve* the quality of life without a comparable effort to assess the ways in which change might be leading to a deterioration in living standards will understate the rate of inflation experienced by consumers.

This tension appears most directly in the treatment of new goods. The commission rightly notes the opportunities provided by the development of computers and the Internet. In an earlier era, it would have cited the development of telephones, cars, or television. While the CPI does not pick up the full gains to consumers resulting from these innovations, all of these products also impose large costs that are left out of the CPI. For example, in the case of telephones, an individual who did not possess a telephone in 1960, when it was a standard method of communication, was much worse off than an individual who did not own a telephone in 1920, when it still was a relative rarity. Similarly, a person who did not own a car in 1980 is much worse off than a person who did not own a car in 1940. In 1940, most people's transportation needs could be met through walking or public transport. By 1980 society had become largely organized around car ownership, and in most parts of the country people lacking cars would have had considerable difficulty carrying through their daily activities. The diffusion of items such as telephones and cars made these items necessities, and a person not buying them was actually made worse off as a result of this development.

These sorts of societal changes go hand in hand with the development of new products: new products create new possibilities, but they also impose new costs. Our society is mobile in a way that would have been unimaginable 50 years ago, and as a result families are dispersed across the country as they never have been before. In such a context, the lack of access to long-distance communication or air travel means losing contact with family and close friends. These are necessary expenses created by a changed social environment. A person unable to afford such expenses in 1997 is unambiguously worse off than a person unable to afford them in 1947, when families stayed closer together. Also, new drugs such as heart medications may vastly extend life expectancies for many people, but the purchase of these drugs becomes a necessary expenditure for the people dependent on them. In such cases, the cost of buying the drug becomes an increase in the cost of living, even if the prices of the drugs themselves are falling.

One final point worth noting in a discussion of the concept of a cost-of-living index is the possibility that poverty and human welfare are inherently relative concepts. (As noted above, this is the only logically consistent way to reconcile the commission's findings with nearly all measurements of poverty rates over the last several decades.) Prominent economists from Thorstein Veblen to Paul Krugman (1996) have argued that perceptions of our own well-being are always relative. This means that whether we consider ourselves to be well-off depends not on the bundle of goods and services we are able to consume but rather on how much we are able to consume relative to others with whom we compare ourselves. Insofar as this provides an accurate description of human behavior, a cost-of-living index would be an impossible construct. No amount of money can guarantee that we will be as well off this year as last year if those with whom we compare ourselves are doing even better. If well-being is inherently relative, then there is nothing for a cost-of-living index to measure.

The idea that well-being is relative is directly at odds with conventional economic theory, which assumes that individuals are only concerned about their own consumption, not the consumption of others. This assumption underlies virtually all of modern economics, and for this reason economists have been reluctant to consider the possibility that welfare really is relative. However, researchers in other social sciences such as psychology and sociology routinely develop theoretical models and carry through research in a framework that assumes that well-being is relative. Certainly economists cannot rule out this possibility *a priori*. But if well-being is relative, and a cost-of-living index can have no real meaning, then economists should stick to a price index.

V. Conclusion: Is the CPI the Best Measure of Consumer Inflation?

There are problems with the CPI as a measure of consumer inflation. Many of these have been correctly identified by the commission, although the size and net impact of the various biases are far more ambiguous than indicated by its report. The finding of a substantial bias in the CPI would have a tremendous impact on both economic research and economic policy. The fact that so much of this research would have to be reexamined or discarded altogether should counsel caution in adopting the commission's report. Also, any basis for concern for the well-being of future generations would disappear if the Boskin Commission's conclusions are accepted.

Although the commission argues that there is upward bias in the CPI resulting from its failure to take account of substitutions away from items that are rising rapidly in price, the impact of this upward bias is currently small, and it will be reduced further in the near future as BLS implements changes in procedures based on research findings. Also, an extremely small bias due to the failure of the CPI to pick up the benefits of discount stores is most likely more than outweighed by an unmeasured deterioration in the quality of service at retail stores.

In its estimates of quality and new goods bias in the index, the commission relied on speculation, misinterpreted findings, and questionable extrapolations, and it ignored important changes in BLS procedures. In fact, an alternative set of estimates, with at least as much evidential basis as the commission's estimates, is able to find an overstatement of quality improvements and *understatement* of inflation by the CPI. Table C gives the estimated size of the bias from the various sources identified by the commission and includes our alternative set of estimates of quality bias. The bottom line shows a negative net bias in the CPI of 0.14 percentage points a year, implying that the CPI is *understating* inflation by 0.14 percentage points annually. This is not intended as a conclusive judgment about the size or direction of any bias in the CPI: like the commission's estimate, it should be seen as a calculation based on a limited and dated body of research. But it is, at the very least, as plausible and consistent with the available evidence as the Boskin Commission's estimate. Whether or not the CPI overstates inflation, it is possible that inflation rates vary for different groups, such as the elderly, the wealthy, and the poor. Efforts to evaluate the accuracy of the index should encompass this issue as well.

It has been suggested that the problem with the CPI is that it is a price index and that what is really needed is a cost-of-living index. The commission noted this distinction, and it pointed out that many factors that affect the cost-of-living index should not be included in a price index. There are obvious opportunities for bias if a determined effort is made to incorporate all the benefits of new goods in the market (e.g., cable television, cellular phones, or ATMs) without a corresponding effort to incorporate the developments that lead to declines in living standards (e.g., congestion, crime, or lawsuits). Focusing exclusively on one side of this ledger will inevitably lead to a biased result.

As a practical matter, there is a basic question about whether the CPI is the best measure of inflation for tax brackets, benefit programs, wage contracts, and various other purposes. The commission's work presents many reasons why the index may be flawed, but not necessarily the most important ones. Further research will be necessary to determine the actual impact of the problems that have been identified. The commission's report may be helpful in directing research and resources toward improving the CPI. However, as was noted in the first section, the implications for both economic research and economic policy of a large CPI overstatement are radical. The commission's report does not provide an adequate basis for calling into question such a large body of economic research. Nor is it sufficiently compelling to warrant a complete refocusing of the nation's policy agenda. For such drastic reorientations, it is reasonable to demand a strong burden of evidence, and the commission's report does not meet this standard.

Endnotes

1. The one estimate that was higher came from W. Erwin Diewart, a professor of economics at the University of British Columbia in Vancouver, Canada.

2. Gordon (1990) documents enormous improvements in the measurement of quality changes in consumer durable goods over the period 1950-83. This study shows that the CPI substantially understated quality improvements at the beginning of the period, and therefore overstated the rate of inflation in the goods examined by more than 2% annually. By the end of the period, the study shows that BLS actually may have been overstating quality improvements and therefore understating the true rate of inflation in these goods.

    The BLS adopted a system of sample rotation in 1980 that allows new goods to be fully incorporated into the sample over a five-year period. While this still leaves a substantial lag between the point when goods first appear on the market and the point where they are fully incorporated into the index, this system constitutes an enormous improvement. Prior to the adoption of sample rotation, new goods could only be introduced into the sample at a major revision of the index, approximately a 14-year interval. As a result of this lag, air travel, clothes dryers, and air conditioners did not appear in the CPI until 1964, long after these items had become major consumption expenditures for millions of families.

3. The lifetime income hypothesis states that individuals will attempt to even out their consumption over their lifetime. This means consuming more than their incomes when they are young and their incomes are low, consuming less than their incomes in their middle years, when their earnings peak, and then consuming more than their incomes in old age, when their income falls due to retirement. The commission's adjustment implies that the real value of consumption in old age is much greater than current measures indicate, and that the real value of consumption in youth is far less.

4. If your salary is currently $20,000 and you know that it rose 25% over the last five years, you can conclude that it was $16,000 five years ago. If instead you are told that it rose by 100%, then your salary must have been just $10,000 five years ago. The more rapid the rate at which it increased, the lower the level from which it started.

5. The PCE deflator does not use a fixed basket of goods and services, so it would not be subject to the upper-level substitution bias that the commission estimated as 0.15% annually.

6. Alternatively, applying the overstatement of inflation, and therefore understatement of real output, only to consumption would mean that real investment has been falling relative to real consumption for most of the last 25 years instead of rising, as indicated by current data.

7. Nakamura (1996) argues that the evidence of a current overstatement in the CPI implies that the reported slowdown in productivity growth is purely an artifact of measurement error. This study presents *no* evidence that the size of any overstatement in the CPI has increased in recent years. The existence of any overstatement in the CPI cannot explain the productivity slowdown; only an *increase* in the size of the overstatement can lead to a slowdown in the reported productivity numbers.

8.   Bryan and Cecchetti find that the size of the substitution bias in the CPI averaged 0.88% in the years from 1967 to 1981 but has been virtually zero in the years since. This finding implies that real wage, GDP, and productivity growth were far higher in the 1967-81 period than had previously been thought, and that the slowdown in the growth of these variables was far larger than current data indicate.

9.   This number is calculated by taking the ratio of per capita GNP in the CBO's balanced budget projection ($35,500) to the per capita GNP projected for a scenario in which the debt-to-GDP ratio remains constant through this period ($34,900) (CBO 1996, p. 90). This number is then multiplied by the average wage projected for 2030 ($38,350). This wage is obtained by using the 1.0% projected annual growth rate in the Social Security trustees report and adjusting it upward by 0.23% to include the adjustments made to the CPI over the last two years. The Social Security Advisory Council made similar adjustments in its calculations, although these have not yet been incorporated into the trustees report.

10.   It is important to note that the size of this bias is not affected by the distance of the current year from the base year. In its interim report, the Boskin Commission claimed that the substitution bias increased as the distance from the base year got larger (SFC 1995, pp. 14-5). Although the research from BLS shows that this is not the case, this mistake in the commission's report has been widely repeated.

11.   The Moulton and Smedley study found that the use of a geometric mean reduced the measured rate of inflation on items in the medical care services category by 47% more than in the index as a whole (1995, attachment 3). This appears to be an area in which the implied substitutions between medical procedures are implausible.

12.   There is some evidence that a deterioration in the quality of service at retail stores has taken place. According to a recent *New York Times* article, analysts of retail stores estimate that service staff has been reduced at retailers by between 10 and 30% in the 1990s ("Whatever Happened to Service?" *New York Times*, March 4, 1997; B1). A national poll cited in this story indicated that only 25% of consumers rate the service in department or discount stores as "very good" or "excellent." By comparison, 37% of consumers gave the same rating to the U.S. Postal Service.

13.   Clearly part of the shift to discount stores is explained on the supply side rather than the demand side. Specifically, many owners of small family businesses may die or retire without being replaced because the skills associated with operating such businesses may command a greater premium elsewhere. Those who already work in owner operated businesses may not want to seek a new job late in their career, but younger people entering the labor market will choose better paying employment opportunities. Insofar as this process is a factor in the shift to discount stores, the shift cannot be attributable to increased consumer choice. Instead this would be a source of an unmeasured decline in quality. The existing research does not provide a basis for determining how large this sort of supply effect might be.

14.   It also worth noting that the retail outlet substitution bias would have almost certainly been larger in the past than it is at present. Prior to 1987, the goods subject to this bias comprised twice as large a share of the index. Also, the CPI did not even sample suburban outlets prior to 1964. This would have limited the extent to which the CPI picked up price reductions by competitors in response to discounters entering the market (Baker 1996A).

15. BLS also used a "class mean" imputation in 0.32% of its price quotes in 1995; these accounted for 0.66 percentage points of quality improvement. This method also does not involve a direct measurement of quality, but it attempts to match up the new item with a more precisely selected group of similar items in the link system. The average rate of price increase for this group of items is then assigned to the new item.

16. It is also not clear how the commission, in an exercise in introspection, could separate out the impact of the other sources of bias and thereby avoid double-counting.

17. The commission does not explain how it was able to determine that the average size of rental units increased by 20% over this period, nor do any of the references listed in this section provide any basis for this conclusion. This increase implies that the average size was growing at the rate of 1.25% annually. Since less than 2.0% of rental units were added each year over the period from 1976 to 1993, the average new unit, to get this growth rate, would have to be more than 75% larger than the average existing unit. The sources cited by the commission indicate that new units might have been at most 25-50% larger on average than existing units.

18. A recent study (Moulton 1995) found large differences in quality-adjusted housing costs across regions. For example, rents in Boston, New York, and Honolulu were more than two and a half times as high as in Houston.

19. When a reporter confronted Michael Boskin with the assessment of professional realtors that housing prices are not proportionate to size, he acknowledged the possibility but added, "For every one of these things someone can quibble about on the downside, we left out many on the upside." ("CPI Report Coming Under Fire," *Washington Post*, December 19, 1996, page E1).

20. This number is derived by assuming that sample rotation bias added approximately 0.3% a year to the CPI measured rate of inflation in these goods for the years from 1980 to 1983. BLS research showed this to be approximately the magnitude of sample rotation bias in those portions of the index subject to this bias (Moulton 1993). This amounts to an average bias of 0.08% over the 1972-83 period.

There are two reasons why Gordon's Sears catalog index is a more appropriate basis of comparison than the "energy and repair cost adjusted" *Consumer Reports* index used to derive the commission's estimate. The first and most obvious reason is that part of the difference between the *Consumer Reports* and Sears index is attributable to retail outlet substitution bias. The prices of products listed in *Consumer Reports* were falling relative to Sears prices throughout this period because new stores were charging lower prices than Sears. This effect should not be counted as quality bias, as the commission correctly noted (SFC 1996, 33).

Second, the energy and repair costs adjustments in Gordon's index are somewhat dubious. The index uses hedonic regressions to measure the value of the quality improvements in the products examined. It then adds in additional quality adjustments to capture expected savings on energy and repair costs. These additional adjustments are large. Without them, Gordon's *Consumer Reports* index would also show that the CPI overstates quality improvement and therefore understates the rate of inflation in the products examined.

Although Gordon did not explicitly add energy and repair cost adjustments to his Sears catalog index, his hedonic regressions included variables that are highly correlated with these variables. For example, among the variables included in the Sears catalog index's refrigerator regressions is a feature called a "powermiser." The Sears air conditioner regressions include a watts variable, which Gordon notes "amounts to an energy-efficiency adjustment for this period" (Gordon 1990, 271). Since the Sears index includes such variables, the large difference between Gordon's Sears catalog index and his energy and repair cost adjusted *Consumer Reports* index makes the latter index appear implausible. For example, one implication of these differences is that quality-adjusted prices at Sears rose in some cases by 200-400% relative to prices at its competitors.

The more plausible explanation is that the energy and repair adjusted *Consumer Reports* index grossly overvalues the savings in energy and repair costs. In order to factor in these savings, the study applied a real discount rate of 3.0% to these savings. There is a considerable body of research that indicates that consumers typically apply discounts of 15-20% or higher to these savings (see A.K. Meier and J. Whittier 1983).

21. Inappropriate weighting would be properly considered an aspect of new goods bias if it is attributable to the fact that the good has not yet been incorporated in the CPI's sample. However, the current procedure used in the CPI should not lead to long delays in the inclusion of new drugs.

22. The average price index for Cephalexin fell an average of 22.05% annually, compared to a decline of 13.07% for the "Tornqvist-Divisia (u), diffusion-adjusted" index. In the case of Cephradine, the annual price decline was 11.21% in the average price index, compared with a decline of 6.40% for the "Tornqvist-Divisia (u), diffusion-adjusted" index (Griliches and Cockburn 1994, 1226).

23. See Berndt et al. (1996), Table 5 (line 6 minus line 4) and Table 6 (line 2 minus line 3). The small quality gain associated with the introduction of new drugs is particularly striking because this category of drugs — antidepressants — was selected because it was considered to be an area in which major innovations had taken place during the period under investigation. The study's findings, that even in this area the innovations did not lead to large quality improvements, might be taken as an indication that the rate of quality improvement among pharmaceuticals more generally is quite slow.

24. Economists record how much consumers value products; they don't tell them how much they *should* value products.

25. Part of the measure of bias in the Berndt et al. study also stems from using a divisia index to aggregate rates of price change rather than the fixed weight index in the CPI. This means that part of the bias recorded in this study is attributable to lower-level substitution bias, not quality bias. It would be double-counting to take the full estimate of bias from this study as quality bias.

26. This data is from the Information Technology Industry Council in Washington, D.C.

27. The BLS procedure in place prior to 1997 would have tracked the price of cataract surgery only. It would not have picked up any savings that might be attributable to shorter hospital stays or fewer subsequent complications.

28. This new methodology raises the potential for a low-side bias if hospitals begin to allow patients shorter recovery periods in the hospital even when the shorter periods are not justified by improvements in procedures.

29. This calculation takes the median sale price for new homes and divides it by the median sale price for existing homes for the years 1976 to 1993 (Statistical Abstract of the United States 1995, Tables 1216 and 1218). The number of new units each year is taken from Table 1212, and the number of existing units is extrapolated from the Census years in Table 1214.

30. This calculation is based on multiplying average hourly compensation (approximately $20) by 1.5, and dividing by the average annual telephone bill ($670 in 1993, according to the Current Expenditure Survey).

31. The commission cites the *Census of Retailing* as showing a 28% decline in the number of gasoline pumps between 1972 and 1982 (SFC 1996, 56 fn).

32. The 1993 CES gave the average annual expenditure for this category as $977.

33. In the table in the report, the commission applied a 2.0-percentage-point bias in this whole category, even though in the text it claimed only that two-thirds of the category was subject to a bias of this magnitude. Therefore, if the estimate in the text was correct, the table should have listed a bias of 1.27 percentage points.

34. In its estimate in this category, the commission grossly exaggerated the importance of small appliances, assigning them 30% of the weight in the category. A category of goods that includes "other toilet goods and small personal care appliances, including hair and dental products" has a relative importance of 0.36, compared to 1.19 for the category of personal care as a whole. Small personal care appliances probably account for no more than one-third of this smaller category, meaning that they would account for 0.10% of the personal care category as a whole.

35. It is important to note that this estimate ignores the potential impact of improper weighting in the CPI index. However, insofar as weighting is a problem, it should be included under lower-level substitution bias, not new goods and quality bias.

36. The two studies were Boskin and Hurd (1985) and Jorgenson and Slesnick (1983). The evidence in the Jorgenson and Slesnick study provides questionable support for the commission's view. This study concluded: "To summarize: ... We find changes in the individual cost of living vary substantially for households with different base levels of welfare and different demographic characteristics over the period 1958-1978." (Jorgenson and Slesnick 1983, 185).

37. The commission did not recommend improving the elderly index or make any specific proposal for further research in this area.

38. This finding is particularly striking since the official measure is moved by the CPI-U, not the CPI-UX1. It is nearly universally accepted that the CPI-U overstated inflation by roughly 8.0 percentage points in the 1970s because of its treatment of owner-occupied housing. The CPI-UX1 applies the CPI's current rental equivalence measure for owner-occupied housing in the period prior to its adoption in 1983. It is generally accepted as the appropriate deflator for real wages and income.

39. Quoted in the *Washington Post,* "Administration Seeks New Panel to Revamp CPI," March 1, 1997.

40. However, the commission did not apply its estimate of new goods and quality bias in the medical care component to the full weight that it believes medical care should have in the index, as it did in its treatment of household appliances.

41. Cowan and McDonnell (1993) show that 42% of all household payments for medical care were for insurance premiums (counting Medicare). However, this does not count copayments to insurers, which could raise the percentage significantly. Also, a large portion of household payments were for prescription and nonprescription drugs, so that the portion of doctor and hospital services paid for directly by individuals was almost certainly less than half.

42. The conventional rule of thumb is that 70% of health care expenditures provide care for 10% of the population.

43. There are other situations in which problems due to mandated cross-subsidization would arise, such as in public transportation, telephone service, and electricity service, but these are not likely to be of as much consequence as the problems in health care.

44. It also is important to note that this sort of treatment is not without precedent in national accounts. At present, productivity growth for government workers is assumed to be zero, so that an increase in productivity that leads to a decline in the size of the workforce is recorded as a decline in output.

45. The question being asked in a cost-of-living context would be, in the year after penicillin or the polio vaccine was widely available, how much money would a person need to be as well off as he or she was in the year prior to these items being available? It is possible, if not likely, that most people would answer 10-30% less, even if other prices had increased somewhat.

46. It is also worth noting that, in other areas, an increase in life expectancy is not treated the same as a decline in the cost of living or an increase in real income. This issue arises most clearly in the context of Social Security, where the projections of future real wages are independent of the projections of future life expectancies. If the correct procedure involves treating an increase in life expectancy as an increase in real income, then future generations will be even richer than current projections indicate in real terms relative to those presently working or retired.

47. Hundreds of elderly people died in a heat wave in Chicago in the summer of 1995. Many of these people died because they were too afraid to leave their homes to go to publicly provided cooling centers. In some cases, they were too afraid even to open their windows.

48. The personal business category of national income accounts does not line up precisely with the personal expenses category of the CPI. The former includes investment-related expenses such as brokerage fees and the costs of administering life insurance policies, which are excluded from the CPI.

APPENDIX A: The Record on Adjusting for CPI Bias in Research by Commission Members

Compiled by Jim Perkins

This appendix lists a large cross section of publications by members of the commission in which the CPI or a related deflator was used in carrying through research. The appendix indicates (1) whether the CPI or other deflator was used without any mention of a possible bias, (2) whether the possibility of bias was noted but not corrected for in the research, or (3) whether the possibility of bias was noted and the deflator was adjusted to take account of this bias.

Boskin Commission Members	No error in price index indicated	Error indicated with no adjustment	Error indicated with adjustment made
BOSKIN			
CPI Used			
Boskin, Michael J. and Michael D. Hurd. 1978a. "The Effect of Social Security on Early Retirement." National Bureau of Economic Research, Working Paper No. 20. Cambridge, Mass.: NBER.	✓	—	—
Boskin, Michael J. 1987d. *Reagan and the Economy.* San Francisco: Institute for Contemporary Studies.	—	✓	—
Related or Unspecified Deflator Used			
Boskin, Michael J. 1977a. "Social Security: The Alternatives Before Us." In Michael J. Boskin, ed., *The Crisis in Social Security: Problems and Prospects.* San Francisco: Institute for Contemporary Studies.	—	✓	—
Boskin, Michael J., and Lawrence J. Lau. 1977b. "Taxation and Aggregate Factor Supply: Preliminary Estimates." National Bureau of Economic Research, Working Paper No. 221.	✓	—	—
Boskin, Michael J. 1978b. "Introduction: Taxation and the Role of Government in the Economy." In Michael J. Boskin, ed., *Federal Tax Reform: Myths and Realities.* San Francisco: Institute for Contemporary Studies.	✓	—	—
Boskin, Michael J., Mark Gertler, and Charles Taylor. 1980b. *The Impact of Inflation on U.S. Productivity and International Competitiveness.* Washington, D.C.: National Planning Association Committee on Changing International Realities.	✓	—	—
Boskin, Michael J. and John B. Shoven. 1984a. "Concepts and Measures of Earnings Replacement During Retirement." National Bureau of Economic Research, Working Paper No. 1360. Cambridge, Mass.: NBER.	✓	—	—
Boskin, Michael J., et al. 1984b. "New Estimates of the Value of Federal Mineral Rights and Land." National Bureau of Economic Research, Working Paper No. 1447. Cambridge, Mass.: NBER.	✓	—	—

Boskin Commission Members	No error in price index indicated	Error indicated with no adjustment	Error indicated with adjust-ment made
BOSKIN			
Related or Unspecified Deflator Used (cont.)			
Boskin, Michael J. 1985a. "Changes in the Age Distribution of Income in the United States." National Bureau of Economic Research, Working Paper No.1766. Cambridge, Mass.: NBER.	✓	—	—
Boskin, Michael J. 1985b. "New Estimates of Federal Government Tangible Capital and Net Investment." National Bureau of Economic Research, Working Paper No. 1774. Cambridge, Mass.: NBER.	✓	—	—
Boskin, Michael J., and Laurence J. Kotlikoff. 1985c. "Public Debt and U.S. Saving: A New Test of the Neutrality Hypothesis." National Bureau of Economic Research, Working Paper No. 1646. Cambridge, Mass.: NBER.	✓	—	—
Boskin, Michael J., and William G. Gale. 1986a. "New Results on the Effects of Tax Policy on the International Location of Investment." National Bureau of Economic Research, Working Paper No. 1862, Cambridge, Mass.: NBER.	✓	—	—
Boskin, Michael J., and John B. Shoven. 1986b. "Poverty Among the Elderly: Where are the Holes in the Safety Net?" National Bureau of Economic Research, Working Paper No. 1923. Cambridge, Mass.: NBER.	✓	—	—
Boskin, Michael J. 1986c. "Budgets, Deficits, Technology, and Economic Growth." In Dale W. Jorgenson and Ralph Landau, eds., *Technology and Economic Policy*. Cambridge: Ballinger Publishing Company.	✓	—	—
Boskin, Michael J., Alan M. Huber, and Marc S. Johnson. 1987a. "Government Saving, Capital Formation, and Wealth in the United States, 1947-1985." National Bureau of Economic Research, Working Paper No. 2352. Cambridge, Mass.: NBER.	✓	—	—
Boskin, Michael J., Alan M. Huber, and Marc S. Robinson. 1987b. "New Estimates of State and Local Government Tangible Capital and Net Investment." National Bureau of Economic Research, Working Paper No. 2131. Cambridge, Mass.: NBER.	✓	—	—
Boskin, Michael J. 1987c. "Deficits, Public Debt, Interest Rates, and Private Saving: Perspectives and Deflections on Recent Analyses and on U.S. Experience." In Michael J. Boskin, John S. Flemming, and Stefano Gorini, eds., *Private Saving and Public Debt*. New York: B. Blackwell.	✓	—	—
Boskin, Michael J. and Laurence J. Lau. 1988a. "An Analysis of Postwar U.S. Consumption and Saving." National Bureau of Economic Research, Working Paper No. 2605. Cambridge, Mass.: NBER.	✓	—	—
Boskin, Michael J. 1988b. "Concepts and Measures of Federal Deficits and Debt and their Impact on Economic Activity." In Michael J. Boskin and Kenneth J. Arrow, eds., *The Economics of Public Debt: Proceedings of a Conference Held By the Inter-national Economic Association at Stanford, CA.* New York: St. Martin's Press.	✓	—	—

Boskin Commission Members	No error in price index indicated	Error indicated with no adjustment	Error indicated with adjust- ment made

BOSKIN
Related or Unspecified Deflator Used (cont.)
Boskin, Michael J., Marc S. Robinson, and John M. Roberts. 1989. "New Estimates of Federal Government Tangible Capital and the Net Investment." In Dale W. Jorgenson and Ralph Landau, eds., *Technology and Capital Formation.* Cambridge: MIT Press. ✓ — —

Boskin, Michael J., and Laurence J. Lau. 1990. "Post-war Economic Growth in the Group-of-five Countries: A New Analysis." National Bureau of Economic Research, Working Paper No. 3521. Cambridge, Mass.: NBER. ✓ — —

Total Boskin   19   2   0

GORDON
CPI Used
Gordon, Robert J. 1982. "Wages and Prices Are Not Always Sticky: A Century of Evidence for the U.S., U.K. and Japan." National Bureau of Economic Research, Working Paper No. 847. Cambridge, Mass.: NBER. ✓ — —

Related or Unspecified Deflator Used
Frye, Jon, and Robert J. Gordon. 1980. "The Variance and Acceleration of Inflation in the 1970's: Alternative Explanatory Models and Methods." National Bureau of Economic Research, Working Paper No. 551. Cambridge, Mass.: NBER. ✓ — —

Gordon, Robert J. 1981. "Inflation, Flexible Exchange Rates, and the Natural Rate of Unemployment." National Bureau of Economic Research, Working Paper No. 708. Cambridge, Mass.: NBER. ✓ — —

Gordon, Robert J., and John M. Veitch. 1984. "Fixed Investment in the American Business Cycle, 1913-1983." National Bureau of Economic Research, Working Paper No. 1426. ✓ — —

Total Gordon   4   0   0

JORGENSON
Related or Unspecified Deflator Used
Jorgenson, Dale W., and Alvaro Panchon. 1980. "The Accumulation of Human and Nonhuman Capital." Harvard Institute for Economic Research, Discussion Paper No. 769. Cambridge, Mass.: Harvard University. ✓ — —

Jorgenson, Dale W., and Peter J. Wilcox. 1989. *Environmental Regulation and U.S. Economic Growth.* Cambridge: Harvard University. ✓ — —

Jorgenson, Dale W., and Kun-Young Yun. 1990. "The Excess Burden of Taxation in the U.S." Harvard Institute of Economic Research, Discussion Paper No. 1528. Cambridge, Mass.: Harvard University. ✓ — —

Boskin Commission Members	No error in price index indicated	Error indicated with no adjustment	Error indicated with adjust-ment made
JORGENSON			
Related or Unspecified Deflator Used			
Jorgenson, Dale W. 1995. *Productivity*. Cambridge: MIT Press.	✓	—	—
Jorgenson, Dale W. 1996. *Investment*. Cambridge: MIT Press.	—	—	✓
Total Jorgenson	**4**	**0**	**1**
GRILICHES			
Related or Unspecified Deflator Used			
Griliches, Zvi, and Jacques Mairesse. 1982. "Comparing Productivity Growth: An Exploration of French and U.S. Industrial and Firm Data." National Bureau of Economic Research, Working Paper No. 961. Cambridge, Mass.: NBER.	—	✓	—
Griliches, Zvi, Bronwyn H. Hall, and Ariel Pakes. 1986. "The Value of Patents as Indicators of Inventive Activity." National Bureau of Economic Research, Working Paper No. 2083. Cambridge, Mass.: NBER.	✓	—	—
Griliches, Zvi. 1989. "Patents: Recent Trends and Puzzles." National Bureau of Economic Research, Working Paper No. 2922. Cambridge, Mass.: NBER.	✓	—	—
Griliches, Zvi. 1991a. "Patent Statistics as Economic Indicators: A Survey." National Bureau of Economic Research, Working Paper No. 3301. Cambridge, Mass.: NBER.	✓	—	—
Griliches, Zvi. 1991b. "The Search for R&D Spillover." National Bureau of Economic Research, Working Paper No. 3768. Cambridge, Mass.: NBER.	—	✓	—
Berman, Eli, John Bound, and Zvi Griliches. 1994a. "Changes in the Demand for Skilled Labor Within U.S. Manufacturing: Evidence from the Annual Survey of Manufactures." *Quarterly Journal of Economics*. Vol. 109, No. 2, pp. 367-397.	✓	—	—
Griliches, Zvi. 1994b. "Productivity, R&D, and the Data Constraint." *American Economic Review*. Vol. 84, No. 1, pp. 1-23.	—	✓	—
Total Griliches	**4**	**3**	**0**
TOTAL BOSKIN COMMISSION	**31**	**5**	**1**

APPENDIX B: Examples of New Car Reliability/Durability Quality Adjustments in the CPI Since 1992

- Improved corrosion protection —
  body, electrical system, fuel tank, pump, shocks, brakes, and cables

- Increased warranties

- Body side cladding

- Sealing improvements

- Stainless steel exhaust

- Longer-life spark plugs — 100,000 mile life

- Improved steering gears

- Powertrain improvements

- Dextron III transmission fluid — 100,000 mile life

- Water pump front face — 150,000 mile life

- Battery saver

- Increased catalyst load — 100,000 mile life

- Rust-resistant fuel injection — 100,000 mile life

- Clearcoat paint

- Sided galvanized steel body panels

- Serpentine drive belt

Source: Bureau of Labor Statistics

References

Abraham, K. 1995. "Prepared Statement." In "Consumer Price Index: Hearings Before the Committee of Finance, United States Senate." Senate Hearing 104-69, Washington, D.C.: U.S. Government Printing Office, pp 107-9.

Aizcorbe, A.M. and P.C. Jackman. 1993. "The Commodity Substitution Effect in CPI Data, 1982-91." *Monthly Labor Review*, December, pp 25-33.

Aizcorbe, A.M. and P.C. Jackman. 1997. Update of "The Commodity Substitution Effect in CPI Data, 1982-91." Unpublished data prepared for the Senate Finance Committee Advisory Commission to Study the Consumer Price Index. Washington, D.C.: BLS.

Anderson, D. 1996. "The Aggregate Burden of Crime and Distrust." Unpublished paper. Centre College, Danville, Ky.

Baker, D. 1997. "The Mismeasurement of Inflation." Appendix in *The State of Working America 1996-97*, by L. Mishel, J. Bernstein, and J. Schmitt. Armonk, NY: M.E. Sharpe.

Baker, D. 1996a. "Getting Prices Right: A Methodologically Consistent Consumer Price Index 1953-94." Washington, D.C.: Economic Policy Institute.

Baker, D. 1996b. "The Overstated CPI — Can It Really Be True?" *Challenge Magazine*, September-October 1996, pp 26-33. *Journal of Econometrics*. V. 68 # 1, pp 243-268.

Berndt, E., I. Cockburn, and Z. Griliches. 1996. "Pharmaceutical Innovations and Market Dynamics: Tracking Effects on Price Indexes for Anti-Depressant Drugs." *Brookings Paper on Economic Activity*.

Berndt, E., Z. Griliches, and J. Rosset. 1993. "Auditing the Producer Price Index: Micro Evidence from Prescription Pharmaceutical Preparations." *Journal of Business and Economic Statistics*. V 11 # 3, pp 251-64.

Berndt, E., Z. Griliches, and N.J. Rappaport. 1995. "Econometric Estimates of Price Indexes for Personal Computers in 1990s." *Journal of Econometrics*, V. 68 # 1, pp 243-268.

Boskin, M., and M. Hurd. 1985. "Indexing Social Security Benefits: A Separate Price Index for the Elderly." *Public Finance Quarterly*, V 13, # 4, pp 436-449.

Bryan, M. and S. Cecchetti. 1993. "The CPI as a Measure of Inflation." *Economic Review*. V 29, # 4, The Federal Reserve Bank of Cleveland, pp 15-24.

Bureau of Labor Statistics. 1995. *Report from the Bureau of Labor Statistics for the House Budget Committee*. Washington, D.C.: U.S. Congress.

Census Bureau, 1995. "What Does It Cost to Mind Our Preschoolers?" by L. Casper. *Current Population Reports*. P70-52. Washington, D.C.: U.S. Department of Commerce.

Congressional Budget Office, 1996. *The Economic and Budget Outlook: Fiscal Years 1997-2006.* Washington, D.C.: Congressional Budget Office.

Cowan, C. and P. McDonnell. 1993. "Business, Households, and Governments: Health Spending, 1991." *Health Care Financing Review.* V 4, # 3, pp 227-248.

Cutler, D., M. McClellan, J. Newhouse, D. Remler. 1996. "Are Medical Prices Declining?" NBER working paper # 5750.

Gordon, R. 1996. "The Sears Catalog Revisited: Apparel and Durable Goods." Unpublished paper. Northwestern University, Evanston, IL.

Gordon, R. 1990. *The Measurement of Durable Goods Prices.* Chicago: University of Chicago Press.

Griliches, Z. and I. Cockburn. 1994. "Generics and New Goods in Pharmaceutical Price Indexes." *American Economic Review,* December, pp 1213-1232.

Hulten, C. 1996. "Quality Change in the CPI: The Neglected Cost Dimension." Unpublished paper. University of Maryland, College Park, MD.

Jorgenson, D. and D. Slesnick. 1983. "Individual and Social Cost-of-Living Indexes." *Price Level Measurement,* W. Diewert and C. Montmarquette (eds.), Ottawa, Statistics Canada, pp 241-336.

Kokoski, M.F. 1987. *Consumer Price Indexes by Demographic Group.* BLS Working Paper # 167. Washington, D.C.: BLS.

Layng, W.J. 1978. "The Revision of the Consumer Price Index." in *The American Statistical Association Proceedings of the Business and Economics Statistics Section,* Part 1. Washington, D.C.: American Statistical Association, pp 195-203.

Maddison, A. 1995. Monitoring the World Economy. Paris: Development Center of The Organization for Economic Co-operation and Development.

Meier, A. and J. Whittier. 1983 "Consumer Discount Rates Implied by Purchases of Energy-Efficient Refrigerators." *Energy* Vol 8, No 12, pp 957-962.

Moulton B.R. 1996. "Bias in the Consumer Price Index: What Is the Evidence?" *Journal of Economic Perspectives.*

Moulton, B.R. 1995. "Interarea Indexes of the Cost of Shelter Using Hedonic Quality Adjustment Techniques." *Journal of Econometrics.* V. 68 # 1, pp 181-205.

Moulton, B.R. 1993. "Basic Components of the CPI: Estimation of Price Changes." *Monthly Labor Review,* December, pp 13-24.

Moulton B.R. and K.E. Smedley. 1995. "A Comparison of Estimators For Elementary Aggregates of the CPI." Unpublished paper. Washington, D.C.: BLS.

Nakamura, L. 1995. "Measuring Inflation In a High-Tech Age." *Business Review of the Federal Reserve Bank of Philadelphia,* November-December, pp 13-26.

National Research Council, 1995. *Measuring Poverty: A New Approach.* C.F. Citro and R.T. Michael, eds. Washington, D.C.: National Academy Press.

Popkin, J. 1995. *"CPI Commission's Findings are Unjustified: An Analysis of Toward a More Accurate Measure of the Cost of Living."* Unpublished Paper, Washington, D.C.: Joel Popkin and Company.

Randolph, W.C. 1988. "Housing Depreciation and Aging Bias in the Consumer Price Index." *Journal of Business and Economic Statistics*, July, pp 359-371.

Schrank, D., and T. Lomax. 1996. *Urban Roadway Congestion — 1982 to 1993, Volume 2: Methodology and Urbanized Area Data.* College Station, Texas: Texas Transportation Institute.

Senate Finance Committee. 1996. *Toward a More Accurate Measure of the Cost of Living.* Final Report to the Senate Finance Committee from the Advisory Commission to Study the Consumer Price Index. Washington, D.C.: U.S. Senate.

Senate Finance Committee. 1995. *Toward a More Accurate Measure of the Cost of Living.* Interim Report to the Senate Finance Committee from the Advisory Commission to Study the Consumer Price Index. Washington, D.C.: U.S. Senate.

Shapiro, M. and D. Wilcox. 1996. "Mismeasurement in the Consumer Price Index: An Evaluation." NBER working paper # 5590.

Smedley, K., and B. Moulton. 1996. "Replication of Armknecht-Weyback Analysis for 1995: Summary of Results." Unpublished paper. Washington, D.C.: BLS.

Zimbalist, A. 1992. *Baseball and Billions.* New York: Basic Books.

PART 3

Additional Views on the Accuracy of the Consumer Price Index

Katharine G. Abraham
Barry P. Bosworth
Martin Feldstein

STATISTICS UNDER THE SPOTLIGHT:
Improving the Consumer Price Index

KATHARINE G. ABRAHAM
Bureau of Labor Statistics
Room 4040, 2 Massachusetts Ave., NE, Washington, D.C. 20212
Paper presented at meeting of the American Statistical Association,
Chicago Ill., August 6, 1996

Given the importance of the consumer price index (CPI), both as an economic indicator that provides timely information on the prices paid by consumers and as a measure used extensively for indexation, not only in a number of large and visible federal programs but also in many private contracts, it's not surprising that measurement issues pertaining to the CPI have garnered substantial attention over the years.

I probably remember more clearly than most of you the specific events that precipitated the recent intensification of interest in the CPI. Back in the early winter of 1995, Federal Reserve Board Chairman Alan Greenspan testified before the Congress that he thought the CPI substantially overstated the rate of growth in the cost of living. His testimony generated a considerable amount of discussion. Soon afterwards, Speaker of the House Newt Gingrich, at a town meeting in Kennesaw, Georgia, was asked about the CPI and responded by saying, "We have a handful of bureaucrats who, all professional economists agree, have an error in their calculations. If they can't get it right in the next 30 days or so, we zero them out, we transfer the responsibility to either the Federal Reserve or the Treasury and tell them to get it right."

I heard about this the next afternoon when I got a call at home from John Berry, a reporter for the *Washington Post,* who read this comment to me and wanted to know if I had any response that I'd like to make. I said to him then the same thing that I would say to you today. If there were problems with the CPI that Bureau of Labor Statistics (BLS) staff knew about and knew how to fix but were just refusing to address, I'd agree with the Speaker: he should zero us out. That is not, however, an accurate characterization of the BLS performance. Indeed, as other speakers have indicated in their comments—and I would like to express my appreciation for their kind words—the staff of the BLS have been at the forefront of trying to identify problems with the way that the CPI is put together, figuring out how to fix those problems, and making improvements in the index.

What I'd like to do in my time this afternoon is to talk about some of the things that the BLS has done recently to improve the CPI, about some of the things that we have planned for the near future, and about some of the things that we'd like to do if we could identify the necessary resources and/or could figure out how to employ them. I'm not going to talk about biases in the CPI, other than to say that I'm considerably more agnostic than the other speakers in my assessment of the overall bias, if any, in the index. There are some things related to the formulas used to construct the CPI on which almost everyone agrees. Most importantly, as an index based upon a fixed market basket, the CPI does not allow for substitution in response to relative price changes and thus has a slight tendency to overstate the growth in the cost of living. There is less basis for agreement around the issues of how well we adjust for changes in the quality of goods and services, how we deal with new goods, and how we treat changes in the relative importance of different kinds of shopping outlets. At this point, there is a great deal that we just don't know about any possible upward or downward biases associated with these things.

Let me turn, then, to talking about the bureau's continuing efforts to improve the CPI. I'm going to talk about three things: first, some very recent changes made to correct the so-called "formula bias" problem; second, our production of a set of alternative measures that answer different questions than does the CPI; and third, some things that we are doing or would like to do in the areas of quality adjustment, the treatment of new goods, and changes in outlet mix.

Let me start with the so-called "formula bias" problem that was in the news this spring, a problem that grew out of the limitations of the data that we have available for use in putting the CPI together. The CPI is designed as a measure of the cost of purchasing a fixed market basket of goods and services. The market basket concept refers to the quantities of goods and services purchased, but the data we have available from our household surveys give us information on the amounts of money consumers spend on different sorts of items at particular stores. After this information has been compiled, our field economists visit stores to collect prices for specific items within each item category. Our procedure for constructing quantity weights for the items whose prices we're tracking used to be, first, to project the initial price collected for each item backwards using information on price trends for similar items and then to divide the appropriate expenditure figure by this backwards-projected price to obtain a base period quantity weight for the item. This may sound pretty straightforward. The problem is that this procedure led us systematically to overweight items that were on sale as of the point in time when we first priced them—expenditure divided by a low price gives you a big quantity weight. The prices of sale items are apt to rise in subsequent months, however, and our procedures thus were imparting an upward bias to the index.

We only began fully to appreciate the existence and nature of this problem with the index during the course of 1994. In January of 1995, we introduced changes to deal with the problem for food-at-home items, and also made some related changes in the way we were putting the housing component of the index together. This summer, we are making further changes that we believe fully correct the problem. Going forward, then, the "formula bias" problem should be a non-problem.

There are, of course, other outstanding issues related to the formulas used to construct the CPI. As David Wilcox emphasized in his remarks, there are a variety of questions that you might use a consumer price measure to answer. The CPI tracks the price of a fixed market basket of goods and services, but, for many purposes, a measure that allowed for substitution among items as their relative prices changed, and thereby more closely approximated a true cost-of-living index, would be more appropriate.

The bureau has done a fair amount of work oriented towards producing alternative indexes that answer different questions than the official CPI. We are in the process of producing an experimental measure that, within the most detailed cells in the index, uses geometric mean aggregation rather than Laspeyres aggregation. This measure may be more appropriate for tracking the cost of living than the CPI if you believe that it is a more reasonable approximation to assume that consumers' preferences exhibit an elasticity of substitution of one between items within item categories rather than an elasticity of substitution of zero. We've also produced experimental superlative measures of the sort originally proposed by Erwin Diewert that take substitution across item categories into account.

There are some issues related to these alternative measures that need to be considered. The key question about using the geometric mean formula for within-cell aggregation is whether assuming an elasticity of substitution of one across the board really is a more reasonable approximation than assuming an elasticity of substitution of zero. Evidence on this issue will be hard to come by.

The superlative measures are theoretically elegant, but are likely to be more difficult than the CPI for the general public to understand. From an operational perspective, production of the superlative measures requires expenditure share data that are available only with a lag. Our experimental superlative measures currently are not available until the fall of the year following the year to which they refer. It would be difficult to shorten that production cycle by very much even for an experimental index, and if we were to produce a superlative index subject to the same sort of review as the official CPI, the necessary lag might well increase. For certain purposes, it is important to have a measure that comes out promptly.

There is also an issue about the precision of our experimental superlative measures. The weights for the superlative measures are constructed using data from the Consumer Expenditure Survey (CEX). For the official CPI, we use three years of CEX data to construct weights that our statisticians have deemed to be of adequate precision. For the superlative measure, only two years of expenditure data are used, because the superlative measure is based on the average of the expenditure shares for a base year and an ending year. To produce superlative measures that were of comparable precision to the official CPI would require a Consumer Expenditure Survey that was about 50% larger than we now have—and that would cost money.

On the general topic of alternative measures, David Wilcox alluded in his remarks to interest in the growth in the cost of living for the elderly. We have for some time now produced an experimental CPI for the elderly, which we construct by reweighting price change data that we already have using information based on the consumption pattern of the elderly. This method has shortcomings, but doing a better job would require selecting a separate sample of outlets and items to reflect where elderly consumers shop and what they buy, and thus would be quite an expensive proposition.

Turning to a third topic, I would like to talk about some things we have been doing or would like to do that relate to our treatment of quality change, new goods, and different kinds of outlets in the index. With respect to the treatment of quality change, the obvious strategy is to try to make more use than we have in the past of hedonic adjustments or other explicit adjustments for changes in the features of the items that we're pricing. How much of this we do is mainly, though not exclusively, a resource issue. Making explicit adjustments for changes in item features requires that we collect information not only on item prices but also on item characteristics. This would not have to be done every month, but we would need substantially more information than we now collect to be able to look systematically, item category by item category, at the relationship between price and item characteristics.

Something that we have planned for implementation as part of the ongoing CPI Revision is the introduction of a new way of updating the CPI outlet and item samples. The current procedure is to update those samples each year for 20% of the areas in which we collect prices. By moving to a telephone survey to compile the underlying sampling frames, we'll be able to change that rotation pattern. Instead of bringing in new outlets and items geographic area by geographic area, we'll be able to bring in new outlets and items for whole item categories in all geographic areas at once. If there are categories of items for which we know that there has been a lot of change in what people are purchasing or where they are shopping, we'll be able to bring in new samples for those item categories on a more frequent basis.

Quite appropriately, there has been a great deal of attention devoted to the way that medical care is treated in the CPI. We're in the process of making some changes there as well. Under the procedures currently in place for constructing the hospital components of the CPI, we sample and collect prices for very specific items when we visit a hospital. We might, for example, end up tracking the price of a unit of blood. The problems with this approach have become clear to all of us. Hospital care really isn't sold specific item by specific item. In January of 1997—that is, this next January—we will be shifting over to an approach to tracking hospital care prices that involves visiting a hospital, picking a patient bill, identifying the key services covered by that bill, and then tracking the cost of providing that bundle of services. This is not, of course, a solution to all of the problems we have with tracking medical care prices, but looking at whole treatment bundles puts us in a better position to begin thinking about how to accommodate changes in treatment protocols in constructing the index.

There are a number of important outstanding issues that I would have to say we don't have good ways to handle. From an operational point of view, for example, we simply don't know how to go about comparing the prices of different items that may satisfy similar needs or even the prices of the same item sold at different types of outlets. Similarly, in an operational context, we don't have any good way to deal with the value consumers may attach to increases or decreases in the variety of items available for sale. We're working on some of these things, but I am not optimistic about our ever arriving at implementable solutions to all of the concerns that have been raised regarding the CPI.

As I've indicated, some of the things we could and would like to be able to do would require additional resources. Money is always tight, and it's even tighter today than in times past. In addition to seeking extra resources to do some of the things I've talked about, we also need to be looking at whether we're using the money we already have in the most efficient possible way. Changing how we put together the area sample for the CPI, for example, might allow us to reduce our costs, and we've begun to look at that. When we update the sample of geographic areas in which we're collecting prices—something that we do roughly every 10 years—it might be possible to have more overlap between the old and the new areas. The largest 30 or so metropolitan areas appear in the sample with certainty, and our area selection procedures already are designed to give some preference to smaller areas from the prior area sample. Most of the smaller geographic areas, however, are replaced during our regular revisions. It's very expensive to go into a totally new area, hire staff, and begin collecting prices. Having more overlap in the geographic areas across area samples thus could save some money.

It also may not be necessary to collect prices for all item categories in all areas. The CPI sample of price quotations currently is structured so that we have a set of geographic areas and a set of item categories. With the exception of certain special cases like postage and used cars, we collect prices for all of the item categories in all of the geographic areas. The prices of items in certain categories, however, may be set in national markets, so that filling in the whole area/item-category matrix isn't necessary.

Moving away from our current approach to sample design would carry some risks. Further increasing the overlap between old and new geographic area samples, for example, might well make it more likely that we would end up with an area sample that was not truly representative of current reality. Similarly, selecting and pricing items nationally rather than locally, even if only in certain item categories, might increase the risk of not representing in our market basket items that account for a significant part of consumers' purchases or of not accurately reflecting price trends in individual areas. These risks are real, but I nonetheless believe that we ought to be looking at and evaluating the sorts of possible changes in our sampling strategy that I've mentioned.

Let me conclude by saying that, as the BLS moves forward, we can use all the help that we can get with continuing to improve the CPI. We are very eager to have ideas from any of you regarding how we could be doing a better job, and I've gotten some good ideas from the other panelists today. We are in the process of constructing research data bases suitable for addressing a wide range of price measurement issues and I'd invite any of you to talk with us if you have a project for which those data bases might be suitable and that might contribute to an improved understanding of price change in our economy.

Testimony of Barry P. Bosworth
Before the Senate Finance Committee

February 11, 1997

First, the Senate Finance Committee and the Advisory Commission to Study the Consumer Price Index are to be congratulated for the attention they have brought to the question of the adequacy of the consumer price index as a measure of inflation. This is an issue that needs to be explored on an even broader basis because I believe that years of neglect and underfunding have resulted in a serious erosion of the quality of the U.S. statistical system. Yet, as we learn in this specific case, the accuracy of the statistics can have major implications for the budget and millions of citizens (in this case, taxpayers and Social Security recipients). Furthermore, the commission's conclusion about the mismeasurement of inflation, if true, radically alters our perception of the course of economic growth and gains in living standards over the past several decades. It would, for example, roughly double the growth in real wages, making it difficult to attribute public complaints about the lack of income growth to anything other than inflated expectations.

With that said, however, I think that the commission exaggerated the evidence on the extent of the upward bias in the CPI and paid too little attention to other areas in which the errors could go in the opposite direction. The tendency to overstate conclusions, however, need not detract from the basic recommendations to implement an expanded and more current set of weights in the CPI and to explore some alternative price indices. Those proposals are unlikely to be met with any opposition. The central issue of dispute is the measurement of quality changes.

The commission argued in its final report that the consumer price index overstates the annual rate of increase in consumer prices by 1.1% per year with a confidence band of from 0.8% to 1.6%. The conclusion that the CPI overstates inflation is consistent with prior research on price indexes, and few analysts would disagree. There is far less empirical basis for, and less professional unanimity with, the commission's estimate of the magnitude of the bias. While it is consistent with a number of other recent surveys, it is important to understand that they are all extrapolating from a common small set of empirical studies, and those underlying studies were not intended to provide an unbiased assessment. Few academic economists have been willing to involve themselves in issues of data collection; and most of the empirical evidence arises out of the research of analysts at the Bureau of Labor Statistics. Those studies focused on very specific problems with the CPI, and were not represented as an assessment of their overall importance. Naturally, the researchers looked in those narrow areas of the CPI where the effect would be largest. At this time, we simply do not know the extent to which the results can be generalized to other parts of the index.

More usefully, the issue of bias in the CPI can be divided into (1) a set of technical issues about how to deal with the aggregation of subcomponents of the index, and (2) quality change. I have no particular quarrel with the commission's recommendations with respect to the technical aspects, including the use of alternative price index formulas to more adequately capture the commodity and substitution bias. They have done what a commission should do in highlighting some basic problems and providing specific suggestions that would go a long way toward resolving them. The Congress should provide the funding to update the index and the BLS should move in the direction proposed by the commission. The result would be a better index.

The crux of the problem with the commission's report is in the chapter on quality change. This discussion, both publicly and professionally, has always been distorted by a failure to appreciate fully the extent to which the current CPI already adjusts for quality change. We can all point to areas where the quality of goods and services has improved; but that is not the question. Instead, we must know if the improvements have been more than are embodied in the current procedures. In this regard, few people outside of the BLS appreciate that the index already reflects a large amount of quality gain. In 1995, the total price increase in a subsample of the CPI, covering about 70% of the total, amounted to 4.7%, but the BLS determined that 2.6 percentage points, or slightly over half of the increase, represented improvements in quality. That is, quality improvements offset about half of the gross price increase, yielding an estimated 2.2% inflation rate. The commission is apparently arguing that the quality adjustment should have been close to 3.2% rather than 2.6%. They could be correct; but, on the basis of existing evidence, we don't know that, and I don't see how anyone can be certain that the number is 3.2, instead of 2.6, or 2.0.

The BLS contributed to the problem until recently by providing little or no information on the magnitude of the existing quality adjustments. However, the commission provides a one-sided view of the problem, and it offers no new procedures to deal with it. We are not going to obtain a solution to the difficulty of measuring quality change with the anecdotal stories and introspective thought experiments provided by the commission's report. There is a need to develop specific procedures that BLS could use to identify instances of quality change and to measure the amount. The most disappointing aspect of the commission's report is the lack of any recommendations about how to deal with quality change.

Within the CPI, most issues of quality change arise in the context of breaks in the collection of price information on a specific item, such as might occur with the introduction of a model year change, that necessitate a substitution. BLS treats those substitutions in a variety of ways.

If the new and old items are judged to be nearly equivalent, *comparable substitutes,* the difference between the price of the item in the prior month and the current price of the new item is all assumed to represent a price change.

If the old and new items are both available in the current month, an *overlap method* is used in which the old item can be used to measure the price change from the prior month and the new product can be used to measure the price change going forward. In effect, any difference in the current month's price of the two items is assumed to represent a quality difference and is excluded from the index. Overlaps are only infrequently available.

If the substitute item is not comparable, the BLS may attempt a *direct quality adjustment* using manufacturer information on the costs of the quality differences, as with new automotive models, or hedonic price regressions that relate price differences to specific product characteristics, as with rent and apparel products.

Finally, a *link method* is used to first calculate the average price change for the strata excluding the item, and use that rate of price change to impute a change for the product in question. A recent innovation, the class-mean imputation, estimates the price change for the link using only the price changes of other items classified as comparable substitutes or those with direct quality adjustments.

Recently, the BLS made available a tabulation of the frequency and size of these adjustments for 1995, 1983, and 1984. A summary of the 1995 data is shown in **Table 1**. The analysis refers to a restricted version of the CPI that excludes rent and a few other small items.

The existing procedures certainly miss small changes in quality where the BLS does not find it necessary to make a substitution, but it is striking that the category of nonsubstitutes (96% of the total sample) accounts for such a small portion of the total increase in the CPI. Whatever quality change is missed does not seem to have much of an impact since it should have biased the price change up. We could give endless examples of gradual improvements in quality that are overlooked, but there are also cases of small decrements as producers reposition items in the marketplace. Consumers frequently complain about deteriorations in products or services that are not captured in the price indexes any more than the small improvements.

At present, adjustments for quality change are largely limited to situations where the agents identify major discontinuities in the nature of the product being priced. The BLS has made some efforts to expand its use of direct adjustment methods, but the majority of the quality adjustments still occur using the link method (1.50 plus 0.67 percentage points of the total of 2.56 in 1995). Linking creates the situation with the greatest potential for overstating the quality change. If producers follow a practice of timing their price increases to coincide with the introduction of new models or other quality changes, the BLS methodology will result in most of the price increase being linked out: the measure of inflation will be biased downward. That is the problem that emerged in autos (where producers clearly introduced price increases at the beginning of the model year and cut prices in subsequent months), and led to the effort to make direct adjustments.

Another example of the problem with the linking method is provided, until recently, by the apparel category. For years, the CPI reported dramatically lower rates of price increase for women's clothing compared to men's and children's. This made little sense when all of the categories should have been subject to similar costs trends. The problem arose because women's clothing underwent major annual style changes that created a break in the pricing and a linking out of all of the price change. Men bought the same clothes year after year, and the same suit could be priced continuously for years.

Thus, much of the dispute over the adequacy of the current estimate of quality change involves different models of how producers go about introducing price and quality changes. If a large portion of the quality improvements are continuous, and independent of the timing of price changes, the current techniques may overlook them. But, if price and quality changes are tied closely together, the link methodology may overestimate the quality improvements and underestimate the amount of price change.

Even in the area of direct adjustment there are problems because, while the criteria of value to the consumer is used to identify significant changes in products such as autos, the BLS normally relies on the producers to provide estimates of the cost of the improvements. They, of course, have an incentive to overstate those costs, as anyone who has dealt with the companies on issues of environment and safety can attest.

Finally, the commission places great emphasis on making the CPI a measure of the cost of living, and that is right in concept. But the Congress should also understand that pushing the idea to its extreme can open a can of worms that exceeds the capacity of the current methodology. Where do we draw the line between economic and noneconomic aspects of the cost of living, and are they separable? Should we include a cost of the time used to shop for the lowest price? That is, how should we value convenience? How should we treat increases in the range of choice?

We should also distinguish between issues of quality and consumer surplus. Since prices are determined by the marginal buyer and seller, there are, in any market, buyers who obtain the product for much less than they would be willing to pay, consumer surplus. Should the gain in their standard of living be computed to include or exclude the change in consumer surplus? In several instances, the commission appears to be focusing on questions of capturing consumer surplus in the index, not just quality change.

Finally, I am not so naive as to believe that the committee and the commission members were interested solely in improving the quality of the nation's statistical system. This issue has large implications for the federal budget and the standard of living of retirees. From a political perspective, a CPI adjustment appears as an immaculate conception version of deficit reduction.

I have no problem with improvements in the procedures of the BLS that result in changed estimates of changes in the CPI. I am troubled, however, by suggestions, such as those of the chairman of the Federal Reserve, that "experts" exist who know what the actual increase in the nation's average cost of living has truly been. And, I am skeptical of suggestions that a commission or its equivalent can produce an additional adjustment to the annual change in benefits of existing retirees that is based on anything other than their own biases.

Were it not for the politics of immaculate conceptions, I don't think we would be considering a benefit reduction that increases with the age of the retiree. The proposal does nothing to the benefits of a new retiree; but, after 20 years, the benefits of an 82-year-old could be reduced by 10-20%. Under the current system, poverty already increases with age, and this proposal would exacerbate that trend. Private pensions have no annual adjustments and the real income of most retirees declines over time. If OASDI benefits are to be reduced, it seems to me that it would be better to concentrate the cuts at the beginning of the retirement period when individuals can take actions to mitigate their effect by working longer, not in their 80s when they have no employment options.

Table 1. Quality and Price Changes in the Consumer Price Index, 1995

Category	Percentage of Price Quotes	Annual Percent Change		
		Quality Change	Pure Price Change	Total Price Change
Comparable substitutions	2.54	0.00	0.54	0.54
Noncomparable substitutions	1.35	2.56	0.45	3.01
Overlap Method	0.05	-0.01	0.10	0.09
Direct Adjustment	0.41	0.40	0.17	0.57
Link Method	0.57	1.50	0.01	1.51
Class-mean Method	0.32	0.67	0.17	0.84
Total Substitutions	3.90	2.56	1.00	3.56
Nonsubstitutions	96.10	0.00	1.16	1.16
Total Covered CPI	100.00	2.56	2.16	4.72
Total CPI			2.50	

Source: Brent R. Moulton and Karin E. Smedley, "Addressing the Quality Change Issue in the Consumer Price Index," Bureau of Labor Statistics (January 1997).

Note: The covered CPI excludes rent, homeowners equivalent rent, used cars, health insurance, and other items with a total relative importance of about 28% in the total CPI.

Statement by Martin Feldstein
Before the Committee on Finance,
United States Senate

Professor of Economics, Harvard University
President, National Bureau of Economic Research
February 11, 1997

Thank you, Mr. Chairman. I am pleased to appear before this committee to discuss the problem of adjusting government outlays and receipts for changes in the cost of living. I have three conclusions to share with the committee:

(1) In my judgment, the current consumer price index overstates the true increase in the cost of living by *at least* the 1.1% per year indicated by the Advisory Commission to Study the Consumer Price Index.

(2) Congress and the President should act *this year* to change the procedure for adjusting government outlays and receipts for inflation.

(3) The appropriate Inflation Adjustment Factor cannot be derived by rigorous statistical methods but requires the exercise of informed judgment. While the Bureau of Labor Statistics should be encouraged to improve the existing CPI measure, Congress should (as recommended by the Advisory Commission) establish a rotating expert advisory committee that will periodically recommend the Inflation Adjustment Factor that, in its judgment, best represents the modification of the CPI needed to measure the increase in the cost of living.

I will now comment briefly on each of these three conclusions.

1. *The CPI currently overstates the increase in the cost of living by at least 1.1% per year.*

The most difficult problems in measuring the cost of living are associated with the introduction of new products and changes in the quality of existing products. There has been substantial research on these problems in recent years, especially among the economists who are associated with the National Bureau of Economic Research. This research has dealt with a very wide range of particular goods and services, including such very different things as prescription drugs, breakfast cereals, and the care of patients who have experienced heart attacks.

In study after study, the researchers have found that the existing CPI procedures substantially overstate the true rise in the cost of living. Sometimes this is because the CPI procedure introduces new products too slowly. More importantly, the CPI procedure generally fails to take into account the value of the new product as such and only captures the change in its price long after it has been introduced.

In the case of health care, the CPI procedure takes into account only the cost of the service and not its improving effectiveness in treating patients. There are also a variety of special problems. For example, the CPI fails to capture the important price decline that occurs when the patent runs out on a prescription drug, causing the same generic drug to be available at a much lower price.

2. *Congress and the President should act this year to change the inflation adjustment procedure.*

There is no reason to delay the legislative change. Indeed, the fact that inflation adjustments in the past have been based on the unadjusted CPI means that the existing benefit levels and tax rates have gone far beyond the appropriate inflation adjustment.

Delaying the legislative change would have only a small effect in the first year but would mean that government outlays and receipts would be permanently and substantially higher than they should be and government receipts would be permanently and substantially lower. On the basis of recent estimates by the Congressional Budget Office, I have calculated that a 1.1 percentage point change in the Inflation Adjustment Factor beginning in fiscal year 1998 would reduce the deficit in that year by $6 billion and the deficit in 2002 by about $60 billion. If the inflation adjustment were postponed by just two years, the deficit reduction in 2002 would be only about half as large (about $33 billion) and the national debt would be more than $90 billion larger.

3. *Because the appropriate Inflation Adjustment Factor cannot be derived by rigorous statistical methods but requires informed judgment, the Congress should appoint a rotating expert advisory committee that will periodically recommend an appropriate Inflation Adjustment Factor.*

Although studies of individual goods and services can indicate that the CPI method overstates the rise in the cost of living, there is no statistically rigorous scientific way to modify the CPI for the quality changes in the millions of products in our economy or to take into account all of the new products that are introduced each year. But that is not a reason for ignoring such changes in deciding how much to adjust benefits and tax brackets each year.

Rather, it tells me that the CPI calculated according to rigorous rules by the Bureau of Labor Statistics should be regarded as only a starting point for deciding on the Inflation Adjustment Factor. To do this, the Congress should establish a rotating expert advisory comniittee that will periodically recommend an Inflation Adjustment Factor that, in its judgment, best represents the modification of the CPI needed to measure the increase in the cost of living.

In her recent testimony to the Senate Budget Committee, BLS Commissioner Katharine Abraham indicated her concern that when "evidence ... is sparse" the recent Advisory Commission was "forced to fall back on its best judgment" and expressed her view that the CPI should instead be based on tested and reliable statistical techniques. I think she is correct both in her characterization of the work of the commission and in the scientific standard to which the official CPI should aspire.

But that is not a reason for the Congress to reject the use of informed judgment in deciding how to adjust benefits and taxes. Indeed the technical standard that the BLS will rightly insist upon means that even if the BLS makes all of the improvements in the CPI that it currently contemplates and that future research may suggest, the resulting estimate will still be certain to overstate the true increase in the cost of living. It is important therefore to go beyond the technical CPI calculation done by the BLS staff and introduce an element of judgment.

In thinking about the separate roles of the BLS and the Advisory Committee, I find it helpful to think of the BLS as similar to an accounting firm. Accountants follow rigorous rules to produce an estimate of the so-called book value of a company. But when another firm wants to buy that company, it doesn't use just the book value. Rather, it looks to experts for advice based on judgments. I think such judgmental decisions are inescapable in the current context and that it is better to rely on the judgment of experts than to use only the BLS methods of inflation accounting that are rigorous and replicable but that inevitably overstate the true increase in the cost of living.

Further Readings

OVERVIEWS

Abraham, K. 1995. "Prepared Statement." In "Consumer Price Index: Hearings Before the Committee of Finance, United States Senate." Senate Hearing 104-69, Washington, D.C.: U.S. Government Printing Office, pp 107-9.

Baker, D. 1997. "The Mismeasurement of Inflation." appendix in *The State of Working America 1996-97*, by L. Mishel, J. Bernstein, and J. Schmitt. Armonk, NY: M.E. Sharpe.

Baker, D. 1996a. "Getting Prices Right: A Methodologically Consistent Consumer Price Index 1953-94." Washington, D.C.: Economic Policy Institute.

Baker, D. 1996b. "The Overstated CPI: Can It Really Be True?" *Challenge Magazine*, September-October 1996, pp 26-33. *Journal of Econometrics*. V. 68 # 1, pp 243-268.

Bureau of Labor Statistics. 1995. *Report from the Bureau of Labor Statistics for the House Budget Committee.* Washington, D.C.: U.S. Congress.

Bureau of Labor Statistics. 1966. *The Consumer Price Index: History and Techniques.* Bulletin 1517. Washington, D.C.: BLS.

Congressional Budget Office. 1994. *Is the Growth of the CPI a Biased Measure of Changes in the Cost of Living?* Washington, D.C.: CBO.

Fixler, D. 1993. "The Consumer Price Index: Underlying Concepts and Caveats." *Monthly Labor Review*, December, pp 3-12.

Gordon, R. 1992. *Measuring the Aggregate Price Level: Implications for Economic Performance and Policy.* National Bureau of Economic Research Working Paper # 3969.

Krugman, P. 1996. "The CPI and the Rat Race." http://www.slate.com/Dismal/96-12-21/Dismal.asp.

Lebow, D.E., J.M. Roberts, and D.J. Stockton. 1994. "Monetary Policy and the Price Level." Washington, D.C.: Board of Governors of the Federal Reserve Board.

Lebow, D.E., J.M. Roberts, and D.J. Stockton. 1992. *Economic Performance Under Price Stability.* Working Paper Series # 125. Washington, D.C.: Board of Governors of the Federal Reserve Board.

Moulton B.R. 1996. "Bias in the Consumer Price Index: What Is the Evidence?" *Journal of Economic Perspectives.*

Nakamura, L. 1995. "Measuring Inflation In a High-Tech Age." *Business Review of the Federal Reserve Bank of Philadelphia*, November-December, pp 13-26.

Popkin, J. 1997. "*Remarks on the CPI and the Boskin Panel Report.*" Paper presented at the American Economics Association Meeting, New Orleans, Louisiana, January 1997.

Popkin, J. 1995. "*CPI Commission's Findings are Unjustified: An Analysis of Toward a More Accurate Measure of the Cost of Living.*" Unpublished Paper, Washington, D.C.: Joel Popkin and Company.

Senate Finance Committee. 1996. *Toward a More Accurate Measure of the Cost of Living.* Final Report to the Senate Finance Committee from the Advisory Commission to Study the Consumer Price Index. Washington, D.C.: U.S. Senate.

Senate Finance Committee. 1995. *Toward a More Accurate Measure of the Cost of Living.* Interim Report to the Senate Finance Committee from the Advisory Commission to Study the Consumer Price Index. Washington, D.C.: U.S. Senate.

Shapiro, M. and D. Wilcox. 1996. "Mismeasurement in the Consumer Price Index: An Evaluation." NBER working paper # 5590.

Wynne, M.A. and F.D. Sigalla. 1994. "The Consumer Price Index." *Economic Review*, Federal Reserve Bank of Dallas, Second Quarter.

INDEX CONSTRUCTION AND SUBSTITUTION BIAS

Aizcorbe, A.M. and P.C. Jackman. 1993. "The Commodity Substitution Effect in CPI Data, 1982-91." *Monthly Labor Review*, December, pp 25-33. (See also BLS updates.)

Armknecht, P.A., B.R. Moulton, and K.J. Stewart. 1995. "Improvements to the Food at Home, Shelter, and Prescription Drug Indexes in the U.S. Consumer Price Index." BLS Working Paper # 263. Washington, D.C.: BLS.

Braithwait, S.D. 1980. "Substitution Bias of the Laspeyres Price Index: An Analysis Using Estimated Cost of Living Indexes." *American Economic Review.* V 90, March, pp 64-77.

Bryan, M. and S. Cecchetti. 1993. "The CPI as a Measure of Inflation." *Economic Review.* V 29, # 4, The Federal Reserve Bank of Cleveland, pp 15-24.

Bureau of Labor Statistics. 1996. "Extending the Improvements in CPI Sample Rotation Procedures and Improving the Procedures for Substitute Items." BLS Press Release. Washington, D.C.: BLS.

Dahlen, J. "Computing Elementary Aggregates in the Swedish Consumer Price Index." *Journal of Official Statistics* V8, pp 129-47.

Diewart, W.E. 1995. "Axiomatic and Economic Approaches to Elementary Price Indexes." NBER working paper # 5104.

Diewart, W.E. 1987. "Index Numbers" in Eatwell, Millgate, Newman (eds), *The New Palgrave Dictionary of Economics.* Volume 2, Macmillian, pp 767-780.

Diewart, W.E. 1976. "Exact and Superlative Index Numbers." *Journal of Econometrics.* V4 # 2, pp 115-45.

Fisher, I. 1922. *The Making of Index Numbers.* Boston: Houghton-Miffin.

Greenlees, J. 1997. "Expenditure Weights and Measured Inflation." Unpublished paper. Washington, D.C.: BLS.

Henderson, S. and K. Smedley. 1994. "Improvements in Estimating the Shelter Indexes in the CPI." *Consumer Price Index Detailed Report*, October, pp 5-6.

Moulton, B.R. 1996. "Estimation of Elementary Indexes of the Consumer Price Index." Unpublished paper. Washington, D.C.: BLS.

Moulton, B.R. 1995. "Interarea Indexes of the Cost of Shelter Using Hedonic Quality Adjustment Techniques." *Journal of Econometrics*. V. 68 # 1, pp 181-205.

Moulton, B.R. 1993. "Basic Components of the CPI: Estimation of Price Changes." *Monthly Labor Review*, December, pp 13-24.

Moulton B.R. and K.E. Smedley. 1995. "A Comparison of Estimators for Elementary Aggregates of the CPI." Unpublished paper. Washington, D.C.: BLS.

Pollak, R.A. 1989. *The Theory of the Cost-of-Living Index*. New York: Oxford University Press.

Reinsdorf, M. 1996. "Formula Bias and Seller Substitution." Unpublished paper. Washington, D.C.: BLS.

Reinsdorf, M. and B.R. Moulton. 1995. "The Construction of Basic Components of Cost of Living Indexes." BLS Working Paper # 261.

Schmidt, M.L. 1993. "Effects of Updating the CPI Market Basket." *Monthly Labor Review*, December, pp 59-62.

Triplett, J. 1988. *Price Index Research and its Influence on Data: A Historical Review*. Conference on Research in Income and Wealth Working Paper.

RETAIL OUTLET SUBSTITUTION BIAS

Oi, W.Y. 1992. "Productivity in the Distributive Trades: The Shopper and the Economies of Massed Resources." In Zvi Griliches (ed.), *Output Measurement in the Service Sectors*. National Bureau of Economic Research Conference on Research in Income and Wealth, Volume 56. Chicago: The University of Chicago Press.

Reinsdorf, M. 1996. "Formula Bias and Seller Substitution." Unpublished paper. Washington, D.C.: BLS.

Reinsdorf, M. 1993. "The Effect of Outlet Price Differentials in the U.S. Consumer Price Index." in M.F. Foss, M.E. Manser and A.H. Young (eds.) *Price Measurements and Their Uses*. National Bureau of Economic Research Conference on Research in Income and Wealth, Volume 57, pp 227-254.

QUALITY AND NEW GOODS BIAS

Armknecht, P.A., W.F. Lane, and K.J. Stewart. 1994. "New Products and the U.S. Consumer Price Index." Paper presented at the NBER Conference on Income and Wealth, Williamsburg, VA. April 1994.

Armknecht, P.A., B.R. Moulton, and K.J. Stewart. 1995. "Improvements to the Food at Home, Shelter, and Prescription Drug Indexes in the U.S. Consumer Price Index." BLS Working Paper # 263. Washington, D.C.: BLS.

Armknecht, P.A. and Daniel H. Ginsburg. 1992. "Measuring Price Changes in Consumer Services." In Zvi Griliches (ed.), *Output Measurement in the Service Sectors*. National Bureau of Economic Research Conference on Research in Income and Wealth, Volume 56. Chicago: The University of Chicago Press.

Armknecht, P.A. and D. Weyback. 1992. "Adjustments for Quality Change in the U.S. Consumer Price Index." *Journal of Official Statistics*, pp 129-147.

Berndt, E., and Z. Griliches. 1993. "Price Indexes for Microcomputers: An Exploratory Study." in M.F. Foss, M.E. Manser and A.H. Young (eds.) *Price Measurements and Their Uses*. National Bureau of Economic Research Conference on Research in Income and Wealth, Volume 57, pp 63-99.

Berndt, E., I. Cockburn, and Z. Griliches. 1996. "Pharmaceutical Innovations and Market Dynamics: Tracking Effects on Price Indexes for Anti-Depressant Drugs." *Brookings Paper on Economic Activity*.

Berndt, E., Z. Griliches, and J. Rosset. 1993. "Auditing the Producer Price Index: Micro Evidence from Prescription Pharmaceutical Preparations." *Journal of Business and Economic Statistics*, V 11 # 3, pp 251-64.

Berndt, E., Z. Griliches, and N.J. Rappaport. 1995. "Econometric Estimates of Price Indexes for Personal Computers in 1990s." *Journal of Econometrics*, V. 68 # 1, pp 243-268.

Bresnahan, T., and R. Gordon. 1997. *The Economics of New Goods*. Chicago: University of Chicago Press.

Cutler, D., M. McClellan, J. Newhouse, D. Remler. 1996. "Are Medical Prices Declining?" NBER working paper # 5750.

Dulberger, E.R. 1993. "Sources of Price Decline in Computer Processors: Selected Electronic Components." in M.F. Foss, M.E. Manser and A.H. Young (eds.) *Price Measurements and Their Uses*. National Bureau of Economic Research Conference on Research in Income and Wealth, Volume 57, pp 103-124.

Gordon, R. 1996. "The Sears Catalog Revisited: Apparel and Durable Goods." Unpublished paper. Northwestern University, Evanston, IL.

Gordon, R. 1990. *The Measurement of Durable Goods Prices*. Chicago: University of Chicago Press.

Griliches, Z. and I. Cockburn. 1994. "Generics and New Goods in Pharmaceutical Price Indexes." *American Economic Review*, December, pp 1213-1232.

Hausman, J. 1994. "Valuation of New Goods Under Imperfect Competition." NBER Working paper # 4970.

Hulten, C. 1996. "Quality Change in the CPI: The Neglected Cost Dimension." Unpublished paper. University of Maryland, College Park, MD.

Lancaster, K. 1977. "The Measurement of Changes in Quality." *Review of Income and Wealth.* June, pp 157-172.

Liegey, P.R. Jr. 1994. "Apparel Price Indexes: Effects of Hedonic Adjustment." *Monthly Labor Review*, May, pp 38-45.

Liegey, P.R. Jr. 1993. "Adjusting Apparel Indexes in the Consumer Price Index for Quality Differences." in M.F. Foss, M.E. Manser and A.H. Young (eds.) *Price Measurements and Their Uses.* National Bureau of Economic Research Conference on Research in Income and Wealth, Volume 57. pp 209-227.

Moulton, B.R. 1995. "Interarea Indexes of the Cost of Shelter Using Hedonic Quality Adjustment Techniques." *Journal of Econometrics*, V. 68 # 1, pp 181-205.

Randolph, W.C. 1988. "Estimation of Housing Depreciation: Short-Term Quality Change and Long-Term Vintage Effects." *Journal of Urban Economics*, V 23, pp 162-78.

Randolph, W.C. 1988. "Housing Depreciation and Aging Bias in the Consumer Price Index." *Journal of Business and Economic Statistics*, July, pp 359-371.

Shapiro, M. and D. Wilcox. 1996. "Mismeasurement in the Consumer Price Index: An Evaluation." NBER working paper # 5590.

Smedley, K., and B. Moulton. 1997. "Replication of Armknecht-Weyback Analysis for 1995: Summary of Results." Unpublished paper. Washington, D.C.: BLS.

Trajtenberg, M. 1990. *Product Innovations, Price Indices, and the (Mis)measurement of Economic Performance.* NBER Working Paper No. 3261.

Triplett, J. 1993. "Review of Robert J. Gordon '*The Measurement of Durable Goods Prices.*' " *Journal of Economic Literature*, V31.

Triplett, J. 1971. "Quality Bias in Price Indexes and New Methods of Quality Measurement." in Z. Griliches (ed.) *Price Indexes and Quality Change: Studies in New Methods of Measurement.* Cambridge, MA.: Harvard University Press.

Triplett, J. and R. McDonald. 1977. "Assessing the Quality Error in Output Measures: The Case of Refrigerators." *Review of Income and Wealth*, June, pp 137-156.

THE COST-OF-LIVING ACROSS DEMOGRAPHIC GROUPS

Amble, N. and Ken Stuart. 1994. "Experimental Price Index for the Elderly." *Monthly Labor Review*, May, pp 11-16. (See also BLS updates.)

Boskin, M., and M. Hurd. 1985. "Indexing Social Security Benefits: A Separate Price Index for the Elderly." *Public Finance Quarterly*, V 13, # 4, pp 436-449.

Jorgenson, D. and D. Slesnick. 1983. "Individual and Social Cost-of-Living Indexes." *Price Level Measurement*, W. Diewert and C. Montmarquette (eds.), Ottawa, Statistics Canada, pp 241-336.

Kokoski, M.F. 1987. *Consumer Price Indexes by Demographic Group.* BLS Working Paper # 167. Washington, D.C.: BLS.

Layng, W.J. 1978. "The Revision of the Consumer Price Index." In *The American Statistical Association Proceedings of the Business and Economics Statistics Section*, Part 1. Washington, D.C.: American Statistical Association, pp 195-203.

Index

About EPI

The Economic Policy Institute was founded in 1986 to widen the debate about policies to achieve healthy economic growth, prosperity, and opportunity in the difficult new era America has entered.

Today, America's economy is threatened by stagnant growth and increasing inequality. Expanding global competition, changes in the nature of work, and rapid technological advances are altering economic reality. Yet many of our policies, attitudes, and institutions are based on assumptions that no longer reflect real world conditions.

Central to the Economic Policy Institute's search for solutions is the exploration of policies that encourage every segment of the American economy (business, labor, government, universities, voluntary organizations, etc.) to work cooperatively to raise productivity and living standards for all Americans. Such an undertaking involves a challenge to conventional views of market behavior and a revival of a cooperative relationship between the public and private sectors.

With the support of leaders from labor, business, and the foundation world, the Institute has sponsored research and public discussion of a wide variety of topics: trade and fiscal policies; trends in wages, incomes, and prices; the causes of the productivity slowdown; labor-market problems; rural and urban policies; inflation; state-level economic development strategies; comparative international economic performance; and studies of the overall health of the U.S. manufacturing sector and of specific key industries.

The Institute works with a growing network of innovative economists and other social science researchers in universities and research centers all over the country who are willing to go beyond the conventional wisdom in considering strategies for public policy.

Founding scholars of the Institute include Jeff Faux, EPI president; Lester Thurow, Sloan School of Management, MIT; Ray Marshall, former U.S. secretary of labor, professor at the LBJ School of Public Affairs, University of Texas; Barry Bluestone, University of Massachusetts-Boston; Robert Reich, U.S. secretary of labor; and Robert Kuttner, author, editor of *The American Prospect,* and columnist for *Business Week* and the Washington Post Writers Group.

For additional information about the Institute, contact EPI at 1660 L Street, NW, Suite 1200, Washington, DC 20036, (202) 775-8810.

About the Editor

DEAN BAKER is a macroeconomist at the Economic Policy Institute. He received a B.A. in history from Swarthmore College (1981), an M.A. in economics from the University of Denver (1983), and a Ph.D. in economics from the University of Michigan (1988). Before joining EPI he was an assistant professor of economics at Bucknell University. His areas of specialization are monetary and financial policy and public finance.

His recent publications include: *Getting Prices Right: A Methodologically Consistent Consumer Price Index 1953-94* (Economic Policy Institute 1996); *Trends in Corporate Profitability: Getting More for Less?* (EPI 1996); *Robbing the Cradle? A Critical Assessment of Generational Accounting* (EPI 1995); "The Myth of the Investment-Led Recovery," which appeared in the November-December 1994 issue of *Challenge* magazine; "Conceptual and Accounting Issues in the Analysis of Saving, Investment and Macroeconomic Activity," which will soon be published in the volume *Issues in Saving and Investment* (University of Michigan Press); and "An Evaluation of Private Alternatives to Social Security" (Twentieth Century Fund).